Neoliberalism's War on Higher Education

Neoliberalism's War on Higher Education

Henry A. Giroux

Haymarket Books
Chicago, Illinois

This paperback edition
published in 2014 by
Haymarket Books
PO Box 180165
Chicago, IL 60618
773-583-7884
www.haymarketbooks.org
info@haymarketbooks.org

ISBN: 978-1-60846-334-3

Trade distribution:
In the US, Consortium Book Sales and Distribution, www.cbsd.com
In Canada, Publishers Group Canada, www.pgcbooks.ca
In the UK, Turnaround Publisher Services, www.turnaround-uk.com
In Australia, Palgrave Macmillan, www.palgravemacmillan.com.au
All other countries, Publishers Group Worldwide, www.pgw.com

Cover design by Rachel Cohen. Cover image of a march during the student strike
throughout Quebec in 2012 by Doug Tanner.

This book was published with the generous support of Lannan Foundation and
the Wallace Global Fund.

Printed in Canada by union labor.

Library of Congress Cataloging-in-Publication data is available.

10 9 8 7 6 5 4 3 2 1

RECYCLED
Paper made from
recycled material
FSC® C103567

Table of Contents

For Wendy Simon

To those brave and committed teachers who are struggling to educate young people for a more just and democratic world

ACKNOWLEDGMENTS

This book could not have been completed without the help of many people. My late dear friend Roger Simon provided a range of insightful ideas regarding the Quebec student protest. I will miss his friendship and the many conversations we had. Susan Searls Giroux, Brad Evans, and Michael Peters all contributed greatly to the articles we co-authored and shared. Grace Pollock once again provided editorial advice and skills that continually improve the quality of my writing. My colleague David L. Clark was enormously generous in reading some chapters and offering a range of insightful ideas. Through his kindness, patience, and professional insight, Dr. Bruno Salena contributed greatly to the conditions that allowed me to write this book. Lynn Worsham has always been a wonderful colleague, and I want to thank her for publishing earlier versions of "Intellectual Violence in the Age of Gated Intellectuals" and "Universities Gone Wild" in *JAC*. I especially want to thank my administrative assistant, Danielle Martak, for reading and editing every word of this book. Her interventions were invaluable, and her insights, editorial help, and administrative skills have greatly improved the quality of the manuscript. This book was written mostly in Hamilton and Toronto, Ontario, during a difficult time in my life—a time made much easier by the continued presence of my two canine companions, Miles and Kaya.

Neoliberalism's War on Democracy

It is certain, in any case, that ignorance, allied with power, is the most ferocious enemy justice can have.

—James Baldwin

Four decades of neoliberal policies have resulted in an economic Darwinism that promotes privatization, commodification, free trade, and deregulation. It privileges personal responsibility over larger social forces, reinforces the gap between the rich and poor by redistributing wealth to the most powerful and wealthy individuals and groups, and it fosters a mode of public pedagogy that privileges the entrepreneurial subject while encouraging a value system that promotes self-interest, if not an unchecked selfishness.[1] Since the 1970s, neoliberalism or free-market fundamentalism has become not only a much-vaunted ideology that now shapes all aspects of life in the United States but also a predatory global phenomenon "that drives the practices and principles of the International Monetary Fund, the World Bank, and World Trade Organization, trans-national institutions which largely determine the economic policies of developing countries and the rules of international trade."[2]

1

With its theater of cruelty and mode of public pedagogy, neoliberalism as a form of economic Darwinism attempts to undermine all forms of solidarity capable of challenging market-driven values and social relations, promoting the virtues of an unbridled individualism almost pathological in its disdain for community, social responsibility, public values, and the public good. As the welfare state is dismantled and spending is cut to the point where government becomes unrecognizable—*except* to promote policies that benefit the rich, corporations, and the defense industry—the already weakened federal and state governments are increasingly replaced by what João Biehl has called proliferating "zones of social abandonment" and "terminal exclusion."[3]

One consequence is that social problems are increasingly criminalized while social protections are either eliminated or fatally weakened. Not only are public servants described as the new "welfare queens" and degenerate freeloaders but young people are also increasingly subjected to harsh disciplinary measures both in and out of schools, often as a result of a violation of the most trivial rules.[4] Another characteristic of this crushing form of economic Darwinism is that it thrives on a kind of social amnesia that erases critical thought, historical analysis, and any understanding of broader systemic relations. In this regard, it does the opposite of critical memory work by eliminating those public spheres where people learn to translate private troubles into public issues. That is, it breaks "the link between public agendas and private worries, the very hub of the democratic process."[5] Once set in motion, economic Darwinism unleashes a mode of thinking in which social problems are reduced to individual flaws and political considerations collapse into the injurious and self-indicting discourse of character. Many Americans are preoccupied less with political and moral outrage over a country whose economic and political system is in the hands of a tiny, exorbitantly rich elite than they are with the challenges of being isolated and surviving at the bottom of a savage neoliberal order. This makes it all the simpler for neoliberalism to convince people to remain attached to a set of ideologies, values, modes of governance, and policies that generate massive suffering and hardships. Neoliberalism's "best trick" is to persuade individuals, as a matter of common sense, that they should "imagine [themselves] as . . . solitary agent[s] who can and must live the good life promised by capitalist culture."[6]

As George Lakoff and Glenn Smith argue, the anti-public philosophy of economic Darwinism makes a parody of democracy by defining freedom as "the liberty to seek one's own interests and well-being, without being responsible for the interests or well-being of anyone else. It's a morality of personal, but not social, responsibility. The only freedom you should have is what you can provide for yourself, not what the Public provides for you to start out."[7] Put simply, we alone become responsible for the problems we confront when we can no longer conceive how larger forces control or constrain our choices and the lives we are destined to lead.

Yet the harsh values and practices of this new social order *are* visible—in the increasing incarceration of young people, the modeling of public schools after prisons, state violence waged against peaceful student protesters, and state policies that bail out investment bankers but leave the middle and working classes in a state of poverty, despair, and insecurity. Such values are also evident in the Republican Party's social Darwinist budget plans that reward the rich and cut aid for those who need it the most. For instance, the 2012 Romney/Ryan budget plan "proposed to cut the taxes of households earning over $1 million by an average of $295,874 a year,"[8] at a cruel cost to those most disadvantaged populations who rely on social programs. In order to pay for tax reductions to benefit the rich, the Romney/Ryan budget would have cut funds for food stamps, Pell grants, health care benefits, unemployment insurance, veterans' benefits, and other crucial social programs.[9] As Paul Krugman has argued, the Ryan budget

> isn't just looking for ways to save money [it's] also trying to make life harder for the poor—for their own good. In March [2012], explaining his cuts in aid for the unfortunate, [Ryan] declared, "We don't want to turn the safety net into a hammock that lulls able-bodied people into lives of dependency and complacency, that drains them of their will and their incentive to make the most of their lives."[10]

Krugman rightly replies, "I doubt that Americans forced to rely on unemployment benefits and food stamps in a depressed economy feel that they're living in a comfortable hammock."[11] An extremist version of neoliberalism, Ryanomics is especially vicious toward US children, 16.1 million of whom currently live in poverty.[12] Marian Wright Edelman captures the harshness and savagery of the Ryan budget passed by the House of Representatives before being voted down in the Senate. She writes:

Ryanomics is an all out assault on our poorest children while asking not a dime of sacrifice from the richest 2 percent of Americans or from wealthy corporations. Ryanomics slashes hundreds of billions of dollars from child and family nutrition, health, child care, education, and child protection services, *in order* to extend and add to the massive Bush tax cuts for millionaires and billionaires at a taxpayer cost of $5 trillion over 10 years. On top of making the Bush tax cuts permanent, the top income bracket would get an additional 10 percent tax cut. Millionaires and billionaires would on average keep at least an additional quarter of a million dollars each year and possibly as much as $400,000 a year according to the Citizens for Tax Justice.[13]

As profits soar for corporations and the upper 1 percent, both political parties are imposing austerity measures that punish the poor and cut vital services for those who need them the most.[14] Rather than raising taxes and closing tax loopholes for the wealthy and corporations, the Republican Party would rather impose painful spending cuts that will impact the poor and vital social services. For example, the 2013 budget cuts produced by sequestration slash $20 million from the Maternal, Infant, and Early Child Home Visiting Program, $199 million from public housing, $6 million from emergency food and shelter, $19 million from housing for the elderly, $116 million from higher education, and $96 million from homeless assistance grants—and these are only a small portion of the devastating cuts enacted.[15] Seventy thousand children will be kicked off of Head Start, ten thousand teachers will be fired, and "the long-term unemployed will see their benefits cut by about 10 percent."[16] Under the right-wing insistence on a politics of austerity, Americans are witnessing not only widespread cuts in vital infrastructures, education, and social protections but also the emergence of policies produced in the spirit of revenge aimed at the poor, the elderly, and others marginalized by race and class. As Robert Reich, Charles Ferguson, and a host of recent commentators have noted, this extreme concentration of power in every commanding institution of society promotes predatory practices and rewards sociopathic behavior. Such a system creates an authoritarian class of corporate and hedge-fund swindlers that reaps its own profits by

placing big bets with other people's money. The winners in this system are top Wall Street executives and traders, private-equity managers and hedge-fund moguls, and the losers are most of the rest of us. The system is largely responsible for the greatest concentration of the nation's income and wealth at the very top since the Gilded Age of the nineteenth century, with the richest 400 Americans owning as much as the bottom 150 million put together. And these multimillionaires and billionaires are now actively buying . . . election[s]—and with [them], American democracy.[17]

Unfortunately, the US public has largely remained silent, if not also complicit in the rise of a neoliberal version of authoritarianism. While workers in Wisconsin, striking teachers in Chicago, and young people across the globe have challenged this politics and machinery of corruption, war, brutality, and social and civil death, they represent a small and marginalized part of the larger movement that will be necessary to initiate massive collective resistance to the aggressive violence being waged against all those public spheres that further the promise of democracy in the United States, the United Kingdom, France, and a host of other countries. The actions of teachers, workers, student protesters, and others have been crucial in drawing public attention to the constellation of forces that are pushing the United States and other neoliberal-driven countries into what Hannah Arendt called "dark times" or what might be described as an increasingly authoritarian public realm that constitutes a clear and present danger to democracy. The questions now being asked must be seen as the first step toward exposing the dire social and political costs of concentrating wealth, income, and power into the hands of the upper 1 percent. What role higher education will play in both educating and mobilizing students is a crucial issue that will determine whether a new revolutionary ideal can take hold in order to address the ideals of democracy and its future.

Neoliberal Ideology and the Rhetoric of Freedom

In addition to amassing ever-expanding amounts of material wealth, the rich now control the means of schooling and other cultural apparatuses in the United States. They have disinvested in critical education while reproducing notions of "common sense" that incessantly replicate the basic values, ideas, and relations necessary to sustain the institutions of economic Darwinism. Both major political parties, along with plutocrat "reformers," support educational reforms that increase conceptual and cultural illiteracy.

Critical learning has been replaced with mastering test-taking, memorizing facts, and learning how *not* to question knowledge or authority. Pedagogies that unsettle common sense, make power accountable, and connect class-room knowledge to larger civic issues have become dangerous at all levels of schooling. This method of rote pedagogy, heavily enforced by mainstream educational reformists, is, as Zygmunt Bauman notes, "the most effective prescription for grinding communication to a halt and for [robbing] it of the presumption and expectation of meaningfulness and sense."[18] These rad-ical reformers are also attempting to restructure how higher education is or-ganized. In doing so, they are putting in place modes of governance that mimic corporate structures by increasing the power of administrators at the expense of faculty, reducing faculty to a mostly temporary and low-wage workforce, and reducing students to customers—ripe for being trained for low-skilled jobs and at-risk for incurring large student loans.

This pedagogy of market-driven illiteracy has eviscerated the notion of freedom, turning it largely into the desire to consume and invest ex-clusively in relationships that serve only one's individual interests. Losing one's individuality is now tantamount to losing one's ability to consume. Citizens are treated by the political and economic elite as restless children and are "invited daily to convert the practice of citizenship into the art of shopping."[19] Shallow consumerism coupled with an indifference to the needs and suffering of others has produced a politics of disengage-ment and a culture of moral irresponsibility. At the same time, the eco-nomically Darwinian ethos that places individual interest at the center of everyday life undercuts, if not removes, moral considerations about what we know and how we act from larger social costs and moral con-siderations. In media discourse, language has been stripped of the terms, phrases, and ideas that embrace a concern for the other. With meaning utterly privatized, words are reduced to signifiers that mimic spectacles of violence, designed to provide entertainment rather than thoughtful analysis. Sentiments circulating in the dominant culture parade either idiocy or a survival-of-the-fittest ethic, while anti-public rhetoric strips society of the knowledge and values necessary for the development of a democratically engaged and socially responsible public.

In such circumstances, freedom has truly morphed into its opposite. Neoliberal ideology has construed as pathological any notion that in a healthy society people depend on one another in multiple, complex, direct, and indirect ways. As Lewis Lapham observes, "Citizens are no longer held in thoughtful regard . . . just as thinking and acting are removed from acts of public conscience."[20] Economic Darwinism has produced a legitimating ideology in which the conditions for critical inquiry, moral responsibility, and social and economic justice disappear. The result is that neoliberal ideology increasingly resembles a call to war that turns the principles of democracy against democracy itself. Americans now live in an atomized and pulverized society, "spattered with the debris of broken interhuman bonds,"[21] in which "democracy becomes a perishable commodity"[22] and all things public are viewed with disdain.

Neoliberal Governance

At the level of governance, neoliberalism has increasingly turned mainstream politics into a tawdry form of money-laundering in which the spaces and registers that circulate power are controlled by those who have amassed large amounts of capital. Elections, like mainstream politicians, are now bought and sold to the highest bidder. In the Senate and House of Representatives, 47 percent are millionaires—the "estimated median net worth of a current US senator stood at an average of $2.56 million while the median net worth of members of Congress is $913,000."[23] Elected representatives no longer even purport to do the bidding of the people who elect them. Rather, they are now largely influenced by the demands of lobbyists, who have enormous clout in promoting the interests of the elite, financial services sector, and megacorporations. In 2012, there were just over fourteen thousand registered lobbyists in Washington, DC, which amounts to approximately twenty-three lobbyists for every member of Congress. Although the number of lobbyists has steadily increased by about 20 percent since 1998, the Center for Responsive Politics found that "total spending on lobbying the federal government has almost tripled since 1998, to $3.3 billion."[24] As Bill Moyers and Bernard Weisberger succinctly put it, "A radical minority of the superrich has gained ascendency over politics, buying the policies, laws, tax breaks, subsidies, and rules that consolidate a permanent state of vast inequality by which they can further help themselves to America's wealth and resources."[25] How else to explain that the 2013 bill designed to regulate the banking and financial sectors was drafted for legislators by Citigroup lobbyists?[26] There is more at stake here than legalized corruption, there is the arrogant dismantling of democracy and the production of policies that extend rather than mitigate human suffering, violence, misery, and everyday hardships. Democratic governance has been replaced by the sovereignty of the market, paving the way for modes of governance intent on transforming democratic citizens into entrepreneurial agents. The language of the market and business culture have now almost entirely supplanted any celebration of the public good or the calls to enhance civil society characteristic of past generations. Moreover, authoritarian governance now creeps into every institution and aspect of public life. Instead of celebrating Martin Luther King for his stands against poverty, militarization, and racism, US society holds him up as an icon denuded of any message of solidarity and social struggle. This erasure and depoliticization of history and politics is matched by the celebration of a business culture in which the US public transforms Bill Gates into a national hero. At the same time, civil rights heroine Rosa Parks cedes her position to the Kardashian sisters, as the prominence of civic culture is canceled out by herd-like public enthusiasm for celebrity culture, reality TV, and the hyper-violence of extreme sports. The older heroes sacrificed in order to alleviate the suffering of others, while the new heroes drawn from corporate and celebrity culture live off the suffering of others.

Clearly, US society is awash in a neoliberal culture of idiocy and illiteracy. It produces many subjects who are indifferent to others and are thus incapable of seeing that when the logic of extreme individualism is extended into the far reaches of the national security state, it serves to legitimate the breakdown of the social bonds necessary for a democratic society and reinforces a culture of cruelty that upholds solitary confinement as a mode of punishment for thousands of incarcerated young people and adults.[27] Is it any wonder that with the breakdown of critical education and the cultural apparatuses that support it, the American public now overwhelmingly supports state torture and capital punishment while decrying the necessity of a national health care system? Fortunately, there are signs of rebellion among workers, young people, students, and teachers, indicating that the US public has not been entirely colonized by the bankers, hedge fund managers, and other apostles of neoliberalism.

For example, in Connecticut, opponents of public-school privatization replaced three right-wing, pro-charter school board members. In Chicago, reform efforts prevented the city from outsourcing the lease of Midway Airport and breast cancer screening for uninsured women. And, in Iowa, as a result of pressure from progressives, the governor rejected corporate bids to purchase Iowa's statewide fiber-optics network.

Neoliberal governance has produced an economy and a political system almost entirely controlled by the rich and powerful—what a Citigroup report called a "plutonomy," an economy powered by the wealthy.[28] I have referred to these plutocrats as "the new zombies": they are parasites that suck the resources out of the planet and the rest of us in order to strengthen their grasp on political and economic power and fuel their exorbitant lifestyles.[29] Power is now global, gated, and driven by a savage disregard for human welfare, while politics resides largely in older institutions of modernity such as nation states. The new plutocrats have no allegiance to national communities, justice, or human rights, just potential markets and profits. The work of citizenship has been set back decades by this new group of winner-take-all global predators.[30] Policies are now enacted that provide massive tax cuts to the rich and generous subsidies to banks and corporations—alongside massive disinvestments in job creation programs, the building of critical infrastructures, and the development of crucial social programs ranging from health care to school meal programs for disadvantaged children.

Neoliberalism's massive disinvestment in schools, social programs, and an aging infrastructure is not about a lack of money. The real problem stems from government priorities that inform both how the money is collected and how it is spent.[31] More than 60 percent of the federal budget goes to military spending, while only 6 percent is allocated toward education. The United States spends more than $92 billion on corporate subsidies and only $59 billion on social welfare programs.[32] John Cavanagh has estimated that if there were a tiny tax imposed on Wall Street stock and derivatives transactions, the government could raise $150 billion annually.[33] In addition, if the tax code were adjusted in a fair manner to tax the wealthy, another $79 billion could be raised. Finally, Cavanagh notes that $100 billion in tax income is lost annually through tax haven abuse; proper regulation would make it costly for corporations to declare "their profits in overseas tax havens like the Cayman Islands."[34]

At the same time, the financialization of the economy and culture has resulted in the poisonous growth of monopoly power, predatory lending, abusive credit card practices, and misuses of CEO pay. The false but central neoliberal tenet that markets can solve all of society's problems grants unchecked power to money and has given rise to "a politics in which policies that favor the rich … have allowed the financial sector to amass vast economic and political power."[35] As Joseph Stiglitz points out, there is more at work in this form of governance than a pandering to the wealthy and powerful: there is also the specter of an authoritarian society "where people live in gated communities," large segments of the population are impoverished or locked up in prison, and Americans live in a state of constant fear as they face growing "economic insecurity, healthcare insecurity, [and] a sense of physical insecurity."[36] In other words, the authoritarian nature of neoliberal political governance and economic power is also visible in the rise of a national security state in which civil liberties are being drastically abridged and violated.

As the war on terror becomes a normalized state of existence, the most basic rights available to American citizens are being shredded. The spirit of revenge, militarization, and fear now permeates the discourse of national security. For instance, under Presidents Bush and Obama, the idea of habeas corpus, with its guarantee that prisoners have minimal rights, has given way to policies of indefinite detention, abductions, targeted assassinations, drone killings, and an expanding state surveillance apparatus. The Obama administration has designated forty-six inmates for indefinite detention at Guantánamo because, according to the government, they can be neither tried nor safely released. Moreover, another "167 men now confined at Guantanamo . . . have been cleared for release yet remain at the facility."[37]

With the passing of the National Defense Authorization Act in 2012, the rule of legal illegalities has been extended to threaten the lives and rights of US citizens. The law authorizes military detention of individuals who are suspected of belonging not only to terrorist groups such as al-Qaida but also to "associated forces." As Glenn Greenwald illuminates, this "grants the president the power to indefinitely detain in military custody not only accused terrorists, but also their supporters, all without charges or trial."[38] The vagueness of the law allows the possibility of subjecting to indefinite detention US citizens who are considered to be in violation of the law. Of course, that might include journalists, writers, intellectuals, and anyone else who might be accused because of their dealings with alleged terrorists. Fortunately, US district judge Katherine Forrest of New York agreed with Chris Hedges, Noam Chomsky, and other writers who have challenged the legality of the law. Judge Forrest recently acknowledged the unconstitutionality of the law and ruled in favor of a preliminary barring of the enforcement of the National Defense Authorization Act.[39] Unfortunately, on July 17, 2013, an appeals court in New York ruled in favor of the Obama administration, allowing the government to detain indefinitely without due process persons designated as enemy combatants.

The antidemocratic practices at work in the Obama administration also include the US government's use of state secrecy to provide a cover for practices that range from the illegal use of torture and the abduction of innocent foreign nationals to the National Security Association's use of a massive surveillance campaign to monitor the phone calls, e-mails, and Internet activity of all Americans. A shadow mass surveillance state has emerged that eschews transparency and commits unlawful acts under the rubric of national security. Given the power of the government to engage in a range of illegalities and to make them disappear through an appeal to state secrecy, it should come as no surprise that warrantless wiretapping, justified in the name of national security, is on the rise at both the federal and state levels. For instance, the New York City Police Department "implemented surveillance programs that violate the civil liberties of that city's Muslim-American citizens [by infiltrating] mosques and universities [and] collecting information on individuals suspected of no crimes."[40] The US public barely acknowledged this shocking abuse of power. Such antidemocratic policies and practices have become the new norm in US society and reveal a frightening and dangerous move toward a twenty-first-century version of authoritarianism.

Neoliberalism as the New Lingua Franca of Cruelty

The harsh realities of a society defined by the imperatives of punishment, cruelty, militarism, secrecy, and exclusion can also be seen in a growing rhetoric of insult, humiliation, and slander. Teachers are referred to as "welfare queens" by right-wing pundits; conservative radio host Rush Limbaugh claimed that Michael J. Fox was "faking" the symptoms of Parkinson's disease when he appeared in a political ad for Democrat Claire McCaskill; and the public is routinely treated to racist comments, slurs, and insults about Barack Obama by a host of shock jocks, politicians, and even a federal judge.[41] Poverty is seen not as a social problem but as a personal failing, and poor people have become the objects of abuse, fear, and loathing. The poor, as right-wing ideologues never fail to remind us, are lazy—and, for that matter, how could they truly be poor if they own TVs and cell phones? Cruel, racist insults and the discourse of humiliation are now packaged in a mindless rhetoric as unapologetic as it is ruthless—this has become the new lingua franca of public exchange.

Republican presidential candidate Mitt Romney echoed the harshness of the new lingua franca of cruelty when asked during the 2012 campaign about the government's responsibility to the 50 million Americans who don't have health insurance. Incredibly, Romney replied that they already have access to health care because they can go to hospital emergency rooms.[42] In response, a *New York Times* editorial stated that emergency room care "is the most expensive and least effective way of providing care" and such a remark "reeks of contempt for those left behind by the current insurance system, suggesting that they must suffer with illness until the point where they need an ambulance."[43] Indifferent to the health care needs of the poor and middle class, Romney also conveniently ignores the fact that, as indicated in a Harvard University study, "more than 62% of all personal bankruptcies are caused by the cost of overwhelming medical expenses."[44] The new lingua franca of cruelty and its politics of disposability are on full display here. To paraphrase Hannah Arendt, we live in a time when revenge has become the cure-all for most of our social and economic ills.

Neoliberalism and the Retreat from Ethical Considerations

Not only does neoliberal rationality believe in the ability of markets to solve all problems, it also removes economics and markets from ethical considerations. Economic growth, rather than social needs, drives politics. Long-term investments are replaced by short-term gains and profits, while compassion is viewed as a weakness and democratic public values are derided. As Stanley Aronowitz points out, public values and collective action have given way to the "absurd notion the market should rule every human activity," including the "absurd neoliberal idea that users should pay for every public good from parks and beaches to highways [and] higher education."[45] The hard work of critical analysis, moral judgments, and social responsibility have given way to the desire for accumulating profits at almost any cost, short of unmistakably breaking the law and risking a jail term (which seems unlikely for Wall Street criminals). Gordon Gekko's "Greed is good" speech in the film *Wall Street* has been revived as a rallying cry for the entire financial services industry, rather than seen as a critique of excess. With society overtaken by the morality of self-interest, profit-seeking weaves its way into every possible space, relationship, and institution. For example, the search for high-end profits has descended upon the educational sector with a vengeance, as private bankers, hedge fund elites, and an assortment of billionaires are investing in for-profit and charter schools while advocating policies that disinvest in public education. At the same time the biotech, pharmaceutical, and defense industries and a range of other corporations are investing in universities to rake in profits while influencing everything from how such institutions are governed and define their mission to what they teach and how they treat faculty members and students. Increasingly, universities are losing their power not only to produce critical and civically engaged students but also to offer the type of education that enables them to refute the neoliberal utopian notion that paradise amounts to a world of voracity and avarice without restrictions, governed by a financial elite who exercise authority without accountability or challenge. Literacy, public service, human rights, and morality in this neoliberal notion of education become damaged concepts, stripped of any sense of reason, responsibility, or obligation to a just society.

In this way, neoliberalism proceeds, in zombie-like fashion, to impose its values, social relations, and forms of social death upon all aspects of civic life. This is marked by not only a sustained lack of interest in the public good, a love of inequitious power relations, and a hatred of democracy. There is also the use of brutality, state violence, and humiliation to normalize a neoliberal social order that celebrates massive inequalities in income, wealth, and access to vital services. This is a social Darwinism without apology, a ruthless form of casino capitalism whose advocates have suggested, without irony, that what they do is divinely inspired.[46] Politics has become an extension of war, just as state-sponsored violence increasingly finds legitimation in popular culture and a broader culture of cruelty that promotes an expanding landscape of selfishness, insecurity, and precarity that undermines any sense of shared responsibility for the well-being of others. Too many young people today learn quickly that their fate is solely a matter of individual responsibility, legitimated through market-driven laws that embrace self-promotion, hypercompetitiveness, and surviving in a society that increasingly reduces social relations to social combat. Young people today are expected to inhabit a set of relations in which the only obligation is to live for oneself and to reduce the obligations of citizenship to the demands of a consumer culture.

Gilded Age vengeance has also returned in the form of scorn for those who are either failed consumers or do not live up to the image of the United States as a white Christian nation. Reality TV's overarching theme, echoing Hobbes's "war of all against all," brings home the lesson that punishment is the norm and reward the exception. Unfortunately, it no longer mimics reality, it is the new reality. There is more at work here than a flight from social responsibility. Also lost is the importance of those social bonds, modes of collective reasoning, and public spheres and cultural apparatuses crucial to the construction of the social state and the formation of a sustainable democratic society. Nowhere is the dismantling of the social state and the transformation of the state into a punishing machine more evident than in the recent attacks on youth, labor rights, and higher education being waged by Republican governors in a number of key states such as Michigan, Wisconsin, Florida, and Ohio.

What is often missed in discussions of these attacks is that the war on the social state and the war on education represent part of the same agenda of destruction and violence. The first war is being waged for the complete control by the rich and powerful of all modes of wealth and income while the second war is conducted on the ideological front and represents a battle over the very capacity of young people and others to imagine a different and more critical mode of subjectivity and alternative mode of politics. If the first war is on the diverse and myriad terrain of political economy the second is being waged though what C. Wright Mills once called the major cultural apparatuses, including public and higher education. This is a struggle to shape indentities, desires, and modes of subjectivity in accordance with market values, needs, and relations. Both of these wars register as part of a larger effort to destroy any vestige of a democratic imaginary, and to relegate the value of the ethical responsibility and the social question to the wasteland of political thought. Paul Krugman is on target in arguing that in spite of massive suffering caused by the economic recession—a recession that produced "once-unthinkable levels of economic distress"— there is "growing evidence that our governing elite just doesn't care."[47] Of course, Krugman is not suggesting that if the corporate and financial elite cared the predatory nature of capitalism would be transformed. Rather, he is suggesting that economic Darwinism leaves no room for compassion or ethical considerations, which makes its use of power much worse than more liberal models of a market-based society.

Politics of Disposability and the Attack on Higher Education

The not-so-hidden order of politics underlying the second Gilded Age and its heartless version of economic Darwinism is that some populations, especially those marginalized by class, race, ethnicity, or immigration status, are viewed as excess populations to be removed from the body politic, relegated to sites of terminal containment or exclusion. Marked as disposable, such populations become targets of state surveillance, violence, torture, abduction, and injury. Removed from all vestiges of the social contract, they have become the unmentionables of neoliberalism. For them, surviving— not getting ahead—marks the space in which politics and power converge. The politics of disposability delineates these populations as unworthy of investment or of sharing in the rights, benefits, and protections of a substantive democracy.[48] Pushed into debt, detention centers, and sometimes prison, the alleged human waste of free-market capitalism now inhabits zones of terminal exclusion—zones marked by forms of social and civil death.[49] Particularly disturbing is the lack of opposition among the US public to this view of particular social groups as disposable—this, perhaps more than anything else, signals the presence of a rising authoritarianism in the United States. Left unchecked, economic Darwinism will not only destroy the social fabric and undermine democracy; it will also ensure the marginalization and eventual elimination of those intellectuals willing to fight for public values, rights, spaces, and institutions not wedded to the logic of privatization, commodification, deregulation, militarization, hypermasculinity, and a ruthless "competitive struggle in which only the fittest could survive."[50] This new culture of cruelty and disposability has become the hallmark of neoliberal sovereignty, and it will wreak destruction in ways not yet imaginable—even given the horrific outcomes of the economic and financial crisis brought on by economic Darwinism. All evidence suggests a new reality is unfolding, one characterized by a deeply rooted crisis of education, agency, and social responsibility.

The current assault threatening higher education and the humanities in particular cannot be understood outside of the crisis of economics, politics, and power. Evidence of this new historical conjuncture is clearly seen in the growing number of groups considered disposable, the collapse of public values, the war on youth, and the assault by the ultra-rich and megacorporations on democracy itself. This state of emergency must take as its starting point what Tony Judt has called "the social question," with its emphasis on addressing acute social problems, providing social protections for the disadvantaged, developing public spheres aimed at promoting the collective good, and protecting educational spheres that enable and deepen the knowledge, skills, and modes of agency necessary for a substantive democracy to flourish.[51] What is new about the current threat to higher education and the humanities in particular is the increasing pace of the corporatization and militarization of the university, the squelching of academic freedom, the rise of an ever increasing contingent of part-time faculty, the rise of a bloated manegerial class, and the view that students are basically consumers and faculty providers of a saleable commodity such as a credential or a set of workplace skills. More striking still is the slow death of the university as a center of critique, vital source of civic education, and crucial public good.

Or, to put it more specifically, the consequence of such dramatic transformations is the near-death of the university as a democratic public sphere. Many faculties are now demoralized as they increasingly lose rights and power. Moreover, a weak faculty translates into one governed by fear rather than by shared responsibilities, one that is susceptible to labor-bashing tactics such as increased workloads, the casualization of labor, and the growing suppression of dissent. Demoralization often translates less into moral outrage than into cynicism, accommodation, and a retreat into a sterile form of professionalism. Faculty now find themselves staring into an abyss, unwilling to address the current attacks on the university or befuddled over how the language of specialization and professionalization has cut them off from not only connecting their work to larger civic issues and social problems but also developing any meaningful relationships to a larger democratic polity.

As faculties no longer feel compelled to address important political issues and social problems, they are less inclined to communicate with a larger public, uphold public values, or engage in a type of scholarship accessible to a broader audience.[52] Beholden to corporate interests, career building, and the insular discourses that accompany specialized scholarship, too many academics have become overly comfortable with the corporatization of the university and the new regimes of neoliberal governance. Chasing after grants, promotions, and conventional research outlets, many academics have retreated from larger public debates and refused to address urgent social problems. Assuming the role of the disinterested academic or the clever faculty star on the make, endlessly chasing theory for its own sake, these so-called academic entrepreneurs simply reinforce the public's perception that they have become largely irrelevant. Incapable, if not unwilling, to defend the university as a crucial site for learning how to think critically and act with civic courage, many academics have disappeared into a disciplinary apparatus that views the university not as a place to think but as a place to prepare students to be competitive in the global marketplace.

This is particularly disturbing given the unapologetic turn that higher education has taken in its willingness to mimic corporate culture and ingratiate itself to the national security state.[53] Universities face a growing set of challenges arising from budget cuts, diminishing quality of instruction, the downsizing of faculty, the militarization of research, and the revamping of the curriculum to fit the interests of the market, all of which not only contradicts the culture and democratic value of higher education but also makes a mockery of the very meaning and mission of the university as a place both to think and to provide the formative culture and agents that make a democracy possible. Universities and colleges have been largely abandoned as democratic public spheres dedicated to providing a public service, expanding upon humankind's great intellectual and cultural achievements, and educating future generations to be able to confront the challenges of a global democracy.

Higher education increasingly stands alone, even in its attenuated state, as a public arena where ideas can be debated, critical knowledge produced, and learning linked to important social issues. Those mainstream cultural apparatuses that once offered alternative points of view, challenged authority, and subordinated public values to market interests have largely been hijacked by the consolidation of corporate power. As Ashley Lutz, Bob McChesney, and many others have noted, approximately 90 percent of the media is currently controlled by six corporations.[54] This is a particularly important statistic in a society in which the free circulation of ideas is being replaced by ideologies, values, and modes of thought managed by the dominant media. One consequence is that dissent is increasingly met with state repression, as indicated by the violence inflicted on the Occupy Wall Street protesters, and critical ideas are increasingly viewed or dismissed as banal, if not reactionary. For many ultra-conservatives, reason itself is viewed as dangerous, along with any notion of science that challenges right-wing fundamentalist world views regarding climate change, evolution, and a host of other social issues.[55] As Frank Rich has observed, the war against literacy and informed judgment is made abundantly clear in the populist rage sweeping the country in the form of the Tea Party, a massive collective anger that "is aimed at the educated, not the wealthy."[56] This mode of civic illiteracy is rooted in racism and has prompted a revival of overtly racist language, symbols, and jokes. Confederate flags are a common feature of Tea Party rallies, as are a variety of racially loaded posters, barbs, and derogatory, racist shouting aimed at President Obama.

Democracy can only be sustained through modes of civic literacy that enable individuals to connect private troubles to larger public issues as part of a broader discourse of critical inquiry, dialogue, and engagement. Civic literacy, in this context, provides a citizenry with the skills for critical understanding while enabling them to actually intervene in society. The right-wing war on education must be understood as a form of organized irresponsibility; that is, it represents a high-intensity assault on those cultures of questioning, forms of literacy, and public spheres in which reason and critique merge with social responsibility as a central feature of critical agency and democratization. As the political philosopher Cornelius Castoriadis insists, for democracy to be vital "it needs to create citizens who are critical thinkers capable of putting existing institutions into question so that democracy again becomes . . . a new type of regime in the full sense of the term."[57]

The right-wing war on critical literacy is part of an ongoing attempt to destroy higher education as a democratic public sphere that enables intellectuals to stand firm, take risks, imagine the otherwise, and push against the grain. It is important to insist that as educators we ask, again and again, how higher education can survive in a society in which civic culture and modes of critical literacy collapse as it becomes more and more difficult to distinguish opinion and emotive outbursts from a sustained argument and logical reasoning. Equally important is the need for educators and young people to take on the challenge of defending the university. Toni Morrison gets it right:

> If the university does not take seriously and rigorously its role as a guardian of wider civic freedoms, as interrogator of more and more complex ethical problems, as servant and preserver of deeper democratic practices, then some other regime or ménage of regimes will do it for us, in spite of us, and without us.[58]

Defending the humanities, as Terry Eagleton has recently argued, means more than offering an academic enclave for students to learn history, philosophy, art, and literature. It also means stressing how indispensable these fields of study are for all students if they are to be able to make any claim whatsoever to being critical and engaged individual and social agents. But the humanities do more. They also provide the knowledge, skills, social relations, and modes of pedagogy that constitute a formative culture in which the historical lessons of democratization can be learned, the demands of social responsibility can be thoughtfully engaged, the imagination can be expanded, and critical thought can be affirmed. As an adjunct of the academic-military-industrial complex, however, higher education has nothing to say about teaching students how to think for themselves in a democracy, how to think critically and engage with others, and how to address through the prism of democratic values the relationship between themselves and the larger world. We need a permanent revolution around the meaning and purpose of higher education, one in which academics are more than willing to move beyond the language of critique and a discourse of both moral and political outrage, however necessary to a sustained individual and collective defense of the university as a vital public sphere central to democracy itself.

We must reject the idea that the university should be modeled after "a sterile Darwinian shark tank in which the only thing that matters is the bottom line."[59] We must also reconsider how the university in a post-9/11 era is being militarized and increasingly reduced to an adjunct of the growing national security state. The public has apparently given up on the idea of either funding higher education or valuing it as a public good indispensable to the life of any viable democracy. This is all the more reason for academics to be at the forefront of a coalition of activists, public servants, and others in both rejecting the growing corporate management of higher education and developing a new discourse in which the university, and particularly the humanities, can be defended as a vital social and public institution in a democratic society.

Beyond Neoliberal Miseducation

As universities turn toward corporate management models, they increasingly use and exploit cheap faculty labor. Many colleges and universities are drawing more and more upon adjunct and nontenured faculty, many of whom occupy the status of indentured servants who are overworked, lack benefits, receive little or no administrative support, and are paid salaries that qualify them for food stamps.[60] Students increasingly fare no better in sharing the status of a subaltern class beholden to neoliberal policies and values. For instance, many are buried under huge debt, celebrated by the collection industry because it is cashing in on their misfortune. Jerry Aston, a member of that industry, wrote in a column after witnessing a protest rally by students criticizing their mounting debt that he "couldn't believe the accumulated wealth they represent—for our industry."[61] And, of course, this type of economic injustice is taking place in an economy in which rich plutocrats such as the infamous union-busting Koch brothers each saw "their investments grow by $6 billion in one year, which is three million dollars per hour based on a 40-hour 'work' week."[62] Workers, students, youth, and the poor are all considered expendable in this neoliberal global economy. Yet the one institution, education, that offers the opportunities for students to challenge these antidemocratic tendencies is under attack in ways that are unparalleled, at least in terms of the scope and intensity of the assault by the corporate elite and other economic fundamentalists.

Casino capitalism does more than infuse market values into every aspect of higher education; it also wages a full-fledged assault on the very notion of public goods, democratic public spheres, and the role of education in creating an informed citizenry. When Rick Santorum argued that intellectuals were not wanted in the Republican Party, he was articulating what has become common sense in a society wedded to narrow instrumentalist values and various modes of fundamentalism. Critical thinking and a literate public have become dangerous to those who want to celebrate orthodoxy over dialogue, emotion over reason, and ideological certainty over thoughtfulness.[63] Hannah Arendt's warning that "it was not stupidity but a curious, quite authentic inability to think"[64] at the heart of authoritarian regimes is now embraced as a fundamental tenet of Republican Party politics.

Right-wing appeals to austerity provide the rationale for slash-and-burn policies intended to deprive governmental social and educational programs of the funds needed to enable them to work, if not survive. Along with health care, public transportation, Medicare, food stamp programs for low-income children, and a host of other social protections, higher education is being defunded as part of a larger scheme to dismantle and privatize all public services, goods, and spheres. But there is more at work here than the march toward privatization and the neverending search for profits at any cost; there is also the issue of wasteful spending on a bloated war machine, the refusal to tax fairly the rich and corporations, and the draining of public funds in order to support the US military presence in Iraq, Afghanistan, and elsewhere. The deficit argument and the austerity policies advocated in its name are a form of class warfare designed largely for the state to be able to redirect revenue in support of the commanding institutions of the corporate-military-industrial complex and away from funding higher education and other crucial public services. The extent of the budget reduction assault is such that in 2012 "states reduced their education budgets by $12.7 billion."[65] Of course, the burden of such reductions falls upon poor minority and other low-income students, who will not be able to afford the tuition increases that will compensate for the loss of state funding.

What has become clear in light of such assaults is that many universities and colleges have become unapologetic accomplices to corporate values and power, and in doing so increasingly regard social problems as either irrelevant or invisible.[66] The transformation of higher education both in the United States and abroad is evident in a number of registers. These include decreased support for programs of study that are not business oriented, reduced support for research that does not increase profits, the replacement of shared forms of governance with business management models, the ongoing exploitation of faculty labor, and the use of student purchasing power as the vital measure of a student's identity, worth, and access to higher education.[67]

As I point out throughout this book, one consequence of this ongoing disinvestment in higher education is the expansion of a punishing state that increasingly criminalizes a range of social behaviors, wages war on the poor instead of poverty, militarizes local police forces, harasses poor minority youth, and spends more on prisons than on higher education.[68] The punishing state produces fear and sustains itself on moral panics. Dissent gives way to widespread insecurity, uncertainty, and an obsession with personal safety. Political, moral, and social indifference is the result, in part, of a public that is increasingly constituted within an educational landscape that reduces thinking to a burden and celebrates civic illiteracy as a prerequisite for negotiating a society in which moral disengagement and political corruption go hand in hand.[69] The assault on the university is symptomatic of the deep educational, economic, and political crisis facing the United States. It is but one lens through which to recognize that the future of democracy depends on the educational and ethical standards of the society we inhabit.[70]

This lapse of the US public into a political and moral coma is induced, in part, by an ever-expanding, mass-mediated celebrity culture that trades in hype and sensation. It is also accentuated by a governmental apparatus that sanctions modes of training that undermine any viable notion of critical schooling and public pedagogy. While there is much being written about how unfair the Left is to the Obama administration, what is often forgotten by these liberal critics is that Obama has aligned himself with educational practices and policies as instrumentalist and anti-intellectual as they are politically reactionary, and therein lies one viable reason for not supporting his initiatives and administration.[71] What liberals refuse to entertain is that the Left is correct in attacking Obama for his cowardly retreat from a number of progressive issues and his dastardly undermining of civil liberties. In fact, they do not go far enough in their criticisms. Often even progressives miss that Obama's views on education are utterly reactionary and provide no space for the nurturance of a radically democratic imagination. Hence, while liberals point to some of Obama's progressive policies—often in a New Age discourse that betrays their own supine moralism—they fail to acknowledge that Obama's educational policies do nothing to contest, and are in fact aligned with, his weak-willed compromises and authoritarian policies. In other words, Obama's educational commitments undermine the creation of a formative culture capable of questioning authoritarian ideas, modes of governance, and reactionary policies. The question is not whether Obama's policies are slightly less repugnant than those of his right-wing detractors. On the contrary, it is about how the Left should engage politics in a more robust and democratic way by imagining what it would mean to work collectively and with "slow impatience" for a new political order outside of the current moderate and extreme right-wing politics and the debased, uncritical educational apparatus that supports it.[72]

The Role of Critical Education

One way of challenging the new authoritarianism is to reclaim the relationship between critical education and social change. The question of what kind of subjects and modes of individual and social agency are necessary for a democracy to survive appears more crucial now than ever before, and this is a question that places matters of education, pedagogy, and culture at the center of any understanding of politics. We live at a time when too few Americans appear to have an interest in democracy beyond the every-four-years ritual performance of voting, and even this act fails to attract a robust majority of citizens. The term "democracy" has been emptied of any viable meaning, hijacked by political scoundrels, corporate elites, and the advertising industry. The promise that democracy exhibits as an ongoing struggle for rights, justice, and a future of hope has been degraded into a misplaced desire to shop and to fulfill the pleasure quotient in spectacles of violence, while the language of democracy is misappropriated and deployed as a rationale for racist actions against immigrants, Muslims, and the poor. Of course, while more and more nails are being put into the coffin of democracy, there are flashes of resistance, such as those among workers in Wisconsin, the Occupy Wall Street movement, and the more recent strike by Chicago teachers. Public employees, fast food workers, Walmart employees, disaffected youth, and others are struggling to expose the massive injustices and death-dealing machinations of the 1 percent and the pernicious effects of casino capitalism. But this struggle is just beginning and only time will tell how far it goes.

The time has come not only to redefine the promise of democracy but also to challenge those who have poisoned its meaning. We have already witnessed such a challenge by protest movements both at home and abroad in which the struggle over education has become one of the most powerful fulcrums for redressing the detrimental effects of neoliberalism. What these struggles, particularly by young people, have in common is the attempt to merge the powers of persuasion and critical, civic literacy with the power of social movements to activate and mobilize real change. They are recovering a notion of the social and reclaiming a kind of humanity that should inspire and inform our collective willingness to imagine what a real democracy might look like. Cornelius Castoriadis rightly argues that "people need to be educated for democracy by not only expanding the capacities that enable them to assume public responsibility but also through active participation in the very process of governing."[73]

As the crucial lens through which to create the formative culture in which politics and power can be made visible and held accountable, pedagogy plays a central role. But as Archon Fung notes, criticism is not the only public responsibility of intellectuals, artists, journalists, educators, and others who engage in critical pedagogical practices. "Intellectuals can also join citizens—and sometimes governments—to construct a world that is more just and democratic. One such constructive role is aiding popular movements and organizations in their efforts to advance justice and democracy."[74] In this instance, understanding must be linked to the practice of social responsibility and the willingness to fashion a politics that addresses real problems and enacts concrete solutions. As Heather Gautney points out,

> We need to start thinking seriously about what kind of political system we really want. And we need to start pressing for things that our politicians did NOT discuss at the conventions. Real solutions—like universal education, debt forgiveness, wealth redistribution, and participatory political structures—that would empower us to decide together what's best. Not who's best.[75]

Critical thinking divorced from action is often as sterile as action divorced from critical theory. Given the urgency of the historical moment, we need a politics and a public pedagogy that make knowledge meaningful in order to make it critical and transformative. Or, as Stuart Hall argues, we need to produce modes of analysis and knowledge in which "people can invest something of themselves . . . something that they recognize is of them or speaks to their condition."[76] A notion of higher education as a democratic public sphere is crucial to this project, especially at a time in which the apostles of neoliberalism and other forms of political and religious fundamentalism are ushering in a new age of conformity, cruelty, and disposability. But as public intellectuals, academics can do more.

First, they can write for multiple audiences, expanding public spheres, especially online, to address a range of social issues including, importantly, the relationship between the attack on the social state and the defunding of higher education. In any democratic society, education should be viewed as a right, not an entitlement, and this suggests a re-ordering of state and federal priorities to make that happen. For instance, the military budget could be cut by two-thirds and those funds invested instead in public and higher education. There is nothing utopian about this demand, given the excess of military power in the United States, but addressing this task requires a sustained critique of the militarization of American society and a clear analysis of the damage it has caused both at home and abroad. Brown University's Watson Institute for International Studies, with the efforts of a number of writers such as Andrew

Bacevich, has been doing this for years and offers a treasure trove of information that could be easily accessed and used by public intellectuals in and outside of the academy. A related issue, as Angela Davis, Michelle Alexander, and others have argued, is the need for public intellectuals to become part of a broader social movement aimed at dismantling the prison-industrial complex and the punishing state, which drains billions of dollars in funds to put people in jail when such funds could be used to fund public and higher education or other social supports that may help prevent criminalized behaviors in the first place. The punishing state is a dire threat not only to public and higher education but also, more broadly, to democracy itself. It is the pillar of the authoritarian state, undermining civil liberties, criminalizing a range of social behaviors related to concrete social problems, and intensifying the legacy of Jim Crow against poor people of color. The US public does not need more prisons; it needs more schools.

Second, academics, artists, journalists, and other cultural workers need to connect the rise of subaltern, part-time labor in the university as well as the larger society with the massive inequality in wealth and income that now corrupts every aspect of American politics and society. Precarity has become a weapon both to exploit adjuncts, part-time workers, and temporary laborers and to suppress dissent by keeping them in a state of fear over losing their jobs. Insecure forms of labor increasingly produce "a feeling of passivity born of despair."[77] Multinational corporations have abandoned the social contract and any vestige of supporting the social state. They plunder labor and perpetuate the mechanizations of social death whenever they have the chance to accumulate capital. This issue is not simply about restoring a balance between labor and capital, it is about recognizing a new form of serfdom that kills the spirit as much as it depoliticizes the mind. The new authoritarians do not ride around in tanks; they have private jets, they fund right-wing think tanks, and they lobby for reactionary policies that privatize everything in sight while filling their bank accounts with massive profits. They are the embodiment of a culture of greed, cruelty, and disposability.

Third, academics can fight for the rights of students to get a free education, a formidable and critical education not dominated by corporate values, to have a say in its shaping, and to experience what it means to expand and deepen the practice of freedom and democracy. Young people have been left out of the discourse of democracy. They are the new disposable individuals, a population lacking jobs, a decent education, and any hope of a future better than the one their parents inherited. They are a reminder of how finance capital has abandoned any viable vision of the future, including one that would support future generations. This is a mode of politics and capital that eats its own children and throws their fate to the vagaries of the market. If a society is in part judged by how it views and treats its children, US society by all accounts has truly failed in a colossal way and, in doing so, provides a glimpse of the heartlessness at the core of the new authoritarianism.

Last, public intellectuals should also address and resist the ongoing shift in power relations between faculty and the managerial class. Too many faculty are now removed from the governing structures of higher education and as a result have been abandoned to the misery of impoverished wages, excessive class loads, no health care, and few, if any, social benefits. This is shameful and is not merely an issue of the education system but a deeply political matter, one that must address how neoliberal ideology and policy have imposed on higher education an antidemocratic governing structure that mimics the broader authoritarian forces now threatening the United States.[78]

I want to conclude by quoting from James Baldwin, a courageous writer who refused to let the hope of democracy die in his lifetime, and who offered that mix of politics, passion, and courage that deserves not just admiration but emulation. His sense of rage was grounded in a working-class sensibility, eloquence, and heart that illuminate a higher standard for what it means to be a public and an engaged intellectual. His words capture something that is missing from the US cultural and political landscape, something affirmative that needs to be seized upon, rethought, and occupied by intellectuals, academics, artists, and other concerned citizens—as part of both the fight against the new authoritarianism and its cynical, dangerous, and cruel practices, and the struggle to reclaim a belief in justice and mutuality that seems to be dying in all of us. In *The Fire Next Time*, Baldwin writes:

> One must say Yes to life, and embrace it wherever it is found—and it is found in terrible places. . . . For nothing is fixed, forever and forever,

it is not fixed; the earth is always shifting, the light is always changing, the sea does not cease to grind down rock. Generations do not cease to be born, and we are responsible to them because we are the only witnesses they have. The sea rises, the light fails, lovers cling to each other, and children cling to us. The moment we cease to hold each other, the moment we break faith with one another, the sea engulfs us and the light goes out.

CHAPTER ONE

Dystopian Education in a Neoliberal Society

I n the United States and abroad, public and higher education is under assault by a host of religious, economic, ideological, and political fundamentalists. As regards public schools, the most serious attack is being waged by religious conservatives and advocates of neoliberalism whose reform efforts focus narrowly on high-stakes testing, skill-based teaching, traditional curriculum, and memorization drills.[1] Ideologically, the pedagogical emphasis is the antithesis of a critical approach to teaching and learning, emphasizing a pedagogy of conformity and a curriculum marked by a vulgar "vocationalist instrumentality."[2] At the level of policy, the assault is driven by an aggressive attempt to disinvest in public schools, replace them with charter schools, and remove state and federal governments completely from public education in order to allow education to be organized and administered by a variety of privatizing, market-driven forces and for-profit corporations.[3] In this instance, public schools are defined through practices of repression, removed from any larger notion of the public good, reduced to "simply another corporate asset bundled in credit default swaps," valuable solely for their rate of exchange and trade value on the open market.[4] Clearly, public education should not be harnessed to the script of cost-benefit analyses, the national security state, or the needs of corporations, which often leads to the loss of egalitarian and democratic values, ideals, and responsibilities.

At the same time, a full-fledged assault is also being waged on higher education in North America, the United Kingdom, and various European countries. While the nature of the assault varies across countries, there is a common set of assumptions and practices driving the transformations of higher education into an adjunct of corporate power and values. The effects of the assault are not hard to discern. Universities are being defunded, tuition fees are skyrocketing, faculty salaries are shrinking as workloads are increasing, and faculty are being reduced to a subaltern class of migrant laborers. Corporate management schemes are being put in place, "underpinned by market-like principles, based on metrics, control, and display of performance."[5] The latter is reinforcing an audit culture that mimics the organizational structures of a market economy. In addition, class sizes are ballooning, curriculum is stripped of liberal values, research is largely assessed for its ability to produce profits, administrative staffs are being cut back, governance has been handed over to paragons of corporate culture, and valuable services are being either outsourced or curtailed.

The neoliberal paradigm driving these attacks on public and higher education abhors democracy and views public and higher education as a toxic civic sphere that poses a threat to corporate values, power, and ideology. As democratic public spheres, colleges and universities are allegedly dedicated to teaching students to think critically, take imaginative risks, learn how to be moral witnesses, and procure the skills that enable one to connect to others in ways that strengthen the democratic polity, and this is precisely why they are under attack by the concentrated forces of neoliberalism.[6] Self-confident citizens are regarded as abhorrent by conservatives and evangelical fundamentalists who, traumatized by the campus turmoil of the sixties, largely view dissent, if not critical thought itself, as a dire threat to corporate power and religious authority.[7] Similarly, critical thought, knowledge, dialogue, and dissent are increasingly perceived with suspicion by the new corporate university that now defines faculty as entrepreneurs, students as customers, and education as a mode of training.[8]

Welcome to the dystopian world of corporate education, in which learning how to think, appropriate public values, and become an engaged critical citizen is viewed as a failure rather than a success. Instead of producing "a generation of leaders worthy of the challenges,"[9] the dystopian mission of public and higher education is to produce robots, technocrats, and trained workers. There is more than a backlash at work in these assaults on public and higher education; there is a sustained effort to dismantle education from the discourse of democracy, public values, critical thought, social responsibility, and civic courage. Put more bluntly, the dystopian shadow that has fallen on public and higher education reveals the coming darkness of a counterrevolution that is putting into place a mode of corporate sovereignty constituting a new, updated form of authoritarianism. During the Cold War, US officials never let us forget that authoritarian countries put their intellectuals into prison. While such practices do not prevail in the United States or other capitalist democracies, the fate of critical intellectuals today is no better, since they are either fired or denied tenure for being too critical, or relegated to an intolerable state of dire poverty and existential impoverishment in part-time appointments that pay low wages.[10]

Education within the last three decades has been removed from its utopian possibilities of educating young people to be reflective, critical, and socially engaged agents. The post-WWII Keynesian period up to the civil rights movement and the campus uprisings in the 1960s witnessed an ongoing expansion of public and higher education as democratic public spheres. Democratic ideals were never far from the realms of public and higher education, though they often lacked full support of both the public and the university administration. While not all educators willingly addressed matters of equity, inclusion, racism, and the role of education as a public good, such issues never disappeared from public view. Under neoliberal regimes, however diverse, the notion of public and higher education, as well as the larger notion of education as the primary register of the greater culture, are viewed as too dangerous by the apostles of free-market capitalism. Critical thought and the imaginings of a better world present a direct threat to a neoliberal paradigm in which the future replicates the present in an endless circle, with capital and the identities that legitimate it merging with each other into what might be called the dead zone of casino capitalism. This dystopian impulse thrives on producing myriad forms of violence embracing the symbolic and the structural as part of a broader attempt to define education in purely instrumental and anti-intellectual terms. It is this replacement of educated hope with an aggressive dystopian project in particular that characterizes the current assault on higher education in various parts of the globe extending from the United States and the United Kingdom to Greece and Spain.

In light of this dystopian attempt to remove education from any notion of critique, dialogue, and empowerment, it would be an understatement to suggest that there is something very wrong with US public and higher education. For a start, this counterrevolution is giving rise to punitive evaluation schemes, harsh disciplinary measures, and the ongoing deskilling of many teachers that together are reducing many excellent educators to the debased status of technicians and security personnel. Additionally, as more and more wealth is distributed to the richest Americans and corporations, states are drained of resources and are shifting the burden of their deficits onto public schools and other vital public services. With 40 percent of wealth going to the top 1 percent, public services are drying up from lack of revenue, and more and more young people find themselves locked out of the dream of getting a decent education or a job, robbed of any hope for the future.[11]

While the nation's schools and infrastructure suffer from a lack of resources, right-wing politicians are enacting policies that lower the taxes of the rich and megacorporations. For the elite, taxes are seen as constituting a form of class warfare waged by the state against the rich, who view the collection of taxes as a form of state coercion. What is ironic in this argument is the startling fact that not only are the rich not taxed fairly but they also receive billions in corporate subsidies. But there is more at stake here than untaxed wealth and revenue; there is also the fact that wealth corrupts and buys power. And this poisonous mix of wealth, politics, and power translates into an array of antidemocratic practices that have created an unhealthy society in every major index ranging from infant mortality rates to a dysfunctional political system.[12]

Hidden in this hollow outrage by the wealthy is the belief that the real enemy is any form of government that needs to raise revenue in order to build and maintain infrastructures, provide basic services for those who need them, and develop investments such as a transportation system and schools that are not tied to the logic of the market. One consequence of this vile form of actual class warfare is a battle over crucial resources, a battle that has dire political and educational consequences especially for the poor and middle classes, if not democracy itself. This battle in the United States is particularly fierce over the issue of taxes. As David Theo Goldberg points out, neoliberal ideology makes clear—as part of its project of hollowing out public institutions—that "paying taxes has devolved from a central social responsibility to a game of creative work-arounds. Today, taxes are not so much the common contribution to cover the costs of social benefits and infrastructure relative to one's means, as they are a burden to be avoided."[13]

Money no longer simply controls elections; it also controls policies that shape public education, if not practically all other social, cultural, and economic institutions.[14] One indicator of such corruption is that hedge fund managers now sit on school boards across the country, doing everything in their power to eliminate public schools and punish union-ized teachers who do not support charter schools. In New Jersey hundreds of teachers have been sacked because of alleged budget deficits. Not only is Governor Christie using the deficit argument to fire teachers, he also uses it to break unions and balance the budget on the backs of students and teachers. How else to explain Christie's refusal to endorse reinstitut-ing the "millionaires' taxes," or his craven support for lowering taxes on the top twenty-five hedge fund officers in New Jersey, who in 2009 raked in $25 billion, enough to fund 658,000 entry-level teachers?[15]

In this conservative right-wing reform culture, the role of public and higher education, if we are to believe the Heritage Foundation and bil-lionaires such as Bill Gates, is to produce students who laud conformity, believe job training is more important than education, and view public values as irrelevant. While Gates, former DC education chancellor Michelle Rhee, and secretary of education Arne Duncan would argue they are the true education reformers, the fact of the matter is that education in their view is tied to job training, quantitative measurements, and the development of curricula to prepare students for particular occupations. Teaching to the test, undercutting the power of teachers, and removing subjects such as art, literature, music, and critical thinking from the school curriculum are at the core of their conservative vision for reform. More-over, their relentless attempts to turn public schools into charter schools are in direct opposition to their claims that their policies serve the public good and empower young people, especially poor minorities. Students in this corporate-driven world view are no longer educated for democratic citizenship. On the contrary, they are being trained to fulfill the need for human capital.[16] At the same time, this emphasis on defining schools through an audit culture and various accountability regimes conveniently allows the financial elite to ignore those forces that affect schools such as poverty, unemployment, poor health care, inequality, and other important social and economic forces. Removing matters of equity from issues of excellence and learning also makes it easier for right-wing foundations and conservative foundations to blame teachers and unions for the failure of schools, making it all the easier to turn public schools, universities, and colleges over to for-profit forces.

What is lost in this approach to schooling is what Noam Chomsky describes as "creating creative and independent thought and inquiry, challenging perceived beliefs, exploring new horizons and forgetting external constraints."[17] At the same time, public schools and colleges are under assault not because they are failing (though some are) but because they are one of the few public spheres left where people can learn the knowledge and skills necessary to allow them to think critically and hold power and authority accountable. It is worth repeating that not only are the lines between the corporate world and public and higher education blurring, but all modes of education (except for the elite) are being reduced to what Peter Seybold calls a "corporate service station," in which the democratic ideals at the heart of public and higher education are up for sale.[18] At the heart of this crisis of education are larger questions about the formative culture necessary for a democracy to survive, the nature of civic education and teaching in dark times, the role of educators as civic intellectuals, and what it means to understand the purpose and meaning of education as a site of individual and collective empowerment.

This current right-wing emphasis on low-level skills distracts the US public from examining the broader economic, political, and cultural forces that bear down on schools. Matters concerning the influence on schools of corporations, textbook publishers, commercial industries, and the national security state are rendered invisible, as if schools and the practices they promote exist in a bubble. At work here is a dystopian pedagogy that displaces, infantilizes, and depoliticizes both students and large segments of the US public. Under the current regime of neoliberalism, schools have been transformed into a private right rather than a public good. Students are being educated to become consumers rather than thoughtful, critical citizens. Increasingly, as public schools are put in the hands of for-profit corporations, hedge fund elites, and other market-driven sources, their value is derived from their ability to turn a profit and produce compliant students eager to join the workforce.[19]

What is truly scandalous about the current dismantling of and disinvestment in public schooling is that those who advocate such changes are called the new education reformers. They are not reformers at all. They are reactionaries and financial mercenaries, and resemble dystopian zombies in spewing toxic educational gore. In their wake, teaching is turned into the practice of conformity, and curricula are driven by an anti-intellectual obsession with student test scores. In addition, students are educated to be active consumers and compliant subjects, increasingly unable to think critically about themselves and their relationship to the larger world. This virus of repression, conformity, and instrumentalism is turning public and higher education into a repressive site of containment, devoid of poetry, critical learning, or soaring acts of curiosity and imagination. As Diane Ravitch sums it up, what is driving the current public school reform movement is a profoundly anti-intellectual project that promotes "more testing, more privately managed schools, more deregulation, more firing of teachers, [and] more school closings."[20]

At the level of higher education, the script is similar with a project designed to defund higher education, impose corporate models of governance, purge the university of critical thinkers, turn faculty into a low-wage army of part-time workers, and allow corporate money and power to increasingly decide course content and determine what faculty get hired. As public values are replaced by corporate values, students become clients, faculty are deskilled and depoliticized, tuition rises, and more and more working-class and poor minority students are excluded from the benefits of higher education. There are no powerful and profound intellectual dramas in this view of schooling, just the noisy and demonstative rush to make schools another source of profit for finance capital with its growing legion of bankers, billionaires, and hedge fund scoundrels.

Public schooling and higher education are also increasingly harnessed to the needs of corporations and the warfare state. One consequence is that many public schools, especially those occupied by poor minority youth, have become the equivalent of factories for dumbing down the curricula and turning teachers into what amounts to machine parts. At the same time, such schools have become increasingly militarized and provide a direct route for many youth into the prison-industrial complex via the "school-to-prison pipeline."[21] What is buried under the educational-reform rhetoric of hedge fund and casino capitalism is the ideal of offering public school students a civic education that provides the capacities, knowledge, and skills that enable students to speak, write, and act from a position of agency and empowerment. At the college level, students are dazzled with a blitz of spaces that now look like malls, while in between classes they are endlessly entertained by a mammoth sports culture that is often as debasing as it is dangerous in its hypermasculinity, racism, and overt sexism.[22]

Privatization, commodification, militarization, and deregulation are the new guiding categories through which schools, teachers, pedagogy, and students are defined. The current assaults on public and higher education are not new, but they are more vile and more powerful than in the past. Crucial to any viable resistance is the need to understand the historical context in which education has been transformed into an adjunct of corporate power as well as the ways in which the current right-wing reform operates within a broader play of forces that bear down in antidemocratic ways on the purpose of schooling and the practice of teaching itself. Making power visible is important but only a first step in understanding how it works and how it might be challenged. But recognizing such a challenge is not the same thing as overcoming it. Part of this task necessitates that educators anchor their own work in classrooms, however diverse, in projects that engage the promise of an unrealized democracy against its existing, often repressive forms. And this is only a first step.

Public and higher education, along with the pedagogical role of the larger culture, should be viewed as crucial to any viable notion of democracy, while the pedagogical practices they employ should be consistent with the ideal of the good society. This means teaching more than the knowledge of traditional canons. In fact, teachers and students need to recognize that as a moral and political practice pedagogy is about the struggle over identity just as much as it is a struggle over what counts as knowledge. At a time when censorship is running amok in public schools and dissent is viewed as a distraction or unpatriotic, the debate over whether we should view schools as political institutions seems not only moot but irrelevant. Pedagogy is a mode of critical intervention, one that endows teachers with a responsibility to prepare students not merely for jobs but for being in the world in ways that allow them to influence the larger political, ideological, and economic forces that bear down on their lives. Schooling is an eminently political and moral practice because it is directive of and also actively legitimates what counts as knowledge, sanctions particular values, and constructs particular forms of agency.

One of the most notable features of contemporary conservative reform efforts is the way in which they increasingly position teachers as a liability and in doing so align with modes of education that are as demeaning as they are deskilling. These reforms are not innocent and actually promote failure in the classroom. And when that is successful, they open the door for more public schools to be closed, provide another chance at busting the union, and allow such schools to be taken over by private and corporate interests. Under the influence of market-based pedagogies, public school teachers are subjected to what can only be described as repressive disciplinary measures in the school and an increasing chorus of verbal humiliation from politicians outside of the classroom. Academics do not fare much better and are often criticized for being too radical, for not working long hours, and for receiving cushy paychecks—a position at odds with the fact that more than 70 percent of academic labor is now either part-time or on a non-tenure track. Many contingent faculty earn so little income that they are part of the growing new class of workers who qualify for food stamps. With no health insurance and lacking other crucial benefits, they are truly on their own.

Teachers and academics are not only on the defensive in the neoliberal war on schools, they are also increasingly pressured to assume a more instrumentalist and mercenary role. Such approaches leave them with no time to be creative, use their imagination, work with other teachers, or develop classroom practices that are not wedded to teaching to the test and other demeaning empirical measures. Of course, the practice of disinvesting in public schools and higher education has a long history, but it has strengthened since the election of Ronald Reagan in 1980 and intensified in the new millennium. How else to explain that many states invest more in building prisons than educating students, especially those who are poor, disabled, and immersed in poverty? What are we to make of the fact that there are more black men in prison than in higher education in states such as Louisiana and California?[23] The right-wing makeover of public education has resulted in some states, Texas for example, banning the teaching of critical thinking in their classrooms, while in Arizona legislation has been passed that eliminates all curricular material from the classroom that includes the histories of Mexican Americans. The latter case is particularly loathsome. Masquerading as legislation designed to teach students how— no irony intended—to value each other and eliminate the hatred of other ethnic groups and races, Bill HB2281 bans ethnic studies. According to the bill, it is illegal for a school district to have any courses or classes that will "promote the overthrow of the U.S. government, promote resentment of a particular race or class of people, are designed primarily for students of a particular ethnic group or advocate ethnic solidarity instead of the treatment of pupils as individuals."[24] Schools that do not comply with this racist law will lose 10 percent of their monthly share of state aid.

It gets worse. In addition to eliminating the teaching of the history and culture of those ethnic groups considered a threat or disposable, the Arizona Department of Education "began telling school districts that teachers whose spoken English it deems to be heavily accented or ungrammatical must be removed from classes for students still learning English."[25] The targets here include not only ethnic studies but also those educators who inhabit ethnic identities. This is an unadulterated expression of educational discrimination and apartheid, and it is as disgraceful as it is racist. It is worth noting that these states also want to tie the salaries of faculty in higher education to performance measures based on a neoliberal model of evaluation. In this case, these racist reforms share an unholy alliance with neoliberal reforms that make teachers voiceless, if not powerless, to reject them by preoccupying them with modes of pedagogy as repressive as they are anti-intellectual and depoliticized.

Fighting for democracy as an educational project means encouraging a culture of questioning in classrooms, one that explores both the strengths and weaknesses of the current era. This notion of questioning is not simply about airing conflicting points of view, nor is it about substituting dogma for genuine dialogue and critical analysis. Most importantly, it is about a culture of questioning that raises ideas to the status of public values and a broader encounter with the larger social order. At issue here are pedagogical practices that are not only about the search for the truth but also about taking responsibility for intervening in the world by connecting knowledge and power, learning and values to interrelated modes of commitment and social engagement. I think Zygmunt Bauman is right in arguing that "if there is no room for the idea of *a wrong* society, there is hardly much chance for the idea of a good society to be born, let alone make waves."[26] The relevant question in this instance is what kind of future do our teachings presuppose? What forms of literacy and agency do we make available to our students through our pedagogical practices? How do we understand and incorporate in classroom pedagogies the ongoing search for equity and excellence, truth and justice, knowledge and commitment? I believe that this broader project of addressing democratization as a pedagogical practice should be central to any worthwhile attempt to engage in classroom teaching. And this is a political project. As educators, we have to begin with a vision of schooling as a democratic public sphere, and then we have to figure out what the ideological, political, and social impediments are to such a goal and organize collectively to derail them. In other word, educators need to start with a project, not a method. They need to view themselves through the lens of civic responsibility and address what it means to educate students in the best of those traditions and knowledge forms we have inherited from the past and also in terms of what it means to prepare them to be in the world as critically engaged agents.

Educators need to be more forceful and committed to linking their overall investment in democracy to modes of critique and collective action that address the presupposition that democratic societies are never too just or just enough. Moreover, such a commitment suggests that a viable democratic society must constantly nurture the possibilities for self-critique, collective agency, and forms of citizenship in which teachers and students play a fundamental role. Rather than being forced to participate in a pedagogy designed to raise test scores and undermine forms of critical thinking, students must be involved pedagogically in critically discussing, administrating, and shaping the material relations of power and ideological forces that structure their everyday lives. Central to such an educational project is the continual struggle by teachers to connect their pedagogical practices to the building of an inclusive and just democracy, which should be open to many forms, offers no political guarantees, and provides an important normative dimension to politics as an ongoing process that never ends. Such a project is based on the realization that a democracy open to exchange, question, and self-criticism never reaches the limits of justice; it is never just enough and never finished. It is precisely the open-ended and normative nature of such a project that provides a common ground for educators to share their resources with a diverse range of intellectual pursuits while refusing to believe that such struggles in schools ever come to an end.

In order to connect teaching with the larger world so as to make pedagogy meaningful, critical, and transformative, educators will have to focus their work on important social issues that connect what is learned in the classroom to the larger society and the lives of their students. Such issues might include the ongoing destruction of the ecological biosphere, the current war against youth, the hegemony of neoliberal globalization, the widespread attack by corporate culture on public schools, the relentless attack on the welfare system, the increasing rates of incarceration of people of color, the dangerous growth of the prison-industrial complex, the increasing gap between the rich and the poor, the rise of a generation of students who are laboring under the burden of debt, and the increasing spread of war globally.

Once again, educators need to do more than create the conditions for critical learning for their students; they also need to responsibly assume the role of civic educators willing to share their ideas with other educators and the wider public. This suggests writing and speaking to a variety of audiences through a host of public means of expression including the lecture circuit, Internet, radio interviews, alternative magazines, and the church pulpit, to name only a few. Such writing needs to become public by crossing over into spheres and avenues of expression that speak to more general audiences in a language that is clear but not theoretically simplistic. Capitalizing on their role as intellectuals, educators can address the challenge of combining scholarship and commitment through the use of a vocabulary that is neither dull nor obtuse, while seeking to reach a broad audience. More importantly, as teachers organize to assert the importance of their role and that of public schooling in a democracy, they can forge new alliances and connections to develop social movements that include and also expand beyond working with unions.

Educators also need to be more specific about what it means to be self-critical as well as attentive to learning how to work collectively with other educators through a vast array of networks across a number of public spheres. This might mean sharing resources with educators in a variety of fields and sites, extending from other teachers to community workers and artists outside of the school. This also suggests that educators become more active in addressing the ethical and political challenges of globalization. Public schools, teachers, and higher education faculties need to unite across the various states and make a case for public and higher education. At the very least, they could make clear to a befuddled American public that the deficit theory regarding school cutbacks is a fraud.

There is plenty of money to provide quality education to every student in the United States—and this certainly holds true for the United Kingdom and Canada as well. As Salvatore Babones points out, "The problem isn't a lack of money. The problem is where the money is going."[27] The issue is not about the absence of funds as much as it is about where funds are being invested and how more revenue can be raised to support public education in the United States. The United States spends around $960 billion on its wars and defense-related projects.[28] In fact, the cost of war over a ten-year period "will run at least $3.7 trillion and could reach as high as $4.4 trillion, according to the research project "Costs of War" by Brown University's Watson Institute for International Studies."[29] Military spending seems to know no bounds. The United States could spend as much as a trillion dollars for a fleet of F-35 fighter planes with stealth technology. Each plane costs $90 million, and the military is "spending more on this plane than Australia's entire GDP ($924 billion)."[30] Many military experts urged the Pentagon to ditch the project because of cost overruns and a series of technological problems that more recently have resulted in the Pentagon grounding all F-35s. In just this one example, billions are being wasted on faulty military planes when the money could be used to fund food programs for needy children, scholarships for low-income youth, and shelter for the homeless. As Barbones argues, the crucial recognition here is that research consistently shows that education spending creates more jobs per dollar than any other kind of government spending. A University of Massachusetts study ranked military spending worst of five major fiscal levers for job creation. The UMass study ranked education spending the best. A dollar spent on education creates more than twice as many jobs than a dollar spent on defense. Education spending also outperforms health care, clean energy and tax cuts as a mechanism for job creation.[31]

Surely, this budget could be trimmed appropriately to divert much-needed funds to education, given that a nation's highest priority should be investing in its children rather than in the production of organized violence. As capital, finance, trade, and culture become extraterritorial and increasingly removed from traditional political constraints, it becomes all the more pressing to put global networks and political organizations into play to contend with the reach and power of neoliberal globalization. Engaging in intellectual practices that offer the possibility of alliances and new forms of solidarity among public school teachers and cultural workers such as artists, writers, journalists, academics, and others who engage in forms of public pedagogy grounded in a democratic project represents a small, but important, step in addressing the massive and unprecedented reach of global capitalism.

Educators also need to register and make visible their own subjective involvement in what they teach, how they shape classroom social relations, and how they defend their positions within institutions that often legitimate educational processes based on narrow ideological interests and political exclusions. This suggests making one's authority and classroom work the subject of critical analysis with students but taken up in terms that move beyond the rhetoric of method, psychology, or private interests. Pedagogy in this instance can be addressed as a moral and political discourse in which students are able to connect learning to social change, scholarship to commitment, and classroom knowledge to public life. Such a pedagogical task suggests that educators speak truth to power, exercise civic courage, and take risk in their role as public intellectuals. Theodor Adorno is insightful here in arguing that "the undiminished presence of suffering, fear and menace necessitates that thought that cannot be realized should not be discarded."[32] This suggests, in part, that academics must overcome an intense obsession with the demands of their own cir-

cumscribed professional pursuits, rejecting the privatized notion of scholarship and agency that dominates academic life. Too many academics are
willing to depoliticize their work by insulating theory, teaching, and research from the discourse, structures, and experiences of everyday life.
This is not merely a matter of intellectuals selling out but of standing
still, refusing to push against the grain to address the crimes and rubbish
of the new Gilded Age. Of course, there are many academics, teachers,
and right-wing pundits who argue that the classroom should be free of
politics and hence a space where matters of power, values, and social justice should not be addressed. The usual object of scorn in this case is the
charge that teachers who believe in civic education indoctrinate students.
In this ideologically pure world, authority in the classroom is reduced to
a transparent pedagogy in which nothing controversial can be stated and
teachers are forbidden to utter one word related to any of the major problems facing the larger society. Of course, this position is as much a flight
from responsibility as it is an instance of a dreadful pedagogy.

One useful approach to embracing the classroom as a political site
but at the same time eschewing any form of indoctrination is for educators
to think through the distinction between a *politicizing pedagogy*, which insists wrongly that students think as we do, and a *political pedagogy*, which
teaches students by example and through dialogue about the importance
of power, social responsibility, and of taking a stand (without standing
still) while rigorously engaging the full range of ideas about an issue.

Political pedagogy offers the promise of nurturing students to think
critically about their understanding of classroom knowledge and its relationship to the issue of social responsibility. Yet it would also invoke
the challenge of educating students not only to engage the world critically
but also to be responsible enough to fight for those political and economic conditions that make democratic participation in both schools
and the larger society viable. Such a pedagogy affirms the experience of
the social and the obligations it evokes regarding questions of responsibility and transformation. In part, it does this by opening up for students
important questions about power, knowledge, and what it might mean
for them to critically engage the conditions under which life is presented
to them. In addition, the pedagogy of freedom would provide students
with the knowledge and skills to analyze and work to overcome those

social relations of oppression that make living unbearable for those who are poor, hungry, unemployed, deprived of adequate social services, and viewed under the aegis of neoliberalism as largely disposable. What is important about this type of critical pedagogy is the issue of responsibility as both a normative issue and a strategic act. Responsibility not only highlights the performative nature of pedagogy by raising questions about the relationship that teachers have to students but also the relationship that students have to themselves and others.

Central here is the importance for educators to encourage students to reflect on what it means for them to connect knowledge and criticism to becoming agents of social change, buttressed by a profound desire to overcome injustice and a spirited commitment to social agency. Political education teaches students to take risks, challenge those with power, and encourage them to be reflexive about how power is used in the classroom. Political education proposes that the role of the teacher as public intellectual is not to consolidate authority but to question and interrogate it, and that teachers and students should temper any reverence for authority with a sense of critical awareness and an acute willingness to hold it accountable for its consequences. Moreover, political education foregrounds education not within the imperatives of specialization and professionalization but within a project designed to expand the possibilities of democracy by linking education to modes of political agency that promote critical citizenship and address the ethical imperative to alleviate human suffering.

On the other hand, politicizing education silences in the name of orthodoxy and imposes itself on students while undermining dialogue, deliberation, and critical engagement. Politicizing education is often grounded in a combination of self-righteousness and ideological purity that silences students as it enacts "correct" positions. Authority in this perspective rarely opens itself to self-criticism or for that matter to any criticism, especially from students. Politicizing education cannot decipher the distinction between critical teaching and pedagogical terrorism because its advocates have no sense of the difference between encouraging human agency and social responsibility and molding students according to the imperatives of an unquestioned ideological position and sutured pedagogical script. Politicizing education is more religious than secular and more about training than educating; it harbors a great dislike for complicating issues, promoting critical dialogue, and generating a culture of questioning.

If teachers are truly concerned about how education operates as a crucial site of power in the modern world, they will have to take more seriously how pedagogy functions on local and global levels to secure and challenge the ways in which power is deployed, affirmed, and resisted within and outside traditional discourses and cultural spheres. In this instance, pedagogy becomes an important theoretical tool for understanding the institutional conditions that place constraints on the production of knowledge, learning, and academic labor itself. Pedagogy also provides a discourse for engaging and challenging the production of social hierarchies, identities, and ideologies as they traverse local and national borders. In addition, pedagogy as a form of production and critique offers a discourse of possibility, a way of providing students with the opportunity to link meaning to commitment and understanding to social transformation—and to do so in the interest of the greatest possible justice. Unlike traditional vanguardist or elitist notions of the intellectual, critical pedagogy and education should embrace the notion of rooting the vocation of intellectuals in pedagogical and political work tempered by humility, a moral focus on suffering, and the need to produce alternative visions and policies that go beyond a language of sheer critique.

I now want to shift my frame a bit in order to focus on the implications of the concerns I have addressed thus far and how they might be connected to developing an academic agenda for teachers as public intellectuals, particularly at a time when neoliberal agendas increasingly guide social policy.

Once again, in opposition to the privatization, commodification, commercialization, and militarization of everything public, educators need to define public education as a resource vital to the democratic and civic life of the nation. At the heart of such a task is the challenge for teachers, academics, cultural workers, and labor organizers to join together in opposition to the transformation of public education into a commercial sector—to resist what Bill Readings has called a consumer-oriented corporation more concerned about accounting than accountability.[33] As Bauman reminds us, schools are one of the few public spaces left where students can learn the "skills for citizen participation and effective political action. And where there is no [such] institution, there is no 'citizenship' either."[34] Public education may be one of the few sites available in which students can learn about the limits of commercial values, address what it means to learn the skills of social citizenship, and learn how to deepen and expand the possibilities of collective agency and democratic life.

Defending education at all levels of learning as a vital public sphere and public good rather than merely a private good is necessary to develop and nourish the proper balance between democratic public spheres and commercial power, between identities founded on democratic principles and identities steeped in forms of competitive, self-interested individualism that celebrate selfishness, profit-making, and greed. This view suggests that public education be defended through intellectual work that self-consciously recalls the tension between the democratic imperatives and possibilities of public institutions and their everyday realization within a society dominated by market principles. If public and higher education are to remain sites of critical thinking, collective work, and thoughtful dialogue, educators need to expand and resolutely defend how they view the meaning and purpose of their work with young people. As I have stressed repeatedly, academics, teachers, students, parents, community activists, and other socially concerned groups must provide the first line of defense in protecting public education as a resource vital to the moral life of the nation, open to people and communities whose resources, knowledge, and skills have often been viewed as marginal. This demands not only a revolutionary educational idea and concrete analysis of the neoliberal and other reactionary forces at work in dismantling public education but also the desire to build a powerful social movement as a precondition to real change and free quality education for everyone.

Such a project suggests that educators develop a more inclusive vocabulary for aligning politics and the task of leadership. In part, this means providing students with the language, knowledge, and social relations to engage in the "art of translating individual problems into public issues, and common interests into individual rights and duties."[35] Leadership demands a politics and pedagogy that refuses to separate individual problems and experience from public issues and social considerations. Within such a perspective, leadership displaces cynicism with hope, challenges the neoliberal notion that there are no alternatives with visions of a better society, and develops a pedagogy of commitment that puts into place modes of critical literacy in which competency and interpretation provide the basis for actually intervening in the world. Leadership invokes the demand to make the pedagogical more political by linking critical thought to collective action, human agency to social responsibility, and knowledge and power to a profound impatience with a status quo founded upon deep inequalities and injustices.

One of the crucial challenges faced by educators is rejecting the neoliberal collapse of the public into the private, the rendering of all social problems as biographical in nature. The neoliberal obsession with the private not only furthers a market-based politics that reduces all relationships to the exchange of money and the accumulation of capital, it also depoliticizes politics itself and reduces public activity to the realm of utterly privatized practices and utopias, underscored by the reduction of citizenship to the act of purchasing goods. Within this discourse all forms of solidarity, social agency, and collective resistance disappear into the murky waters of a politics in which the demands of privatized pleasures and ready-made individual choices are organized on the basis of market mentalities and moralities that cancel out all modes of social responsibility, commitment, and action. This is a reactionary public pedagogy that finds its vision in the creation of atomized individuals who live in a moral vacuum and regress to sheer economic Darwinism or infantilism. One of the major challenges now facing educators, especially in light of the current neoliberal attack on public workers, is to reclaim the language of the social, agency, solidarity, democracy, and public life as the basis for rethinking how to name, theorize, and strategize a new kind of education as well as more emancipatory notions of individual and social agency, as well as collective struggle.

This challenge suggests, in part, positing new forms of social citizenship and civic education that have a purchase on people's everyday lives and struggles. Teachers and faculty bear an enormous responsibility in opposing neoliberalism—the most dangerous ideology of our time— by bringing democratic political culture back to life. Part of this effort demands creating new locations of struggle, vocabularies, and values that allow people in a wide variety of public spheres to become more than they are now, to question what it is they have become within existing institutional and social formations, and "to give some thought to their experiences so that they can transform their relations of subordination and oppression."[36] One element of this struggle could take the form of resisting attacks on existing public spheres, such as schools, while creating new spaces in clubs, neighborhoods, bookstores, trade unions, alternative media sites, and other places where dialogue and critical exchanges become possible. At the same time, challenging neoliberalism means fighting against the state's ongoing reconfiguration into the role of an enlarged police precinct, designed to repress dissent, regulate immigrant populations, incarcerate youth who are considered disposable, and safeguard the interests of global investors. It also means shifting spending priorities in favor of young people and a sustainable democracy.

Revenue for investing in young people, social services, health care, crucial infrastructures, and the welfare state has not disappeared. It has simply been moved into other spending categories or used to benefit a small percentage of the population. As mentioned above, military spending is bloated and supports a society organized for the mass production of violence. Such spending needs to be cut to the bone and could be done without endangering the larger society. In addition, as John Cavanagh has suggested, educators and others need to fight for policies that provide a small tax on stocks and derivatives, eliminate the use of overseas tax havens by the rich, and create tax policies in which the wealthy are taxed fairly.[37] Cavanagh estimates that the enactment of these three policies could produce as much as $330 billion in revenue annually, enough to vastly improve the quality of education for all children throughout the United States.[38]

As governments globally give up their role of providing social safety nets, maintaining public services, and regulating corporate greed, capital escapes beyond the reach of democratic control, leaving marginalized individuals and groups at the mercy of their own meager resources to survive. In such circumstances, it becomes difficult to create alternative public spheres that enable people to become effective agents of change. Under neoliberalism's reign of terror, public issues collapse into privatized discourses and a culture of personal confessions, greed, and celebrity worship emerges to set the stage for depoliticizing public life and turning citizenship and governance into a form of consumerism. Celebrity has become the principal expression of value in a society in which only commodified objects have any value. The rich and the powerful dislike public education as much as they despise any real notion of democracy and they will do all in their power to defend their narrow ideological and economic interests.

The growing attack on public and higher education in American society, as well as in the United Kingdom and many other neoliberal countries, may say less about the reputed apathy of the populace than about the bankruptcy of old political languages and orthodoxies and the need for new vocabularies and visions for clarifying our intellectual, ethical, and political projects, especially as they work to reabsorb questions of agency, ethics, and meaning back into politics and public life. In the absence of such a language and the social formations and public spheres that make democracy and justice operative, politics becomes narcissistic and caters to the mood of widespread pessimism and the cathartic allure of the spectacle. In addition, public service and government intervention are sneered at as either bureaucratic or a constraint upon individual freedom. Any attempt to give new life to a substantive democratic politics must address the issue of how people learn to be political agents as well as what kind of educational work is necessary within what kind of public spaces to enable people to use their full intellectual resources to provide a profound critique of existing institutions and to undertake a struggle to make the operation of freedom and autonomy achievable for as many people as possible in a wide variety of spheres.

As engaged educators, we are required to understand more fully why the tools we used in the past feel inadequate in the present, often failing to respond to problems now facing the United States and other parts of the globe. More specifically, educators face the challenge posed by the failure of existing critical discourses to bridge the gap between how society represents itself and how and why individuals fail to understand and critically engage such representations in order to intervene in the oppressive social relationships they often legitimate.

Against neoliberalism, educators, students, and other concerned citizens face the task of providing a language of resistance and possibility, a language that embraces a militant utopianism while constantly being attentive to those forces that seek to turn such hope into a new slogan or punish and dismiss those who dare to look beyond the horizon of the given. Hope is the affective and intellectual precondition for individual and social struggle, the mark of courage on the part of intellectuals in and out of the academy who use the resources of theory to address pressing social problems. But hope is also a referent for civic courage that translates as a political practice and begins when one's life can no longer be taken for granted, making concrete the possibility for transforming politics into an ethical space and a public act that confronts the flow of everyday experience and the weight of social suffering with the force of individual and collective resistance and the unending project of democratic social transformation.

There is a lot of talk among educators and the general public about the death of democratic schooling and the institutional support it provides for critical dialogue, nurturing the imagination, and creating a space of inclusiveness and critical teaching. Given that educators and others now live in a democracy emptied of any principled meaning, the ability of human beings to imagine a more equitable and just world becomes more difficult. I would hope educators, of all groups, would be the most vocal and militant in challenging this assumption by making clear that at the heart of any notion of a substantive democracy is the assumption that learning should be used to expand the public good, create a culture of questioning, and promote democratic social change. Individual and social agency become meaningful as part of the willingness to think in oppositional, if not utopian, terms "in order to help us find our way to a more human future."[39] Under such circumstances, knowledge can be used for amplifying human freedom and promoting social justice, not for simply creating profits. The diverse terrains of critical education and critical pedagogy offer some insights for addressing these issues, and we would do well to learn as much as possible from them in order to expand the meaning of the political and revitalize the pedagogical possibilities of cultural politics and democratic struggles. The late Pierre Bourdieu has argued that intellectuals need to create new ways for doing politics by investing in political struggles through a permanent critique of the abuses of authority and power, especially under the reign of neoliberalism. Bourdieu wanted educators to use their skills and knowledge to break out of the microcosm of academia and the classroom, combine scholarship with commitment, and "enter into sustained and vigorous exchange with the outside world (especially with unions, grassroots organizations, and issue-oriented activist groups) instead of being content with waging the 'political' battles, at once intimate and ultimately, and always a bit unreal, of the scholastic universe."[40]

At a time when our civil liberties are being destroyed and public institutions and goods all over the world are under assault by the forces of a rapacious global capitalism, there is a concrete urgency on the horizon that demands not only the most engaged forms of political opposition on the part of teachers but also new modes of resistance and collective struggle buttressed by rigorous intellectual work, social responsibility, and political courage. The time has come for educators to distinguish caution from cowardice and recognize the need for addressing the dire crisis public education is now facing. As Jacques Derrida reminds us, democracy "demands the most concrete urgency . . . because as a concept it makes visible the promise of democracy, that which is to come."[41] We have seen glimpses of such a promise among those brave students and workers who have demonstrated in Montreal, Paris, London, Athens, Toronto, Mexico City, and many other cities across the globe.

As engaged intellectuals, teachers can learn from such struggles by turning the colleges and public schools into vibrant critical sites of learning and unconditional spheres of pedagogical and political resistance. The power of the existing dominant order does not merely reside in the economic or in material relations of power, but also in the realm of ideas and culture. This is why educators must take sides, speak out, and engage in the hard pedagogical work of debunking corporate culture's assault on teaching and learning, orient their teaching for social change, and connect learning to public life. At the very least, educators can connect knowledge to the operations of power in their classroom, providing a safe space for students to address a variety of important issues ranging from the violation of human rights to crimes against humanity. Assuming the role of public intellectual suggests being a provocateur in the classroom; it means asking hard questions, listening carefully to what students have to say, and pushing teaching against the grain. But it also means stepping out of the classroom and working with others to create public spaces where it becomes possible not only to "shift the way people think about the moment but potentially to energize them to do something differently in that moment," to link one's critical imagination with the possibility of activism in the public sphere.[42] This is, of course, a small step, but if we do not want to repeat the present as the future or, even worse, become complicit in the workings of dominant power, it is time for educators to collectively mobilize their energies by breaking down the illusion of unanimity that dominant power propagates while working diligently, tirelessly, and collectively to reclaim the promises of a truly global, democratic future. There is no room for a dystopian pedagogy in a democratic society because it destroys the foundation for a formative culture necessary to provide the modes of shared sociality and social agents who possess the knowledge, skills, and values that support an ongoing collective struggle for democratization. In light of the current neoliberal assault on all democratic public spheres, along with the urgency of the problems faced by those marginalized because of their class, race, age, or sexual orientation, I think it is all the more crucial to imagine a politics that both challenges and rejects the dystopian "dreamworlds" of consumption, privatization, deregulation, and the neverending search for accumulating profits. At the heart of such a struggle is the need for a new radical imagination—in this case, one that is willing to develop new social movements, a fresh language for politics, an intense struggle to preserve the democratic educational possibilities of higher education, and alternative public spheres. All of which are crucial to sustain a democratic formative culture to challenge the neoliberal authoritarianism that generates massive social inequality, deepens market savagery, promotes massive privatization, and unleashes a global war against any viable notion of social citizenship and critical education.

CHAPTER TWO

At the Limits of Neoliberal Higher Education:
Global Youth Resistance
and the American/British Divide

We need a wholesale revision of how a democracy
both listens to and treats young people.

—Andy Mycock

The global reach and destructiveness of neoliberal values and disciplinary controls are not only evident in the widespread hardships and human suffering caused by the economic recession of 2008, they are also visible in the ongoing and ruthless assault on the social state, workers, unions, higher education, students, and any vestige of the social at odds with neoliberal values. Under the regime of market fundamentalism, institutions that were meant to limit human suffering and misfortune and protect the public from the excesses of the market have been either weakened or abolished, as have been many of those public spheres where private troubles can be understood as social problems and addressed as such.[1] Government institutions and policies to protect workers' rights and regulate corporations have been weakened just as the institutional basis of

53

the welfare state has been undermined along with "the ideas of social pro-vision that supported it."[2] Many programs inaugurated during FDR's New Deal and Lyndon Johnson's Great Society eras have either been eliminated or are now under attack by conservative politicians, especially Texas senator Ted Cruz and other adherents of the Tea Party. One startling example of growing inequality is the reinstatement of ability grouping in public schools, which is a blatant return to the old forms of tracking students by class and race.[3] Such tracking already exists in higher education by virtue of the correlation between a student's opportunity to get a quality educa-tion and the ability to pay soaring tuition rates at the best public and pri-vate schools. Under neoliberalism, privatization has run rampant, engulfing institutions as different in their goals and functions as public schools and core public services, on the one hand, and prisons, on the other. This shift from the social contract to savage forms of corporate sov-ereignty is part of a broader process of "reducing state support of social goods [and] means that states—the institutions best placed to defend the gains workers and other popular forces have made in previous struggles—are instead abandoning them."[4] In this brave new world, there is rapidly growing inequality in income and wealth, the financial sector now occu-pies an unprecedented position in the economy, and one consequence is a "scale of worldwide misery not seen since the 1930s."[5]

Faced with massive deficits, the US federal government, along with that of many states, is refusing to raise taxes either on the rich or on wealthy corporations while at the same time enacting massive cuts in everything from Medicaid programs, food banks, and worker retirement funds to higher education and health care programs for children. As one example, Florida governor Rick Scott has

> proposed slashing corporate income and property taxes, laying off 6,700 state employees, cutting education funding by $4.8 billion, and cutting Medicaid by almost $4 billion. Scott's ultimate plan is to phase the Sunshine state's corporate income tax out entirely. He [wants] to gut Florida's unemployment insurance system, leaving unemployed workers "with much less economic protection than unemployed work-ers in any other state in the country."[6]

As social problems are privatized and public spaces are commodified, there has been an increased emphasis on individual solutions to socially produced problems, while at the same time market relations and the commanding institutions of capital are divorced from matters of politics, ethics, and responsibility. Free market ideology, with its emphasis on the privatization of public wealth, the elimination of social protections, and its deregulation of economic activity, now shapes practically every commanding political and economic institution in the United States. In these circumstances, notions of the public good, community, and the obligations of citizenship are replaced by the overburdened demands of individual responsibility and an utterly privatized ideal of freedom.

In the current market-driven society, with its ongoing uncertainties and collectively induced anxieties, core public values that safeguard the common good have been abandoned under a regime that promotes a survival-of-the-fittest economic doctrine. As Jeffrey Sachs points out, "Income inequality is at historic highs, but the rich claim they have no responsibility to the rest of society. They refuse to come to the aid of the destitute, and defend tax cuts at every opportunity. Almost everybody complains, almost everybody aggressively defends their own narrow, short-term interests, and almost everybody abandons any pretense of looking ahead or addressing the needs of others."[7] Shared sacrifice and shared responsibilities now give way to shared fears and a disdain for investing in the common good or, for that matter, the security of future generations of young people. Conservatives and liberals alike seem to view public values as either a hindrance to the profit-seeking goals of the allegedly free market or as an enervating drain on society. Espousing a notion of the common good is now treated as a sign of weakness, if not a dangerous pathology.[8]

Public spheres that once offered at least the glimmer of progressive ideas, enlightened social policies, noncommodified values, and critical exchange have been increasingly commercialized—or replaced by private spaces and corporate settings whose ultimate fidelity is to expanding profit margins. For example, higher education is increasingly defined as an adjunct of corporate power and culture. Public spaces such as libraries are detached from the language of public discourse and viewed increasingly as a waste of taxpayers' money. No longer vibrant political spheres and ethical sites, public spaces are reduced to dead spaces in which it becomes almost impossible to construct those modes of knowledge, communication, agency, and meaningful interventions necessary for an aspiring democracy. What has become clear is that the neoliberal attack on the social state, workers, and unions is now being matched by a full-fledged assault on higher education. Such attacks are not happening just in the United States but in the many other parts of the globe where neoliberalism is waging a savage battle to eliminate all of those public spheres that might offer a glimmer of opposition to and protection from market-driven policies, institutions, ideology, and values. Higher education is being targeted by conservative politicians and governments because it embodies, at least ideally, a sphere in which students learn that democracy, as Jacques Rancière suggests, entails rupture, relentless critique, and dialogue about official power, its institutions, and its never-ending attempts to silence dissent.[9]

The Neoliberal Attack on Higher Education

As Ellen Schrecker observes, "Today the entire enterprise of higher education, not just its dissident professors, is under attack, both internally and externally."[10] In England and the United States, universities and businesses are forming stronger ties, the humanities are being underfunded, student tuition is rising at astronomical rates, knowledge is being commodified, and research is valued through the lens of an audit culture. In England, the Browne Report—an ostensibly independent review of British higher education, released in 2009—has established modes of governance, financing, and evaluation that for all intents and purposes make higher education an adjunct of corporate values and interests.[11] Delivering improved employability has reshaped the connection between knowledge and power while rendering faculty and students as professional entrepreneurs and budding customers. The notion of the university as a center of critique and a vital democratic public sphere that cultivates the knowledge, skills, and values necessary for the production of a democratic polity is giving way to a view of the university as a marketing machine essential to the production of neoliberal subjects.[12] This is completely at odds with the notion that higher education, in particular, is wedded to the presupposition that literacy in its various economic, political, cultural, and social forms is essential to the development of a formative culture that provides the foundation for producing critically engaged and informed citizens.

Clearly, any institution that makes a claim to literacy, critical dialogue, informed debate, and reason is now a threat to a political culture in which ignorance, stupidity, lies, misinformation, and appeals to common sense have become the dominant, if not most valued, currency of exchange. And this seems to apply as well to the dominant media. How else to explain the widespread public support for politicians in the United States such as Herman Cain, who is as much a buffoon as he is an exemplar of illiteracy and ignorance in the service of the political spectacle? In fact, one can argue reasonably that the entire slate of 2012 presidential Republican Party candidates, extending from Cain to Rick Santorum to Rick Perry and Michele Bachmann, embodied not simply a rejection of science, evidence, informed argument, and other elements associated with the Enlightenment but a deep-seated disdain and hatred for any vestige of a critical mind. During the 2012 campaign, almost every position taken by the Republican primary candidates harked back to a pre-Enlightenment period when faith and cruelty ruled the day and ignorance was the modus operandi for legitimating political and ethical impotence. Mitt Romney, the eventual Republican Party front-runner, not only supported such views but also appeared to have little regard for the truth, as he constantly changed his positions on a number of issues to simply fit the demands of his various audiences. Even the post-election attempt by the Republican Party to find new faces of leadership, such as Florida senator Marco Rubio, perpetuated the legacy of ignorance and denial that plagues the party. For example, Rubio, in his response to Obama's state of the union address, "dismissed the idea that the U.S. government could do anything to combat climate change," crassly implying that climate change was not man-made and was not a vital political and environmental issue.[13] Rubio has also made comments about hearing what he called "reasonable debate" from both sides about whether climate change is man-made. In this regressive, neoliberal worldview, ignorance and scientific evidence are weighed equally, as if one balances the other. This type of ideological fundamentalism buttressed by a willful ignorance is especially disingenuous in light of a large number of scientific studies that affirm the existence of man-made global warming. "In fact, a study, published in 2010 in the *Proceedings of the National Academy of Sciences*, surveyed 1,372 climate researchers and found that 97 to 98 percent of them agree that climate change is anthropogenic."[14]

Beneath the harsh rule of a neoliberal sovereignty, education, if not critical thought itself, is removed from its civic ties and rendered instrumental, more closely tied to the production of ignorance and conformity than informed knowledge and critical exchange. Under such circumstances, it is not surprising that higher education, or for that matter any other critical public sphere in the United States and increasingly in England, occupies a high-profile target for dismantlement and reform by neoliberal and right-wing politicians and other extremists. While there is ample commentary on the dumbing down of the culture as a result of the corporate control of the dominant media, what is often missed in this argument is how education has come under a similar attack, and not simply because there is an attempt to privatize or commercialize such institutions.

Under casino capitalism, higher education matters only to the extent that it promotes national prosperity and drives economic growth, innovation, and transformation. But there is more at stake here in turning the university into an adjunct of the corporation: there is also an attempt to remove it because it is one of the few remaining institutions in which dissent, critical dialogue, and social problems can be critically engaged. Young people in the United States now recognize that the university has become part of a Ponzi scheme designed to impose on students an unconscionable amount of debt while subjecting them to the harsh demands and power of commanding financial institutions for years after they graduate. Under this economic model of subservience, there is no future for young people, there is no time to talk about advancing social justice, addressing social problems, promoting critical thinking, cultivating social responsibility, or engaging noncommodified values that might challenge the neoliberal world view.

One of the most flagrant examples of how the university as a place to think is being dismantled can be seen in the Browne Report. Chaired by Lord Browne of Madingley, the former chief executive of BP, the Browne Report recommended a series of deeply conservative changes to British higher education, including raising the cap on fees that universities could charge students. The report's guiding assumptions suggest that "student choice," a consumer model of pedagogy, an instrumentalist culture of auditing practices, and market-driven values are at the core of the new neoliberal university. Like most neoliberal models of education, higher education matters only to the extent that it promotes national prosperity and drives economic growth, innovation, and transformation.[15] Tuition will be tripled in some cases. Numerous schools will be closed. Higher education will be effectively remade according to the dictates of a corporate culture.

On March 26, 2011, students in London joined with labor union activists, public service employees, and others in a massive demonstration protesting the savage cuts in jobs, services, and higher education proposed by the Conservative-Liberal Democratic coalition government formed in May 2010. Yet the government appears indifferent to the devastating consequences its policies will produce. Simon Head has suggested that the Browne policies represent a severe threat to academic freedom. In actuality, the neoliberal policies outlined in the report represent a fundamental threat to the future of democracy as well as the university—one of the few remaining institutions left in which dissent, critical dialogue, and social problems can be critically engaged.[16] What is often lost in critiques of the neoliberal university is the connection to broader society. Democracy necessitates a culture of questioning and a set of institutions in which complicated ideas can be engaged, authority challenged, power held accountable, and public intellectuals produced.

In the United States, the neoliberal model takes a somewhat different form since states control the budgets for higher education. Under the call for austerity, states have begun the process of massively defunding public universities while simultaneously providing massive tax breaks for corporations and the rich. At the same time, higher education in its search for funding has "adopted the organizational trappings of medium-sized or large corporations."[17] University presidents are now viewed as CEOs, faculty as entrepreneurs, and students as consumers. In some universities, college deans are shifting their focus beyond the campus in order to take on "the fund-raising, strategic planning, and partner-seeking duties that were once the bailiwick of the university president."[18] Academic leadership is now defined in part through the ability to partner with corporate donors. In fact, deans are increasingly viewed as the heads of complex businesses, and their job performance is rated according to their fundraising capacity.

College presidents now willingly and openly align themselves with corporate interests. The *Chronicle of Higher Education* has reported that "presidents from 19 of the top 40 research universities with the largest operating budges sat on at least one company board."[19] As business culture permeates higher education, all manner of school practices—from food service and specific modes of instruction to the hiring of temporary faculty—is now outsourced to private contractors. In the process of adopting market values and cutting costs, classes have ballooned in size, matched only by a top-heavy layer of managerial elites, who now outnumber faculty at American universities. For faculty and students alike, there is an increased emphasis on rote learning and standardized testing. Tuition fees have skyrocketed, making it impossible for thousands of working-class youth to gain access to higher education. Moreover, the value of higher education is now tied exclusively to the need for credentials. Disciplines and subjects that do not fall within the purview of mathematical utility and economic rationality are seen as dispensable.

Among the most serious consequences facing faculty in the United States under the reign of neoliberal austerity and disciplinary measures is the increased casualization of academic labor. As universities adopt models of corporate governance, they are aggressively eliminating tenure positions, increasing part-time and full-time positions without the guarantee of tenure, and attacking faculty unions. In a number of states such as Ohio and Utah, legislatures have passed bills outlawing tenure, while in Wisconsin the governor has abrogated the bargaining rights of state university faculty.[20] At a time when higher education is becoming increasingly vocationalized, the ranks of tenure-track faculty are being drastically depleted in the United States, furthering the loss of faculty as stakeholders. Currently, only 27 percent of faculty are either on a tenure track or in a full-time tenure position.[21] As faculty are demoted to contingency forms of labor, they lose their power to influence the conditions of their work; they see their work load increase; they are paid poorly, deprived of office space and supplies, and refused travel money; and, most significantly, they are subject to policies that allow them to be fired at another's will.[22] The latter is particularly egregious because, when coupled with an ongoing series of attacks by right-wing ideologues against left-oriented and progressive academics, many nontenured faculty begin to censor themselves in their classes. At a time when critical faculty might be fired for their political beliefs, have their names posted on right-wing web sites, be forced to turn over their e-mail correspondence to right-wing groups,[23] or face harassment by the conservative press, it is crucial that protections be put in place that safeguard their positions and enable them to exercise the right of academic freedom.[24]

Neoliberal and right-wing political attacks on higher education and the rise of student protests movements in England and the United States, in particular, must be viewed within a broader political landscape that goes far beyond a critique of massive increases in student tuition. A broader analysis is needed to provide insights into how neoliberal policies and modes of resistance manifest themselves in different historical contexts while also offering possibilities for building alliances among different student groups across a range of countries. What both the United Kingdom and the United States share is a full-fledged attack by corporate and market-driven forces to destroy higher education as a democratic public sphere, despite the ongoing "desirability of an educated population to sustain a vibrant democracy and culture that provides a key component of the good life."[25]

Students Against Neoliberal Authoritarianism

In the face of the mass uprisings in England, Europe, Canada, and the Middle East, many commentators have raised questions about why comparable forms of widespread resistance did not take place earlier among US youth. Before the California student movement of 2009–2010 and the Occupy Wall Street protests, everyone from left critics to mainstream radio commentators voiced surprise and disappointment that US youth appeared unengaged by the collective action of their counterparts in other countries. In a wave of global protests that indicted the lack of vision, courage, and responsibility on the part of their elders and political leaders, young people in London, Paris, Montreal, Tunis, Quebec, and Athens were taking history into their own hands, fighting not merely for a space to survive but also for a society in which matters of justice, dignity, and freedom are objects of collective struggle. These demonstrations have created a new stage on which young people once again are defining what John Pilger calls the "theater of the possible."[26] Signaling a generational and political crisis that is global in scope, young people sent a message to the world that they refuse to live any longer under repressive authoritarian regimes sustained by morally bankrupt market-driven policies and repressive governments. Throughout Europe, students protested the attack on the social state, the savagery of neoliberal policies, and the devaluation of higher education as a public good. In doing so, they defied a social order in which they could not work at a decent job, have access to a quality education, or support a family—a social order that offered them a meager life stripped of self-determination and dignity. In London, students have been at the forefront of a massive progressive movement protesting against a Cameron-Clegg government that has imposed, under the ideological rubric of austerity-driven slash-and-burn policies, drastic cuts to public spending. These draconian policies are designed to shift the burden and responsibility of the recession from the rich to the most vulnerable elements of society, such as the elderly, workers, lower-income people, and students.

While young people in the United States did not take to the streets as quickly as their European counterparts, they have embraced the spirit of collective protests with the Occupy Wall Street movement. In the United States young people are not simply protesting tuition increases, the defunding of academia, and the enormous debt many of them are laboring under, they are also situating such concerns within a broader attack on the fundamental institutions and ideology of casino capitalism in its particularly virulent neoliberal form. Claiming that they are left out of the discourse of democracy, student protesters have not only made clear that inequality is out of control but that power largely resides in the hands of the top 1 percent, who control almost every aspect of society, from the government and the media to the schools and numerous cultural apparatuses. The Occupy Wall Street movement, taking a lesson from the Quebec student movement, is leading the move away from a focus on isolated issues in an attempt to develop a broader critique as the basis for an energized social movement less interested in liberal reforms than in a wholesale restructuring of US society under more radical and democratic values, social relations, and institutions of power. Ironically, very few progressives saw this movement coming and had for all intents and purposes written off the possibility of a new youth movement protesting against the savage policies of neoliberalism.

Some commentators, including Courtney Martin, a senior correspondent for *The American Prospect*, suggested that the problem is one of privilege. In a 2010 article for the magazine titled "Why Class Matters in Campus Activism," Martin argues that US students are often privileged and view politics as something that happens elsewhere, far removed from local activism.[27]

> Many of us from middle- and upper-income backgrounds have been socialized to believe that it is our duty to make a difference, but undertake such efforts abroad—where the "real" poor people are. We found nonprofits aimed at schooling children all over the globe while rarely acknowledging that our friend from the high school football team can't afford the same kind of opportunities we can. Or we create Third World bicycle programs while ignoring that our lab partner has to travel two hours by bus, as he is unable to get a driver's license as an undocumented immigrant. We were born lucky, so we head to the bars—oblivious to the rising tuition prices and crushing bureaucracy inside the financial aid office.[28]

This theme is taken up in greater detail in Martin's latest book, *Do It Anyway: A New Generation of Activists*. Sadly, however, the analysis Martin provides in that book suffers, like her piece in *The American Prospect*, from the same sort of privilege it critiques. It suggests not only that privileged middle-class kids are somehow the appropriate vanguard of change for this generation but also that they suffer from both a narcissistic refusal to look inward and a narrow, ego-driven sense of politics that is paternalistic and missionary in focus. This critique is too simplistic, overlooks complexity, and ignores social issues in a manner as objectionable as the attitudes it purports to find so misguided.

The other side of the overprivileged youth argument is suggested by longtime activist Tom Hayden, who argues that many students are so saddled with financial debt and focused on what it takes to get a job that they have little time for political activism.[29] According to Hayden, student activism in the United States, especially since the 1980s, has been narrowly issues-based, ranging from a focus on student unionization and gender equity to environmental topics and greater minority enrollment, thus circumscribing in advance youth participation in larger political spheres.[30] While Martin and Haydén both offer enticing narratives to explain the belated onslaught of student resistance, Simon Talley, a writer for *Campus Progress*, may be closer to the truth in claiming that students in the United States have had less of an investment in higher education than European students because for the last thirty years they have been told that higher education neither serves a public good nor is a valuable democratic public sphere.[31]

These commentators, however much they sometimes got it right, still underestimated the historical and current impacts of the conservative political climate on American campuses and the culture of youth protest. This conservatism took firm hold with the election of Ronald Reagan and the emergence of both neoconservative and neoliberal disciplinary apparatuses since the 1980s. Youth have in fact been very active in the last few decades, but in many instances to deeply conservative ends. As Susan Searls Giroux has argued, a series of well-funded, right-wing campus organizations have made much use of old and new media to produce bestselling screeds as well as interactive websites for students to report injustices in the interests of protesting the alleged left-totalitarianism of the academy. In her book *Between Race and Reason: Violence, Intellectual Responsibility and the University to Come,* Susan Searls Giroux writes:

> Conservative think tanks provide $20 million annually to the campus Right, according to the People for the American Way, to fund campus organizations such as Students for Academic Freedom, whose credo is "You can't get a good education if they're only telling you half the story" and boasts over 150 campus chapters. Providing an online complaint form for disgruntled students to fill out, the organization's website monitors insults, slurs and claims of more serious infractions that students claim to have suffered. Similarly, the Intercollegiate Studies Institute, founded by William F. Buckley, funds over 80 right-wing student publications through its Collegiate Network, which has produced such media darlings as Dinesh D'Souza and Ann Coulter. There is also the Leadership Institute, which trains, supports and does public relations for 213 conservative student groups who are provided with suggestions for inviting conservative speakers to campus, help starting conservative newspapers, or training to win campus elections. Or the Young Americans for Freedom, which sponsors various campus activities such as "affirmative action bake sales" where students are charged

variously according to their race or ethnicity, or announcements of "whites only" scholarships.[32]

Resistance among young people has not always been on the side of freedom and justice. Many liberal students for the past few decades, for their part, have engaged in forms of activism that also tend to mimic neoliberal rationalities. The increasing emphasis on consumerism, immediate gratification, and the narcissistic ethic of privatization took its toll in a range of student protests developed over issues such as "a defense of the right to consume alcohol."[33] As Mark Edelman Boren points out in his informative book on student resistance, alcohol-related issues caused student uprisings on a number of American campuses. He recounts one telling example: "At Ohio University, several thousand students rioted in April 1998 for a second annual violent protest over the loss of an hour of drinking when clocks were officially set back at the beginning of daylight savings time; forced out of area bars, upset students hurled rocks and bottles at police, who knew to show up in full riot gear after the previous year's riot. The troops finally resorted to shooting wooden 'knee-knocker' bullets at the rioters to suppress them."[34]

Widening the Lens

All of these explanations have some merit in accounting for the lack of resistance among American students until the Occupy Wall Street movement, but I'd like to shift the focus of the analysis. Student resistance in the United States should be viewed within a broader political landscape, especially for what it might tell us about the direction the current Wall Street protests might take; yet, with few exceptions, this landscape still remains unexamined. First, we have to remember that students in England, in particular, were faced with a series of crises that were more immediate, bold, and radical in their assault on young people and the institutions that bear down heavily on their lives than those in the United States. In the face of the economic recession, educational budgets were and continue to be cut in an extreme, take-no-prisoners fashion; the social state is being radically dismantled; tuition costs have spiked exponentially; and unemployment rates for young people are far higher than in the United States (with the exception of youth in poor minority communities). Students in England have experienced a massive and bold assault on their lives, educational opportunities, and their future. Moreover, these students live in a society where it becomes more difficult to collapse public life into largely private considerations. Students in these countries have access to a wider range of critical public spheres, politics in many of these countries has not collapsed entirely into the spectacle of celebrity/commodity culture, left-oriented political parties still exist, and labor unions have more political and ideological clout than they do in the United States. Alternative newspapers, progressive media, and a profound sense of the political constitute elements of a vibrant, discerning formative culture within a wide range of public spheres that have helped nurture and sustain the possibility to think critically, engage in political dissent, organize collectively, and inhabit public spaces in which alternative and critical theories can be developed.

In the United States, by contrast, the assault on colleges and universities has been less uniform. Because of the diverse nature of how higher education is financed and governed, the cuts to funding and services have been differentially spread out among community colleges, public universities, and elite colleges, thus US students are lacking a unified, oppressive narrative against which to position resistance. Moreover, the campus "culture wars" narrative fueled by the Right has served to galvanize many youth around a reactionary cultural project while distancing them from the very nature of the economic and political assault being waged against their future. All this raises another set of questions. The more important questions, ones that do not reproduce the all-too-commonplace demonization of young people as merely apathetic, are twofold. First, the issue should not be why there have been no student protests until recently, but why previous protests have been largely ignored. Evidence of such nascent protests, in fact, has been quite widespread. The student protests against the draconian right-wing policies attempting to destroy the union rights and collective bargaining power of teachers, promoted by Republican governor Scott Walker in Wisconsin, is one example indicating that students were in fact engaged and concerned. There were also smaller student protests taking place at various colleges, including Berkeley, CUNY, and other campuses throughout the United States. Until recently, student activists constituted a minority of US students, with very few enrolled in professional programs. Most student activists have come from the arts, social sciences, and humanities (the conscience of the college). Second, there is the crucial issue regarding what sort of disabling conditions young people have inherited in American society. What political and cultural shifts have worked together to undermine their ability to be critical agents capable of waging a massive protest movement against the growing injustices they face on a daily basis? After all, the assault on higher education in the United States, while not as severe as in Europe, still provides ample reason for students to be in the streets protesting.

Close to forty-three states have pledged major cuts to higher education in order to compensate for insufficient state funding. This means an unprecedented hike in tuition rates is being implemented, enrollments are being slashed, salaries are being reduced, and need-based scholarships are being eliminated in some states. Pell grants, which enable poor students to attend college, are also being cut. Robert Reich has chronicled some of the specific impacts on university budgets, which include cutting state funding for higher education by $151 million in Georgia, reducing student financial aid by $135 million in Michigan, raising tuition by 15 percent in Florida's eleven public universities, and increasing tuition by 40 percent in just two years in the University of California system.[35] As striking as these increases are, tuition has been steadily rising over the past several decades, becoming a disturbingly normative feature of postsecondary education in the United States.

A further reason that US students took so long to begin to mobilize may be because by the time the average US student now graduates, he or she has not only a degree but also an average debt of about $23,000.[36] As Jeffrey Williams points out in a 2008 article for *Dissent,* "Student Debt and the Spirit of Indenture," this debt amounts to a growing form of indentured servitude for many students. Being burdened by excessive debt upon graduation only to encounter growing rates of unemployment—"unemployment for recent college graduates rose from 5.8 percent to 8.7 percent in 2009"[37]—surely undercuts the opportunity to think about, organize, and engage in social activism. In other words, crippling debt plus few job prospects in a society in which individuals are relentlessly held as being solely responsible for the problems they experience leaves little room for rethinking the importance of larger social issues or the necessity for organized collective action against systemic injustice. In addition, as higher education increasingly becomes a fundamental requirement for employment, many universities have been able to justify the reconfiguration of their mission exclusively in corporate terms. They have replaced education with training while defining students as consumers, faculty as a cheap form of subaltern labor, and entire academic departments as revenue-generating units.[38] No longer seen as a public good or a site of social struggle, higher education is increasingly viewed as a credential mill for success in the global economy.

Meanwhile, not only have academic jobs been disappearing, but given the shift to an instrumentalist education that is decidedly technicist in nature, the culture of critical thinking has been slowly disappearing on US campuses as well. As universities and colleges emphasize market-based skills, students are learning neither how to think critically nor how to connect their private troubles with larger public issues. The humanities continue to be downsized, eliminating some of the most important opportunities many students will ever have to develop a commitment to public values, social responsibilities, and the broader demands of critical citizenship. Moreover, critical thinking has been devalued as a result of the growing corporatization of higher education. Under the influence of corporate values, thought in its most operative sense loses its modus operandi as a critical mediation on "civilization, existence, and forms of evaluation."[39]

It has become increasingly difficult for students to recognize how their formal education and social development in the broadest sense have been systematically devalued, and how this not only undercuts their ability to be engaged critics but contributes to the further erosion of what is left of US democracy. How else to explain the reticence of students within the last decade toward protesting against tuition hikes? The forms of instrumental training they receive undermine any critical capacity to connect the fees they pay to the fact that the United States puts more money into the funding of wars, armed forces, and military weaponry than the next twenty-five countries combined—money that could otherwise fund higher education.[40] The inability to be critical of such injustices and to relate them to a broader understanding of politics suggests a failure to think outside of the prescriptive sensibilities of a neoliberal ideology that isolates knowledge and normalizes its own power relations. In fact, one recent study by Richard Arum and Josipa Roksa found that "45 percent of students show no significant improvement in the key measures of critical thinking, complex reasoning and writing by the end of their sophomore years."[41]

The corporatization of schooling and the commodification of knowledge over the last few decades have done more than make universities into adjuncts of corporate power. They have produced a culture of critical illiteracy and further undermined the conditions necessary to enable students to become truly engaged, political agents. The value of knowledge is now linked to a crude instrumentalism, and the only mode of education that seems to matter is that which enthusiastically endorses learning marketable skills, embracing a survival-of-the-fittest ethic, and defining the good life solely through accumulation and disposal of the latest consumer goods. Academic knowledge has been stripped of its value as a social good. To be relevant, and therefore adequately funded, knowledge has to justify itself in market terms or simply perish.

Enforced privatization, the closing down of critical public spheres, and the endless commodification of all aspects of social life have created a generation of students who are increasingly being reared in a society in which politics is viewed as irrelevant, while the struggle for democracy is being erased from social memory. This is not to suggest that Americans have abandoned the notion that ideas have power or that ideologies can move people. Progressives pose an earnest challenge to right-wing ideologies and policies, but they seem less inclined to acknowledge the diverse ways in which the pedagogical force of the wider culture functions in the production, distribution, and regulation of both power and meaning. By contrast, the conservative willingness to use the educational force of the culture explains in part both the rapid rise of the Tea Party movement and the fact that it seemed to have no counterpart among progressives in the United States, especially young people. This is now changing, given the arrogant, right-wing attacks being waged on unions, public sector workers, and public school educators in Wisconsin, Florida, Ohio, New Jersey, and other states where Tea Party candidates have come to power.[42]

Progressives, largely unwilling to engage in a serious manner the educational force of the larger culture as part of their political strategy, have failed to theorize how conservatives successfully seize upon this element of politics in ways that far outstrip its use by the left and other progressive forces. Missing from their critical analyses is any understanding of how public pedagogy has become a central element of politics itself.

Public pedagogy in this sense refers to the array of different sites and technologies of image-based media and screen culture that are reconfiguring the very nature of politics, cultural production, knowledge, and social relations. Market-driven modes of public pedagogy now dominate major cultural apparatuses such as mainstream electronic and print media and other elements of screen culture, whose one-sided activities, permeated by corporate values, proceed more often than not unchallenged. Left to their own devices by progressive movements, which for decades have largely refused to take public pedagogy seriously as part of their political strategy, the new and old media with their depoliticized pedagogies of consumption may finally be encountering some resistance from the rising student protests around the globe.

Higher Education and the Erasure of Critical Formative Cultures

In a social order dominated by the relentless privatization and commodification of everyday life and the elimination of critical public spheres, young people find themselves in a society in which the formative cultures necessary for a democracy to exist have been more or less eliminated, or reduced to spectacles of consumerism made palatable through a daily diet of talk shows, reality TV, and celebrity culture. What is particularly troubling in US society is the absence of the vital formative cultures necessary to construct questioning persons who are capable of seeing through the consumer come-ons, who can dissent and act collectively in an increasingly imperiled democracy. Sheldon Wolin is instructive in his insistence that the creation of a democratic formative culture is fundamental to enabling both political agency and a critical understanding of what it means to sustain a viable democracy. According to Wolin,

Democracy is about the conditions that make it possible for ordinary people to better their lives by becoming political beings and by making power responsive to their hopes and needs. What is at stake in democratic politics is whether ordinary men and women can recognize that their concerns are best protected and cultivated under a regime whose actions are governed by principles of commonality, equality, and fairness, a regime in which taking part in politics becomes a way of staking out and sharing in a common life and its forms of self-fulfillment. Democracy is not about bowling together but about managing together those powers that immediately and significantly affect the lives and circumstances of others and one's self.[43]

Instead of public spheres that promote dialogue, debate, and arguments with supporting evidence, US society offers young people a conservatizing, consumer-driven culture through entertainment spheres that infantilize almost everything they touch, while legitimating opinions that utterly disregard evidence, reason, truth, and civility. The "Like" button has replaced the critical knowledge and the modes of education needed for long-term commitments and the search for the good society. Intimate and committed social attachments are short-lived, and the pleasure of instant gratification cancels out the interplay of freedom, reason, and responsibility. As a long-term social investment, young people are now viewed in market terms as a liability, if not a pathology. No longer a symbol of hope and the future, they are viewed as a drain on the economy, and if they do not assume the role of functioning consumers, they are considered disposable.

Within the last thirty years, the United States under the reign of market fundamentalism has been transformed into a society that is more about forgetting than learning, more about consuming than producing, more about asserting private interests than democratic rights. In a society obsessed with customer satisfaction and the rapid disposability of both consumer goods and long-term attachments, US youth are not encouraged to participate in politics. Nor are they offered the help, guidance, and modes of education that cultivate the capacities for critical thinking and engaged citizenship. As Zygmunt Bauman points out, in a consumerist society, "the tyranny of the moment makes it difficult to live in the present, never mind understand society within a range of larger totalities."[44] Under such circumstances, according to Theodor Adorno, thinking loses its ability to point beyond itself and is reduced to mimicking existing certainties and modes of common sense. Thought cannot sustain itself and becomes short-lived, fickle, and ephemeral. If young people do not display a strong commitment to democratic politics and collective struggle, then, it is because they have lived through thirty years of what I have elsewhere called "a debilitating and humiliating disinvestment in their future," especially if they are marginalized by class, ethnicity, and race.[45]

What sets this generation of young people apart from past generations is that today's youth have been immersed since birth in a relentless, spreading neoliberal pedagogical apparatus with its celebration of an unbridled individualism and its near pathological disdain for community, public values, and the public good. They have been inundated by a market-driven value system that encourages a culture of competitiveness and produces a theater of cruelty that has resulted in what Bauman calls "a weakening of democratic pressures, a growing inability to act politically, [and] a massive exit from politics and from responsible citizenship."[46] And, yet, they refuse to allow this deadening apparatus of force, manufactured ignorance, and ideological domination to shape their lives. Reclaiming both the possibilities inherent in the political use of digital technologies and social media, US students are now protesting in increasing numbers the ongoing intense attack on higher education and the welfare state, refusing a social order shaped by what Alex Honneth describes as "an abyss of failed sociality," one in which "the perceived suffering [of youth] has still not found resonance in the public space of articulation."[47]

Young people, students, and other members of the 99 percent are no longer simply enduring the great injustices they see around them, they are now building new public spaces, confronting a brutalizing police apparatus with their bodies, and refusing to put up with the right-wing notion that they are part of what is often called a "failed generation." Young people, especially, have flipped the script and are making clear that the failures of casino capitalism lie elsewhere, pointing to the psychological and social consequences of growing up under a neoliberal regime that goes to great lengths to enshrine ignorance, privatize hope, derail public values, and reinforce economic inequality and its attendant social injustices. What the Occupy Wall Street protesters, like their counterparts in London, Montreal, Athens, Cairo, and elsewhere, have made clear is that not only is casino capitalism the site of political corruption and economic fraud, but it also reproduces a "failed sociality" that hijacks critical thinking and agency along with any viable attempt of democracy to deliver on its promises.

In the face of a politically organized ignorance on the part of right-wing anti-public intellectuals, think tanks, media organizations, and politicians, the Occupy Wall Street protesters have refused to provide recipes and blueprints about a longed-for utopian future. Instead, they have resurrected the most profound elements of a radical politics, one that recognizes that critical education, dialogue, and new modes of solidarity and communication serve as conditions for their own autonomy and for the sustainability of democratization as an ongoing social movement. This is evident in their embrace of participatory democracy, a consensus model of leadership, the call for direct action, the development of co-op food banks, free health care clinics, and the development of a diverse model of multimedia communication, production, and circulation. What terrifies the corporate rich, bankers, media pundits, and other bloviators about this movement is not that it has captured the attention of the broader public but that it constantly hammers home the message that a substantive democracy requires citizens capable of self-reflection and social criticism, and that such citizens, through their collective struggles, are the products of a critical formative culture in which people are provided with the knowledge and skills to participate effectively in developing a radically democratic society. And this fear on the part of ruling classes and the corporate elite has gone global.

When we see fifteen-year-olds battling against established oppressive orders in the streets of Montreal, Paris, Cairo, and Athens in the hope of forging a more just society, we are being offered a glimpse of what it means for youth to enter "modernist narratives as trouble."[48] This expression of "trouble" exceeds the dominant society's eagerness to view youth as a pathology, as monsters, or as a drain on the market-driven order. Instead, trouble in this sense speaks to something more suggestive of what John and Jean Comaroff call the "productive unsettling of dominant epistemic regimes under the heat of desire, frustration, or anger."[49] The expectations that frame market-driven societies are losing their grip on young people, who can no longer be completely seduced or controlled by the tawdry promises and failed returns of corporate-dominated and authoritarian regimes.

What is truly remarkable about this movement is its emphasis on connecting learning to social change and its willingness to do so through new and collective modes of education. Equally encouraging is that this movement views its very existence and collective identity as part of a larger struggle for the economic, political, and social conditions that give meaning and substance to what it means to make democracy possible. In the United States, the Occupy Wall Street protests have made clear that the social visions embedded in casino capitalism and deeply authoritarian regimes have lost both their utopian thrust and their ability to persuade and intimidate through manufactured consent, threats, coercion, and state violence. Rejecting the terrors of the present along with the modernist dreams of progress at any cost, young people have become, at least for the moment, harbingers of democracy, fashioned through the desires, dreams, and hopes of a world based on the principles of equality, justice, and freedom. One of the most famous slogans of May 1968 was "Be realistic, demand the impossible." The spirit of that slogan is alive once again. But what is different this time is that it appears to be more than a slogan—it now echoes throughout the United States and abroad as both a discourse of critique and as part of a vocabulary of possibility and long-term collective struggle. The current right-wing politics of illiteracy, exploitation, and cruelty can no longer hide in the cave of ignorance, legitimated by their shameful accomplices in the dominant media. The lights have come on all over the United States and young people, workers, and other progressives are on the move. Thinking is no longer seen as an act of stupidity, acting collectively is no longer viewed as unimaginable, and young people are no longer willing to be viewed as disposable. Of course, how this movement plays out over time remains to be seen.

In the United States, the most important question to be raised about US students is no longer why they do not engage in massive protests or why have they not continued the massive protests that characterized the first year of the Occupy Wall Street protest movement, but *when will they join* their youthful counterparts protesting in London, Montreal, Athens, Istanbul, and elsewhere in building a global democratic order in which they can imagine a future different from the present? The test of these movements will be their ability to develop national associations and international alliances that can be sustained for the long run. But this will only happen when young people and others begin to organize collectively in order to develop the formative cultures, public spheres, and institutions that are crucial to helping them confront neoliberalism and the threats it poses to the environment, public goods, and those dispossessed by race, class, and age. Only then will they join together in individual and collective efforts to reclaim higher education as a public good vital for creating new imaginaries and democratic social visions.

CHAPTER THREE

Intellectual Violence in the Age of Gated Intellectuals:
Critical Pedagogy and a Return to the Political

BRAD EVANS AND HENRY A. GIROUX

> *The more radical the person is, the more fully he or she enters into reality so that, knowing it better, he or she can transform it. This individual is not afraid to confront, to listen, to see the world unveiled. This person is not afraid to meet the people or to enter into a dialogue with them. This person does not consider himself or herself the proprietor of history or of all people, or the liberator of the oppressed; but he or she does commit himself or herself, within history, to fight at their side.*
> **—Paulo Freire**

Introduction

Proverbial wisdom warns that while sticks and stones shall inflict pain, words will never kill us. Yet nothing is further from the truth: inflammatory rhetoric has *always* been a strategic precursor to the drums of warfare. This was perhaps most obvious in recent years in the discursive

77

violence used by the Bush administration to justify the invasions of Iraq and Afghanistan. Moreover, the periodic militaristic pronouncements employed by Israel and the United States as a precursor for a potential attack on Iran demonstrate that discourse can continually authenticate the meaning of violent encounters and produce organized violence. Intellectual discourse is also a veritable minefield littered with the corpses of radical pioneers who dared to venture into uncharted fields. One does not have to look too far to find the most sophisticated regimes of truth being used to offer the surest moral backbone to the most reasoned forms of human atrocities. Recent memory provides sufficient testimony here: we only have to look to the gradual buildup for each of the so-called wars on terror for evidence of "discursive creep." As we seamlessly moved through the various stages of securitization, civil liberties were shredded, terrorism became a term that justified the most violent actions, and the seemingly impossible became the altogether inevitable state of affairs. Among both academic and public intellectuals the paths to recognition, resources, and credibility have become dependent upon one's willingness to shamefully compromise with the utility of force and its compulsion to embed all things potentially subversive.

The university has not in any way been immune to these strategies of absorption, as the lines between the times of civic peace and militarism have become increasingly blurred to the latter's normalization. Increasingly, research and the production of knowledge within the university have become militarized as the role of the university has in fact given way to various methods of intellectual policing, with the main strategic function becoming the need to think how to wage war better. For such reasons academics occupy a somewhat (in)enviable position when it comes to the study of intellectual violence. We remain empirical objects and principal stakeholders due to the political stakes. Drawing upon personal experiences, many critical scholars in the post-9/11 moment have publically attested to and critiqued deeply embedded institutional forms of intellectual violence that have shaped their everyday working relations. They have also been highly critical of what they perceive as state violence around the world, a mode of violence that provides cover for the role that higher education often plays in legitimating such violence. Consequently, various critical scholars, such as Ward Churchill, Patricia Adler,

Norman Finklestein, Abu-Manneh, Terri Ginsburg, David Graeber, and, more recently, Samer Shehata, have been refused promotions, or, more severely, denied tenure.[1]

All too frequently positions of academic authority have been awarded to opportunistic careerists who remain completely untroubled by the burdens of complicated thought and the fight for ethical and political responsibility. While it is somewhat easier to come to terms with the usual suspects, who remain openly hostile to any form of post-1968 criticality as it challenges the simple comforts of rehearsed orthodoxy, it is the institutionally sanctioned violence that tends to take more subtle forms, frequently masked by the collegiate language of "consensus," "playing the game," and "majoritarianism," that is of greater concern. Such consensus-building majorities brazenly offer the most fantastic appropriation of democratic terms. What passes for the majority here is not a numeric expression but a particularistic relation of force that provides a sure glimpse into the authoritarian personality so apt to Theodor Adorno's sense of inquiry.[2] Some may invariably call this leadership. The dark and poisonous influence of authoritarianism often wraps itself in the discourse of patriotism, rights, duty, and—most shamefully—the mantle of democracy. Yet if leadership is to reclaim its political and ethical standing and have any collegiate relevance whatsoever, it must be afforded by those who are meant to be inspired by the example and not made to feel coerced into submission.

We are not suggesting a uniform experience. Nor do we refuse to acknowledge the many forms of resistance to this mode of creeping academic authoritarianism. Some schools, faculties, and globally reputable institutions still take great pride in their commitment to the opening of possibilities for thinking the political anew and reclaiming a link between the production of knowledge and social change. Such resistance needs to be celebrated and vigorously defended. And so do the principles of a significant number of scholars who still recognize that the essential function of the university is to continue to hold power to account. The neoliberal assault on global academia is, however, now so pervasive and potentially dangerous in its effects that it is must be viewed as more than a "cause for concern." While the system in the United States has been at the forefront of policies that have tied academic merit to market-driven performance indicators, the ideologically driven transformations under way in the United Kingdom point in an equally worrying direction as the need for policy entrepreneurship increasingly becomes the norm.

The closures of entire philosophy programs signify the most visible shift away from reflective thinking to the embrace of a dumbed-down approach to humanities education with no time for anything beyond the objectively neutralizing and politically compromising deceit of pseudo-scientific paradigms that replace education with training and emphasize teaching to the test. Instrumentalism in the service of corporate needs and financial profit now dominates university modes of governance, teaching, research, and the vocabulary used to describe students and their relationship to each other and the larger world. What is most disturbing about the hyper-militarization of the university and of knowledge is the militarization of pedagogy itself. No longer viewed as a political and ethical practice that provides the conditions for critical thought and engaged modes of democratic action, pedagogy has become repressive. That is, this market-driven pedagogy "mobilizes people's feelings primarily to neutralize their senses, massaging their minds and emotions so that the individual succumbs to the charisma of vitalistic power,"[3] if not the normalization of violence itself. Increasingly within the university, thinking critically and embracing forceful new angles of vision are all too frequently viewed as heresy. One consequence is that those who dare challenge institutional conformity through a commitment to academic freedom and intellectual inquiry often find that insightful ideas emerge only to die quickly.

Discourses, ideas, values, and social relations that push against the grain, redefine the boundaries of the sensible, and reclaim the connection between knowledge and power in the interest of social change too often not only become inconvenient but also rapidly accelerate to being viewed as dangerous. If the dissent is pressed too far, it can lead to being fired, prison time, and possibly death. As Gilles Deleuze once maintained, nobody is ever intellectually put into prison for powerlessness or pessimism. It is the courage to articulate the truth that so perturbs. For thought to be "meaningful," then, it has to become empty, inhabiting a "no-fly" space utterly policed by the apologists for conformity. Any pedagogy that aims at turning out informed citizens makes one immediately suspect.

And it is not simply academics but all cultural workers who now suffer under this rising tide of ignorance that has become a hallmark of a repressive neoliberal ideology. This leaves us, in part, wondering how any author or artist in the current climate could ever create anything remotely comparable to oft-cited historical masterpieces that were not subjected to intellectually compromised performance deadlines. But we are also left to question whether the term "university" itself is appropriate for certain institutions that declare open hostility to the very academic discipline and forms of intellectual inquiry that gave original meaning to the idea of public education.

Despite their provocative intentions, our concerns take us beyond those all-too-familiar vitriolic forms of extremism that seek to publicly shut down points of difference through good old-fashioned bullying techniques. However abhorrent they appear, it is better that such inflammatory thoughts are put into the public arena so that nothing is subject to misinterpretation or counterfactual claims of misrepresentation. Indeed, although it is undoubtedly the case that the center ground for global politics more generally has moved to the extreme right of the spectrum in all its various ontotheological, faith-based expressions, the symbolic violence of the vitriolic leaves enough visible traces to be openly condemned with an even greater degree of intellectual effort. Yet our concern is with the more sophisticated forms of intellectual violence that, although sometimes openly condescending in their patronizing churlishness, nevertheless present a formidable challenge due to the weight of their reasoning. Such violence is a familiar neoliberal deceit. It emanates from a progressive constituency that draws upon the virtues of enlightened praxis and its normalizing tendencies to make us desire that which even the most momentary forms of conscious and reflective political thought will deem particularly intolerable. These normalizing tendencies can be seen in the support of progressives for the wars in Iraq and Afghanistan, indifference to the corporatization of higher education, and utter silence about the status of the United States as "one of the biggest open-air prisons on earth."[4] And such intellectual violence occasions with either personal displays of utmost courteousness or talks to a much wider claim of humanitarianism.

There is a bankrupt civility at work here, disingenuous in its complicity with violence and disillusioned about the social costs it promotes and the moral coma it attempts to impose on those considered rudely uncivil, code for those who take intellectual risks and are willing to think critically and hold power accountable. The very notion that the university might have a role to play in either promoting or resisting authoritarian politics, state and corporate-sponsored violence, and war is often met with a condescending lifting of the head or wave of the hand that bespeaks the violence and deep order of politics lurking beneath this banalized appropriation of civility as code for a flight from moral, political, and pedagogical responsibility. This is the civility of authoritarians who flee from open conflict and mask their intellectual violence with weak handshakes, forced smiles, and mellowed voices. Like the punishment dished out to a recalcitrant child, however, through reason of seductive persuasion or reason of a more brutal force, more "mature" (the authoritarian default) ways of thinking about the world must eventually be shown to be the natural basis for authority and rule.

The concept of violence is not taken lightly here. Violence remains poorly understood if it is accounted for simply in terms of how and what it kills, the scale of its destructiveness, or any other element of its annihilative power. Intellectual violence is no exception as its qualities point to a deadly and destructive conceptual terrain. As with all violence, there are two sides to this relation. There is the annihilative power of nihilistic thought that seeks, through strategies of domination and practices of terminal exclusion, to close down the political as a site for differences. Such violence appeals to the authority of a peaceful settlement, though it does so in a way that imposes a distinct moral image of thought that already maps out what is reasonable to think, speak, and act. Since the means and ends are already set out in advance, the discursive frame is never brought into critical question. And there is an affirmative counter that directly challenges authoritarian violence. Such affirmation refuses to accept the parameters of the rehearsed orthodoxy. It brings into question that which is not ordinarily questioned. Foregrounding the life of the subject as key to understanding political deliberation, it eschews intellectual dogmatism with a commitment to the open possibilities in thought. However, as we shall argue in this chapter, rather than countering intellectual violence with a "purer violence" (discursive or otherwise), there is a need to maintain the language of critical pedagogy. By "criticality," we insist upon a form of thought that does not have war or violence as its object. If there is destruction, this is only apparent when the affirmative is denied. And by criticality we also insist upon a form of thought that does not offer its intellectual soul to the seductions of militarized power. Too often we find that while the critical gestures toward profane illumination, it is really the beginning of violence that amounts to a death sentence for critical thought. Our task is to avoid this false promise and demand a politics that is dignified and open to the possibility of nonviolent ways of living.

The Tyranny of Reason

Michel Foucault introduced the concept of the biopolitical to denounce the illusion of institutional peace and the inevitability of freedom despite the existence of free-flowing power relations. As he put to question, "When, how and why did someone come up with the idea that it is a sort of uninterrupted battle that shapes peace, and that the civil order— its basis, its essence, its essential mechanisms—is basically an order of battle?"[5] There are two important aspects to deal with here. First, when Foucault refers to "killing" in a biopolitical sense he does not simply refer to the vicious and criminal act of physically taking a life: "When I say 'killing,' I obviously do not mean simply murder as such, but also every form of indirect murder: the fact of exposing someone to death, increasing the risk of death for some people, or, quite simply, political death, expulsion, rejection and so on."[6] And second, despite any semblance of peace, it is incumbent upon the critical cartographer to bring into question normalized practices so as to reveal their scars of battle:

> [My methodology] is interested in rediscovering the blood that has dried in the codes, and not, therefore, the absolute right that lies beneath the transience of history; it is interested not in referring the relativity of history to the absolute of law, but in discovering beneath the stability of the law or the truth, the indefiniteness of history. It is interested in the battle cries that can be heard beneath the formulas of right.[7]

This represents an important shift in our understanding of violence. No longer simply content with exploring extrajuridical forms of violent abuse, attentions instead turn toward those forms of violence that take place in the name of human progress and the emancipatory subject. This type of violence takes place through a hidden order of politics concealed beneath the circuits of discursive regimes of truth, civility, and representations of a commodified culture that is fully and uncritically absorbed in the modernist notion of progress.

The dominant institutions for social progress today are no longer sovereign in any popular sense of the term. State sovereignty has been compromised by corporate sovereignty just as state power now more closely resembles the workings of a carceral state. At the same time, politics has become local and power is now global, unrestricted by the politics of the nation-state and indifferent to the specificity of its practices and outcomes. Power and violence have been elevated into the global space of flows.[8] The most evident development of this has been the veritable "capitalization of peace" in which the global ravages of poverty, war, and violence are tied to neoliberal policies that, proceeding in the name of human togetherness/progress/unity, conceal an inner logic of biopolitical separation and social containment.[9]

As politics is emptied of its ability to control global power, the bankruptcy of biocapitalism becomes evident in the hollowing out of the social state and the increasing force of the dominant discourses and policies that legitimate its extinction. For example, when the Bush and Obama administrations argued that the banks were too big to fail, we were presented with more than another neoliberal conceit regarding supply-side economics and its practice of distributing wealth and income away from the already impoverished to the already enriched. The more dangerous conceit paved the way for the destruction of even the most minimal conditions for a sustainable democracy. This subterfuge at one level argues that the victims of casino capitalism are guilty of waging class warfare while at the same time the ruling elite destroy all those public spheres capable of providing even minimal conditions for individuals to engage the capacities to think, feel, and act as engaged and critical citizens. And they do it in the midst of a decrepit and weakened state of politics that holds corporate power unaccountable, while endlessly repeating the poisonous mantra of deregulation, privatization, and commodification. The banking elite and the mega-financial services openly serve the rich while engaging in widespread ecological devastation as well as destroying the safety nets that serve the poor and the middle class. But since the banking sector is seen to be integral to the vision of planetary peace, its surviv-ability is morally tied to humanity's potential for self-ruination.

The ruinous logic of militarization now provides global finance with the mad machinery of violence in order to dispense with the power of reason and the demands of global social responsibility. To put it another way, since global finance is openly presented to be central to the neolib-eral security *dispositif*, we should be under no illusions where military al-legiance lies. George W. Bush certainly didn't send troops into Iraq and Afghanistan for the betterment of the victims of market fundamentalism at home or those Iraqis suffering under the ruthless dictatorship of Sad-dam Hussein. Neither was the more recent securitization of the London Olympics carried out to protect immigrant populations living on the margins in the capital's run-down areas. There is therefore no hegemonic discourse in any conventional sovereign geo-strategic sense of the term. Instead, what appears is a neoliberal will to rule that is upheld by a for-midable school of intellectual thought and takes direct aim at the criti-cally minded as a dangerous community to be vanquished. Reason in this sense is unmoored from its emancipatory trappings, reduced to a le-gitimating discourse for a notion of progress that embraces a mode of technological rationality that operates in the service of repression and the militarization of thought itself.[10]

The contemporary tyranny of reason is not exclusively tied to state power and now works within modes of sovereignty constructed through the logics of biocapitalism and its growing banking and financial sectors. Reason embraces such tyranny through an ossified logic of the market and its principle of risk. It is most revealing to find that economic agencies are at the forefront of this policy that has made economic questions of prime political significance. During the 1990s organizations such as the World Bank increasingly became interested in political concerns as the focus of their work (along with economics more generally) changed from the managed recoveries of national crises to the active promotion of better lives.[11] Transforming their remit from economic management to security governance, such organizations became moral agents in their own right, advocating economic solutions to the ravages of civil wars, criminality, shadow economies, poverty, endemic cultural violence, and political cor-ruption. This was matched by a particular revival in the ideas of political economists such as Friedrich Von Hayek and Milton Friedman, who long equated neoliberalism with marketable freedoms. Neoliberalism in this case becomes a source of political and moral legitimacy, determined not only to institute market-based structural reforms but also to establish the conditions for producing particular types of agency, subjects, and social relations that are said to thrive by embracing a logic of risk that promotes insecurity as a principal design for existence.

The unchecked celebration of a neoliberal subject willing to take market-based risks—either financial or through acts of consumption—does more than provide a rationale for the corrupt trading practices of investment bankers and hedge fund power brokers, it also points to the closer connection between those considered the producers of capital and those who are now the new at-risk, disposable populations. The financial elite now view themselves as corporate missionaries promoting policies, practices, and ideas that are not only designated as universal but take their inspiration from God. How else to interpret Goldman Sachs's chief executive Lloyd Blankfein's comment that he is just a banker "doing God's work."[12] Needless to say, those individuals and populations who are outside the accumulation, possession, and flow of capital are considered the new parasites, excess, and global human waste. That is, those considered failed consumers—"enemy combatants," unpatriotic dissidents, poor minority youth, low-income white kids, immigrants, and others inhabiting the margins of global capital and its intellectual ecosystem of vast inequality and ruthless practices of disposability. Capital is not only wedded to the production of profits, it is also invested in a form of intellectual violence that legitimates its savage market-driven practices and the exercise of ruthless power. When applied to the intellectual terrain, to paraphrase C. Wright Mills, we are seeing the breakdown of democracy, the disappearance of critical thought, and "the collapse of those public spheres which offer a sense of critical agency and social imagination."[13] Since the 1970s, we have seen the forces of market fundamentalism strip education of its public values, critical content, and civic responsibilities as part of its broader goal of creating new subjects wedded to the logic of privatization, efficiency, flexibility, consumerism, and the destruction of the social state.

Tied largely to instrumental purposes and measurable paradigms, many institutions of higher education are now committed almost exclusively to economic growth, instrumental rationality, and the narrow civically deprived task of preparing students strictly for the workforce. The question of what kind of education is needed for students to be informed and active citizens is now rarely asked.[14] Hence, it is no surprise, for example, to read that "Thomas College, a liberal arts college in Maine, advertises itself as Home of the Guaranteed Job!"[15] Within this discourse, faculty are largely understood as a subaltern class of low-skilled entrepreneurs, removed from the powers of governance and subordinated to the policies, values, and practices within a market model of the university that envisages pure instrumentality.[16]

Within both higher education and the educational force of the broader cultural apparatus—with its networks of knowledge production in the old and new media—we are witnessing the emergence and dominance of a form of a powerful and ruthless, if not destructive, market-driven notion of governance, teaching, learning, freedom, agency, and responsibility. Such modes of education do not foster a sense of organized responsibility central to a democracy. They corrupt any commitment to critical pedagogy. As David Harvey insists, "The academy is being subjected to neoliberal disciplinary apparatuses of various kinds [while] also becoming a place where neoliberal ideas are being spread."[17]

Not only does neoliberalism undermine civic education and public values as well as confuse education with training, it also treats knowledge as a product, promoting a neoliberal logic that views schools as malls, students as consumers, and faculty as entrepreneurs. Just as democracy appears to be fading throughout the liberal world, so is the legacy of higher education's faith in and commitment to democracy. As the humanities and liberal arts are downsized, privatized, and commodified, higher education finds itself caught in the paradox of claiming to invest in the future of young people while offering them few intellectual, civic, and ethical supports. One such measure of the degree to which higher education has lost its ethical compass can be viewed in the ways in which it disavows any relationship between equity and excellence, eschews the discourse of democracy, and reduces its commitment to learning to the stripped-down goals of either preparing students for the workforce or teaching them the virtues of measurable utility. While such objectives are not without vocational merit, they have little to say about the role that higher education might play in influencing the fate of future citizens and the state of democracy itself, nor do they say much about what it means for academics to be more than technicians or hermetic scholars.

Gated Academics

Giorgio Agamben came to prominence during the immediate aftermath of 9/11 as his work on the state of exception seemed to strike a precise chord.[18] Central then to Agamben's work was his concern with the spatial figuration of the camp and how sites such as Guantánamo Bay removed any semblance of political, legal, and ethical rights. Bare life thus became a defining critical motif for many who were concerned with the perceived lawlessness of the US administration and its allies as they deployed excessive force against enemies real or newly provoked. We have never been entirely convinced by Agamben's understanding of the modern *nomos* or stripping away of political agency for the globally oppressed. Neither have we been content to focus our attentions simply on the violence that takes place in distinct sites of social abandonment as if all things within law (especially violence) are devoid of complementary relations.

While we do accept that policies of containment are sometimes a preferred method for dealing with troublesome populations who need to be curtailed, along with disposable populations that have nothing meaningful to exploit, encamped life has always been situated within a much wider terrain of market-driven processes that give secondary consideration to surplus lives. What is more, as neoliberal governmentality faces a global crisis of its own making, we are in fact encountering a logical inversion to Agamben's modeling as the politically *included* are increasingly being forced into fortified compounds and gated protectorates that link together the nodal points of a privatized sovereignty within the global space of flows. Having said this, Agamben's insistence that biopolitical marks of separation reveal a distinct violence has merit. It is not, however, that the human condition needs violence in order to resolve its differences. Imposed universality takes hold of difference to produce a violent cartography of human separation.

It is often said that the days when intellectuals could live in an ivory tower are gone. While this is true (and is partly driven by the market's need to have a distinct intellectual identity), contemporary intellectuals, mirroring the world of which they are part, increasingly inhabit a radically interconnected world in which corporate-driven, networked, structured relations define how they mediate their relationship both to the university and the broader world of global flows. A number of critical scholars and academics have been dismayed by this development, as the pursuit of knowledge once central to the creation of epistemic communities gives way to various risk-based assessments. Others openly embrace the idea of "the gated intellectual."[19] Replicating the structural logic of privately owned, fortified strongholds evident in all global megacities, gated intellectuals—walled off from growing impoverished populations—are also cut loose from any ethical mooring or sense of social responsibility as understood in a reciprocal sense of the term. Instead they voice their support for what might be called gated or border pedagogy—one that establishes boundaries to protect the rich, isolates citizens from each other, excludes those populations considered disposable, and renders invisible young people, especially poor youth of color, along with others marginalized by class and race. Such intellectuals play no small role in legitimating what David Theo Goldberg has called a form of neoliberalism that promotes a "shift from the caretaker or pastoral state of welfare capitalism to the 'traffic cop' or 'minimal' state, ordering flows of capital, people, goods, public services and information."[20]

Gated intellectuals and the privately funded institutions or marketed forms of finance that support them believe in societies that stop questioning themselves, engage in a history of forgetting, and celebrate the progressive "decomposition and crumbling of social bonds and communal cohesion."[21] Policed borders, surveillance, state secrecy, targeted assassinations, armed guards, and other forces provide the imprimatur of dominant power and containment, making sure that no one can trespass onto gated property, domains, sites, protected global resources, and public spheres. On guard against any claim to the common good, the social contract, or social protections for the underprivileged, gated intellectuals spring to life in universities, news programs, print media, charitable foundations, churches, think tanks, and other cultural apparatuses, aggressively surveying the terrain to ensure that no one is able to do the crucial pedagogical work of democracy by offering resources and possibilities for resisting the dissolution of sociality, reciprocity, and social citizenship itself. Such guarded consolidation and retrenchment of positions does not entertain paranoiac entropy. It has already amassed an arsenal of preemptive intellectual strikes that allegedly document the demise of the public intellectual as an unfortunate side effect or collateral damage to a wider war effort into which we are all openly recruited. If gated communities are the false registers of safety, gated intellectuals have become the new registers of conformity.

The gated mentality of market fundamentalism has walled off, if not disappeared, those spaces where dialogue, critical reason, and the values and practices of social responsibility can be engaged. The armies of antipublic intellectuals who appear daily on television, radio talk shows, and other platforms work hard to create a fortress of indifference and manufactured stupidity. They ask that intellectualism remain a private affair. Public life is therefore reduced to a host of substanceless politicians, embedded experts, and gated thinkers who pose a dire threat to those vital public spheres that provide the minimal conditions for citizens who can think critically and act responsibly. Higher education is worth mentioning because, for engaged and public intellectuals, it is one of the last strongholds of democratic action and reasoning and one of the most visible targets along with the welfare state.

As is well known, higher education is increasingly being removed from the discourse of public values and the ideals of a substantive democracy at a time when it is most imperative to defend the institution against an onslaught of forces that are as anti-intellectual as they are antidemocratic in nature. Many of the problems in higher education can be linked to the evisceration of funding, the intrusion of the security apparatus of the state, the lack of faculty self-governance, and a wider culture that appears increasingly to view education as a private right rather than a public good. Within the wider sociopolitical environment, corporate power and interests are all too willing to define higher education as a business venture, students as consumers and investors, and faculty as a cheap source of labor. Left to the logic of the market, education is something that consumers and investors now purchase for the best price, deal, and profit. All of these disturbing trends, left unchecked, are likely to challenge the very meaning and mission of the university as a democratic public sphere.

Gated intellectualism points to new forms of intellectual violence—violence(s) that is/are markedly different from the old colonial pursuit of "redeeming savages" through brutalizing subservience, the suppression of women's rights, and the often violent attacks on homosexuals. Although it is fully appreciated that the outside can no longer be left to chance, the veritable distancing between the gated intellectual and his or her precarious surroundings points to a form of inclusive exclusion whose violence employs the preferred technologies of the time. Not only is drone violence the preeminent technology for contemporary forms of violence in which war is seldom declared, it is also the apt metaphor for the twenty-first-century intellectual violence of the gated intellectual.

Abandoning any attempts at making the world more enlightened, what takes its place is a short, sharp, and speedy intellectual attack that points to a purely immanent conception of thought. Such thinking has no time to reflect upon the significance of events. It has no patience for contested memories or excavating the complex histories that make our present. Neither does it entertain the possibility that the world may be thought and lived otherwise. What remains is a politically settled intellectual environment that deems everything alternative to be potentially hostile. There is nothing in this relationship that suggests any reciprocal attempt at establishing better ethical relations among the world of peoples. Instead, fully removed from the realities of contested political spaces, neoliberal risk assessment measures, along with their highly biotechnologized performance indicators, become the surest way to create alternative conditions of the real. This is nothing but simulacrum. It proposes nothing but a manufactured reality that is virtually conceived within the highly policed nodal protectorates of neoliberal governance without any concern to experience the world.

Violence to Memory

History remains the biggest casualty of intellectual violence. The past is written so that the present course of action appears both natural and timeless. What is at stake here is the question of memorialization and how this relates to a politics of events. We have no concern here with those various speculative attempts at offering a definitive philosophical proof for the meaning of events in order to stupefy publics with another form of intellectual violence. There is no poetic joy to reading such hyperstructural technicism, whose language is akin to a perpetual motion machine whose only purpose is its own activity. Political events are now framed in order to debunk any notion of critical analyses on account of the fact that they break open what false semblance of peace exists to the creation of new ways of thinking and relating to the world. Not, of course, to suggest that the conditions that give rise to a revolutionary impetus cannot be critically understood as we seek to explain systemic oppression. But it is to acknowledge that political events have to be understood in terms of their own specificity, and that they forever appear *untimely* (to echo Nietzsche's claim) to us at their moment of arising. Who, for instance, could have anticipated the impact of Rosa Parks's simple yet profound disruption of elements that sent into permanent flux the conventional order of things? Or that the first visible signs of resistance to the New World Order would come from the Zapatistas—an incredibly poor indigenous population in an unknown land?

Our concern with intellectual violence brings us directly to the closing down of the historical space as the multiple experiences of political events are subsumed within the one "true" narrative. September 11, 2001, showed how imposing a uniform truth on the event represented a profound failure of the political imaginary. Judith Butler accounts for this in terms of the framing of the problem:

> The "frames" that work to differentiate the lives we can apprehend from those we cannot (or that produce lives across a continuum of life) not only organize visual experience but also generate specific ontologies of the subject. Subjects are constituted through norms which, in their reiteration, produce and shift the terms through which subjects are recognized.[22]

Importantly, for Butler, since what matters here is the subsequent production of certain truthful subjectivities out of the ashes of devastation, we must bring into question the framing of life as a seemingly objective ontological and epistemological fact:

> To call the frame into question is to show that the frame never quite contained the scene it was meant to limn, that something was already outside, which made the very sense of the inside possible, recognizable. The frame never quite determined precisely what it is we see, think,

recognize, and apprehend. Something exceeds the frame that troubles our sense of reality; in other words, something occurs that does not conform to our established understanding of things.[23]

This call to break with the dominating content of the time is more than an attempt to draw attention to the multiplicity of the experiences of events. It is to open up the space of the political by breaking apart the myth that there is a universal experience of truth. In the hours and days that followed the tragic events of September 11, 2001, the unfolding sense of trauma and loss drew people together in a fragile blend of grief, shared responsibility, compassion, and a newfound respect for the power of common purpose and commitment.[24] The translation of such events into acts of public memory, mourning, and memorializing are ambivalent and deeply unsettling. They offered no certainty. We must recall that they do not only bring about states of emergency and the suspension of civil norms and order: they can, and did, give birth to enormous political, ethical, and social possibilities. Yet, such enlightened moments proved fleeting. A society has to move with deliberate speed from the act of witnessing to the responsibility of just memorializing; put simply, to the equally difficult practice of reconfiguring what politics, ethics, and civic engagement should mean after 9/11. On the tenth anniversary of that tragic day, the struggle to remember and reclaim those moments in good faith was constantly challenged, and in ways that few of us would dare to have imagined a decade later. Public memory became the enemy of a state immersed in a culture of fear as dissent and civil liberties were sacrificed on the altar of security, and ethics and justice gave way from the state legitimation of torture under George W. Bush to the state's right, under President Obama, to murder those considered an enemy of the state, regardless of the due process of law.[25]

The events of 9/11 show how loss, memory, and remembrance share an uneasy, if not unsettled, embrace. Remembrance can become dysfunctional, erasing the most important elements of history and trivializing what survives of the event through either crass appeals to an untroubled celebration of patriotism or a crass commercialization of 9/11 as just another commodity for sale. But remembrance can also recover what is lost to this historical amnesia. It can both produce difficult thoughts, bringing forth not only painful memories of personal loss and collective vulnerability but also new understandings of how specific events infuse the present, and become a force for how one imagines the future, including, to quote Roger Simon, how "one imagines oneself, one's responsibility to others, and one's civic duty to a larger democratic polity and range of diverse communities."[26] Memory can be an instigator of both despair and hope, often in ways in which the division between desperation and hope becomes blurred. For instance, the spectacular shock and violence of 9/11 ruptured an arrogant and insular period in American history that had proclaimed the triumph of progress and the end of ideology, history, and conflict, all the while imposing an unbearable experience of loss, grief, sorrow, and shock on large segments of the world's population.

The collective fall from grace is now well known. Instead of being a threshold to a different future and a register for a restored democratic faith, the decade following 9/11 became an era of buried memories and monumentalization. Rather than initiating a period of questioning and learning, the war on terror morphed into a war without end, producing abuses both at home and abroad, all of which resembled an unending fabric of normalizing violence. America's particular status as a symbol of freedom that elicited worldwide respect was fatefully diminished, giving way to a culture of fear, mass hysteria, and state secrecy. At the same time that the Bush administration waged war overseas, it unleashed ruthless market forces at home, along with a virulent propaganda machine in which public issues collapsed into private concerns, and the future—like the futures market that drove it—was detached from any viable notion of ethical and social responsibility. Finance capital replaced human capital, economics was detached from ethics, youth were viewed as *a* risk rather than *at* risk, and the formative culture necessary for a democracy collapsed into a rampaging commercialism as citizens became defined exclusively as consumers and the notion of the social along with collaborative social bonds were viewed as a liability rather than as a public good central to any viable notion of civic engagement and democracy itself. Finance capital replaced the social debt—based on the obligations we owe to each other—with financial debt, in which creditors now savagely rule a generation of debtors chained to contractual relations marked by persistent deficits, hardships, surveillance, and subordination.[27]

Shared trauma of violence doesn't, however, necessarily translate into discourses of revenge. Counter-violence is simply the option most preferred by certain political ways of thinking. Undoubtedly the history of modern politics has been marked out by the normality of violence. Therefore, what the United States and its allies did in the immediate aftermath of 9/11 was not in any way exceptional. Doing nothing violent in response would have been exceptional. Instead, the response followed the all-too-familiar conventional norm of using violence to reason the world, serve justice, and avert future catastrophes. But it *must* be remembered that none of this is inevitable. Indeed, despite this violent weight of historical reasoning, at the human level it is increasingly clear that the experience of the tragedy was far more complex. What 9/11 made apparent is that memory as a moral, critical, and informed practice requires those elements of counter-memory that challenge the official narratives of 9/11 in order to recover the most valuable and most vulnerable elements of democratic culture too often sacrificed in tragedy's aftermath.

In the hours and days that bled out from the tragic events of 9/11, the unfolding sense of trauma and loss drew us together in a fragile blend of grief, shared responsibility, compassion, and a newfound respect for the power of common purpose and commitment. Hence, if we truly wished to honor the victims of 9/11, we should not be reluctant to engage in a public dialogue about both the legacy and the politics that precipitated and emerged from the events that took place on that tragic day. Such uncomfortable moments of consciousness provide the basis for a form of witnessing that refuses the warmongering, human rights violations, xenophobia, and violations of civil liberties that take shape under the banner of injury and vengeance. Simon Critchley dared to think the "impossible":

> What if the government had simply decided to turn the other cheek and forgive those who sought to attack it, not seven times, but seventy times seven? What if the grief and mourning that followed 9/11 were allowed to foster a nonviolent ethics of compassion rather than a violent politics of revenge and retribution? What if the crime of the Sept. 11 attacks had led not to an unending war on terror, but the cultivation of a practice of peace — a difficult, fraught and ever-compromised endeavour, but perhaps worth the attempt?[28]

Critchley's provocation offers more than a warning against the political ruination of violent responses. He is challenging us to think how we may have a political ethics adequate to such events. This shift toward a politics of forgiveness is no doubt a remarkable task. Perhaps that is the precise point. Ours remains a history marked by a violent humanism so often masquerading under the name of security, peace, and justice. Advocating a politics of forgiveness when faced with such crises is that which passes for something truly exceptional—an affirmative politics of real exceptionalism. Critchley's affinity with Derridean ethics is striking here. As Jacques Derrida maintained, an act of forgiveness worthy of the name must be offered in event of something altogether unforgiveable: "It *should not be* normal, normative, normalizing. It should remain exceptional and extraordinary, in the face of impossible: as if it interrupted the ordinary course of historical temporality."[29] This forgiveness as we currently see it presents itself as an aporia of the impossibility of forgiving unforgivable acts.

And yet, as Derrida reminds us, it is precisely when the aporetic moment arrives that it becomes both possible and necessary. He writes: "It only becomes possible from the moment that it appears impossible."[30] The fact that such a proposition still appears altogether impossible is indicative of the continuum of violence. And yet, the normalized alternative, so common to the history of modern life, illustrates with devastating and politically debilitating surety why Nietzsche was insistent that nihilistic behavior was tied to a spirit of revenge. Once we begin to act out of resentment, so the catastrophic cycle of violence continues to the evacuation of political alternatives. At a time when neoliberalism has turned governance into a legitimation for war, surveillance, and terror, the spirit of revenge and a culture of cruelty do more than permeate everyday lives; the discourse of revenge also reinforces the power of the national security state and contributes to the expansion of its punishing apparatuses, extending from the prison to the schoolroom. And increasingly, the punitive nature of the practices produced by the national security state bear down heavily on those intellectuals now labeled as whistle blowers, "unprivileged enemy belligerents," unpatriotic critical academics, and so on. In the midst of the production of such violence, collective fear serves to silence intellectuals, force them into gated and safe citadels where they do not have to fear being wiretapped, targeted, kidnapped, or subject to state of emergency laws such as the Patriot Act or the National Defense

Authorization Act (NDAA). Or it seduces them into either silence or complicity with the rewards of power, regardless of how tainted ethically and politically such rewards might be.

Radical Criticality

One of the consequences of thinking about threats in global terms has been the collapse of the space/time continuum that once held together the linear world of sovereign reasoning.[31] While we may rejoice, in part, at the breaking open of the former Westphalia semblance of peace that effectively served already established colonial powers by rewriting the rules in their favor, its displacement by a full-spectrum catastrophic imaginary of endangerment has been politically disastrous. As times of war and times of peace merge without any meaningful distinction, so there has been a collapse of the private into the public, the militaristic into the civic, and the authoritarian into the humanitarian. An intellectual casualty of this has been the merger between the radical and the fundamental. While each of these terms once retained a very distinct and oppositional meaning, their coming together is indicative of a social terrain that is violently hostile to political difference. Any thought that seeks to affirm alternative ways of thinking or service to the world is treated as either some immature posturing (the unreason of youth) or the surest indication of a pathological dysfunction (reasoned hostility). So our question therefore becomes, How may we reclaim the terms of radical criticality without succumbing to a violent reasoning that propels us to mimic dominant ways of thinking politics?

We need to learn to live with violence less through the modality of the sacred than through the critical lens of the profane. By this we mean that we need to appreciate our violent histories and how our subjectivities have been formed through a history of physical bloodshed. This requires more of a willingness to interrogate violence in a variety of registers (ranging from the historical and concrete to the abstract and symbolic) than it does a bending to the neoliberal discourses of fate and normalization. We need to acknowledge our own shameful compromises with the varied forces of violence. And we need to accept that intellectualism shares an intimate relationship with violence both in its complicity with violence and as an act of violence. There is an echo of the pornographic here not just in the ethical detachment that now accompanies state violence, particularly with drone technologies, but also in the recuperation of the pleasure principle in the increasing maximization of the spectacle of violence. We need then to reject what Leo Lowenthal has called the imperative to believe that "thinking becomes a stupid crime."[32] This does not require a return to the language of Benjamin's idea of divine violence as a pure expression of force regardless of its contestable claims to non-violent violence.[33] We prefer instead to deploy the oft-abused term "critical pedagogy" as a meaningful political counter to vicissitudes of intellectual violence.

Intellectuals are continually forced to make choices (sometimes against our better judgments). The truth, of course, is that there are no clear lines drawn in the sand neatly separating what is left from what is right. And yet as Paulo Freire insisted, one is invariably drawn into an entire history of struggle the moment our critical ideas are expressed as force and put out into the public realm to the disruption of orthodox thinking. There is, however, a clear warning from history: our intellectual allegiances should be less concerned with ideological dogmatism. There is, after all, no one more micro-fascist or intellectually violent than the authenticating militant whose self-imposed vanguardism compels allegiance through the stupidity of unquestioning loyalty and political purity. To the charges here that critical pedagogy merely masks a retreat into cultural relativism, we may counter that there is no reciprocal relationship with that which doesn't respect difference while at the same time recognizing that pedagogy is an act of intervention. Pedagogy always represents a commitment to the future, and it remains the task of educators to make sure that the future points the way to a more socially just world, a world in which the discourses of critique and possibility in conjunction with the values of reason, freedom, and equality function to alter, as part of a broader democratic project, the grounds upon which life is lived. This is hardly a prescription for either relativism or political indoctrination, but it is a project that gives education its most valued purpose and meaning, which in part is "to encourage human agency, not mould it in the manner of Pygmalion."[34]

Critical pedagogy has a responsibility to mediate the tension between a respect for difference and the exercise of authority that is directive, that is, a mode of authority capable of taking a position while not standing still. Central to its understanding as a moral and political practice, pedagogy as a form of cultural politics contests dominant forms of symbolic production while constantly opening a space to question its own authority and the ever-present danger of fetishizing its own practices. An ethics of difference is central to such a pedagogy, especially at a historical conjuncture in which neoliberalism arrogantly proclaims that there are no alternatives. Within this regime of common sense, neoliberalism eliminates issues of contingency, struggle, and social agency by celebrating the inevitability of economic laws in which the ethical ideal of intervening in the world gives way to the idea that we "have no choice but to adapt both our hopes and our abilities to the new global market."

An ethics of difference, as Foucault critically maintained, requires waging an ongoing fight against fascism in all its forms: "not only historical fascism, the fascism of Hitler and Mussolini—which was able to use the desire of the masses so effectively—but also the fascism in us all, in our heads, and in our everyday behaviour, the fascism that causes us to love power, to desire the very thing that dominates and exploits us."[35] Or as Deleuze once put it, "In every modernity and every novelty, you find conformity and creativity; an insipid conformity, but also 'a little new music'; something in conformity with the time, but also something untimely—separating the one from the other is the task of those who know how to love, the real destroyers and creators of our day."[36]

Academics then are required to speak a kind of truth, but as Stuart Hall points out, "maybe not truth with a capital T, but . . . some kind of truth, the best truth they know or can discover [and] to speak that truth to power."[37] Implicit in Hall's statement is the awareness that to speak truth to power is not a temporary and unfortunate lapse into politics on the part of academics: it is central to opposing all those modes of ignorance, whether they are market-based or rooted in other fundamentalist ideologies that make judgments difficult and democracy dysfunctional. Our view is that academics have an ethical and pedagogical responsibility not only to unsettle and oppose all orthodoxies, to make problematic the commonsense assumptions that often shape students' lives and their understanding of the world, but also to energize them to come to terms with their own power as individual and social agents. Higher education, in this instance, as Pierre Bourdieu, Paulo Freire, Edward Said, Stanley Aronowitz, Susan Searls Giroux, and other intellectuals have reminded us, cannot be removed from the hard realities of those political, economic, and social forces that both support it and consistently, though in diverse ways, attempt to shape its sense of mission and purpose.[38] Politics is not alien to higher education but central to comprehending the institutional, economic, ideological, and social forces that give it meaning and direction. Politics also references the outgrowth of historical conflicts that mark higher education as an important site of struggle. Rather than the scourge of either education or academic research, politics is a primary register of their complex relation to matters of power, ideology, freedom, justice, and democracy.

Talking heads who proclaim that politics have no place in the classroom can, as Jacques Rancière points out, "look forward to the time when politics will be over and they can at last get on with political business undisturbed," especially as it pertains to the political landscape of the university.[39] In this discourse, education as a fundamental basis for engaged citizenship, like politics itself, becomes a temporary irritant to be quickly removed from the hallowed halls of academia. In this stillborn conception of academic labor, faculty and students are scrubbed clean of any illusions about connecting what they learn to a world "strewn with ruin, waste and human suffering."[40] As considerations of power, politics, critique, and social responsibility are removed from the university, balanced judgment becomes code, as C. Wright Mills suggests, for "surface views which rest upon the homogeneous absence of imagination and the passive avoidance of reflection. A vague point of equilibrium between platitudes."[41] Under such circumstances, the university and the intellectuals who inhabit it disassociate higher education from larger public issues, remove themselves from the task of translating private troubles into social problems, and undermine the production of those public values that nourish a democracy. Needless to say, pedagogy is always political by virtue of the ways in which power is used to shape various elements of classroom identities, desires, values, and social relations, but that is different from being an act of indoctrination.

Instead of accepting the role of the gated intellectual, there is an urgent need for public intellectuals in the academy, art world, business sphere, media, and other cultural apparatuses to move from negation to hope. Now more than ever we need reasons to believe in this world. This places renewed emphasis on forms of critical pedagogy that move across different sites—from schools to the alternative media—as part of a broader attempt to construct a critical formative culture in the Western world that enables citizens to reclaim their voices, speak out, exhibit ethical outrage and create the social movements, tactics, and public spheres that will reverse the growing tide of neoliberal fascism. Such intellectuals are essential to democracy, even as social well-being depends on a continuous effort to raise disquieting questions and challenges, use knowledge and analytical skills to address important social problems, alleviate human suffering where possible, and redirect resources back to individuals and communities who cannot survive and flourish without them. Engaged public intellectuals are especially needed at this time to resist the hollowing out of the social state, the rise of a governing-through-crime complex, and the growing gap between the rich and poor that is pushing all liberal democracies back into the moral and political abyss of the Gilded Age—characterized by what David Harvey calls the "accumulation of capital through dispossession," which he claims is "is about plundering, robbing other people of their rights" through the dizzying dreamworlds of consumption, power, greed, deregulation, and unfettered privatization that are central to a neoliberal project.[42]

Under the present circumstances, it is time to remind ourselves that critical ideas are a matter of critical importance. Ideas are not empty gestures, and they do more than express a free-floating idealism. Ideas provide a crucial foundation for assessing the limits and strengths of our senses of individual and collective agency and what it might mean to exercise civic courage in order to not merely live in the world but to shape it in light of democratic ideals that would make it a better place for everyone.

Critical ideas and the technologies, institutions, and public spheres that enable them matter because they offer us the opportunity to think and act otherwise, challenge common sense, cross over into new lines of inquiry, and take positions without standing still—in short, to become border-crossers who refuse the silos that isolate the privileged within an edifice of protections built on greed, inequitable amounts of income and wealth, and the one-sided power of neoliberal governance. Gated intellectuals refute the values of criticality. They don't engage in debates; they simply offer already rehearsed positions in which unsubstantiated opinion and sustained argument collapse into each other. Yet, instead of simply responding to the armies of gated intellectuals and the corporate money that funds them, it is time for critical thinkers with a public interest to make pedagogy central to any viable notion of politics. It is time to initiate a cultural campaign in which the positive virtues of radical criticality can be reclaimed, courage to truth defended, and learning connected to social change. The current attack on public and higher education by the armies of gated intellectuals is symptomatic of the fear that reactionaries have of critical thought, quality education, and the possibility of a generation emerging that can both think critically and act with political and ethical conviction. Our task is to demand a return to the political as a matter of critical urgency.

CHAPTER FOUR

Universities Gone Wild:
Big Sports, Big Money, and the Return
of the Repressed in Higher Education

HENRY A. GIROUX AND SUSAN SEARLS GIROUX

The ever-expanding, ever-deepening nature of the scandal that took place at Pennsylvania State University in 2012 reveals a broad constellation of forces that contributed to the lurid events that sent shock waves through Happy Valley. Comprehending all of the factors that enabled Jerry Sandusky to perpetrate the decade-long serial sexual abuse of young boys is very challenging to say the least—like finding an intellectual foothold in a bottomless pit. One thing is certain, the sordid details constituting the evidence of abuse, the subsequent cover-up and the firing of legendary coach Joe Paterno, along with a number of high-ranking administrators including the university's president, add credence to the rising concern among many Americans that political democracy and the institutions and values that support it are in jeopardy. Although influential media commentators, including journalists such as Paul Krugman of the *New York Times*, have sounded alarms about the collapse of public values, few have connected this horrific scandal to the larger war on youth in America and the continuing collapse of higher education as a democratic public sphere.

This absence of concern regarding youth represents more than a failure of the imagination, particularly given the growing numbers of young people across the United States who are calling attention to a national crisis in education—one that cannot be separated from the radical retreat from social responsibility by an adult citizenry charged with the dual guardianship of its children and the institutions that sustain democratic public life. When placed in this broader context, the Penn State scandal must be seen as a tragic, but not an isolated, incident. Rather, the conditions that have made this revolting series of events possible are replicated on university campuses across the country, derailing the academic mission that has historically defined the enterprise of higher education and compromising the moral leadership and integrity of many postsecondary institutions. Young people have suffered not only the degradation of quality education at all levels but also its increasing inaccessibility for much of their generation. Tuition hikes have gone fist in glove with the defunding of public education, and those who attend university are more often than not saddled with massive debt. In fact, "student private loan debt topped 1 trillion dollars, beating out credit card debt as the highest form of consumer debt, with the exception of mortgage loans."[1] States, in turn, have used their dwindling financial resources as an effective alibi to abet the transformation of universities into commodified knowledge factories or refashion them into extensions of the military-industrial complex.[2] The corporatization and militarization of higher education are not new processes, but they were sharply accelerated during the decade that followed the September 11, 2001, terrorist attacks and have continued unchecked through the recession that commenced with the global financial crisis of 2008.

When students, such as those recently on the campus of University of California, Davis, organized peacefully to challenge these processes and their objectionable impacts on higher education, they have directly experienced—or have borne witness to their friends and peers—being arrested, pepper-sprayed at point-blank range, and assaulted by baton-wielding police on a number of campuses across the country. All the while, the very politicians who support permanent war whatever the costs—and refuse to fund job programs for young people facing record unemployment as they slash financial aid for higher education—taunt the student protesters to take showers and find work. In an irony that invariably escapes the notice of the "liberal media," peaceful protesters are now criminalized and subject to the ruthless dictates of the punishing state, while Wall Street executives and bankers who engaged in various forms of financial fraud, causing savage and ruinous injury to many Americans, roam free and unscathed by the criminal justice system. Given that young people will bear the burden of a multitrillion-dollar deficit, disappearing social safety nets, stagnant job growth, and decrepit educational institutions at all levels, it is no longer hyperbolic to suggest that the war effort has come home—and its primary targets are youth, especially the most vulnerable.[3]

Consider that the conservative politician and former Republican Party presidential candidate Newt Gingrich advocates rewarding the rich with generous tax cuts while exploiting young people by revoking child labor laws in order to allow them to work as janitors in their own schools. He has justified this ludicrous plan by alleging that poor young people grow up in neighborhoods where they are not taught much-needed work habits, and they don't know how to show up for work on Monday. Encouraged by this line of thought, an expansive Gingrich proclaims that poor Black kids don't have to become "pimps, prostitutes, or drug dealers"; to the contrary, they can learn good work habits when they go to school by mopping floors and cleaning toilets. That such youth would take over the unionized janitorial jobs of members of their communities is an added bonus in Gingrich's eyes. One of the few to condemn his racist logic was Comedy Central's Larry Wilmore, whose satirical skit on *The Daily Show* sums up Gingrich's position with the comment: "Dream big, black people! You don't have to be a pimp, prostitute or drug dealer, just clean toilets." In mock juxtaposition with Obama's 2008 "campaign of hope," a banner appears across the Republican candidate's bully pulpit reading "Yes, We Clean!"[4] There is no room in Gingrich's benevolent racism for the concept of the *working* poor, nor for policy reforms calling for job creation for young people, decent employment for their parents, adequate childcare, a living wage, or quality schools for all children. In fact, Gingrich is also against extending unemployment insurance because, as he says, "I am opposed to giving people money for doing nothing."[5] And yet many of the wealthy today have made their fortunes not by creating jobs but by destroying them—a charge he did not fail to level at his arch-rival for the 2012 Republican nomination, Mitt Romney.

As the 2012 Republican presidential candidate race made clear, the poisonous values and power relations that animated the corrupt Wall Street financiers and bankers who produced the financial meltdown and subsequent recession have been embraced by those vying for political leadership in this country.[6] But these market-driven values and power relations have also seeped into a range of public institutions, including higher education. Challenging the pervasive influence of unfettered capitalism across a variety of social institutions has become a central tenet of the student protesters, who argue that such institutions no longer serve the educational, intellectual, economic, and social interests of young people. Too many universities are now beholden to big business, big sports, and big military contracts. And it is within this set of contexts that we must read the Penn State scandal. Much media attention has been drawn to the fact that Penn State pulls in tens of millions of dollars in football revenue annually, but nothing has been said of the fact that it also receives millions from Defense Department contracts and grants, ranking sixth among universities and colleges receiving funds for military research.

The lure of such lucrative partnerships is all the more irresistible given the cumulative consequences of decades of ever-receding state financial support for higher education. The drivers for the cuts in governmental support arise not only from the neoliberal desire to defund all things public, but also from certain demographic shifts that exacerbate such pressures, like the population's changing age distribution, which pits the young and the aged, along with the institutions and policies that serve them, against one another. Consider that "by 2030, for every retired person there will be only two persons in the labor force. When Social Security was introduced in the 1930s, the ratio was 20:1."[7] The postsecondary sector has also been losing the competition for state funding given the increased demand for health care and other forms of care for an aging population. The criminal justice system has been another beneficiary of increased state support, the fiscal consequences of which have been particularly felt in the state of California. But these shifts only account for part of the financial challenges confronting the postsecondary sector. Indeed, higher education now faces a wave of revolutionary changes similar to those in the period of significant upheaval from 1940–1970.

These are the result of the increasing internationalization of higher education and new competition for students coming from Asia, India, and elsewhere. In addition, the proliferation of digital technologies, which has in turn enabled the phenomenon of online universities, has brought with it greater competition for students from the for-profit educational sector. In large part, the result of these considerable financial pressures has been that the academic mission of the university is now less determined by internal criteria established by faculty researchers with knowledge, expertise, and a commitment to the public good than by external market forces concerned with achieving fiscal stability and, if possible, increasing profit margins. One has only to look closely at the tragedy at Penn State University to understand the potentially catastrophic consequences of this decades-long transformation in higher education.

The Penn State crisis may well prove one of the most serious scandals in the history of college athletics and university administration, while it also reinforces the claim by Paul Krugman that "democratic values are under siege in America."[8] Jerry Sandusky, who coached the Nittany Lions for more than thirty years, used his position of authority at the university as well as at his Second Mile Foundation, a foster home, to lure vulnerable minors into situations in which he preyed on them sexually, having gained unfettered access to male youths through a range of voluntary roles.[9] Sandusky was charged with sexually abusing at least a dozen boys, all of whom were twelve years old or younger when they were attacked. In fact, his adopted son announced during the trial that he was also abused by Sandusky.

On at least three occasions, extending from 1998 to 2002, Sandusky was caught abusing young boys on the Penn State campus. These incidents have been the consistent focus of media attention. In 1998, a distraught mother of a boy who had showered with Sandusky reported the incident to the campus police. A janitor also observed Sandusky performing oral sex on a young boy in a Penn State gym in 2000. Finally, according to the grand jury report in the Sandusky case, Mike McQueary, then a twenty-eight-year-old graduate assistant for the Penn State football team, alleged that in 2002 he saw Sandusky raping a young boy in the shower in the Lasch Football Building on the University Park campus. It therefore took nine years for the police to investigate and finally arrest Sandusky, who was eventually charged with and convicted of forty-five charges of sexual abuse. In October 2012, Judge John Cleland ruled Sandusky a dangerous sexual offender and sentenced him to thirty to sixty years in prison for sexually abusing ten boys—"all of the boys were from disadvantaged homes"—over a fifteen-year period.[10]

As tantalizingly sensational as the media have found these events, the scandal is about much more than a person of influence using his power to sexually assault young boys. This tragic narrative is as much about the shocking lengths to which rich and powerful people and institutions will go in order to cover up their complicity in the most horrific crimes, and to refuse responsibility for egregious violations that threaten their power, influence, and brand names.[11] The desecration of public trust is all the more vile when the persons and institution in question have been assigned the intellectual and moral stewardship of generations of youth. Nor is this the first time that Penn State's senior administration and their beloved Coach Paterno have been guilty of inaction when confronted with evidence of escalating harassment and actual threats to young people's lives on campus—and subsequent efforts to conceal such events.

Beginning in 2000, coterminous with the unfolding Sandusky affair but an altogether separate incident, Black students and football players on the main campus in the town of State College began receiving hate mail and actual death threats. The team's Black quarterback was singled out (it was assumed) for much of the vitriol because he had been arrested off-season for assaulting a white police officer in his home town of Hoboken, New Jersey.[12] The events came to a painful head when the body of a Black male was found near the main campus by police, as one of the death threats had warned. Very little was known about the threats to students on campus—though many appeared at their May 2001 graduation ceremony wearing bullet-proof vests—because neither Penn State officials nor its legendary coach would risk the negative publicity such media attention would inevitably bring.

More than ten years later, when news of the coach's firing broke, the former president of the campus's Black Student Caucus, LaKeisha Wolf, recalled a chilling 2001 meeting with Paterno in which she and other students asked him to talk with the players who were concerned for their safety. Paterno's reply to the students was that he would never do anything to risk the university's reputation. Wolf recalled, "To me that said that even if he had specific knowledge of football players' or students' lives in danger that he wouldn't allow that to risk Penn State's image being tainted and that this is something that has stuck in my mind for the last ten years."[13]

The most recent cover-up appears to have begun in 1998 when the Centre County district attorney, Ray Cricar, did not file charges against Sandusky, in spite of obtaining credible evidence that Sandusky had molested two young boys in a shower at Penn State. Then, in 2000, the janitor who witnessed similar abuse and his immediate superior whom he told about it both failed to report the incident to the police for fear of losing their jobs, only to reveal the story years later. But the cover-up that has attracted the most attention took place in 2003 after Mike McQueary reported to celebrated coach Joe Paterno that he saw Sandusky having anal intercourse with a ten-year-old boy in one of the football facility's showers. Paterno reported the incident to his athletic director, Tim Curley, who then notified Gary Schultz, a senior vice president for finance and business. Both informed President Spanier about the incident. In light of the seriousness of a highly credible and detailed report alleging that a child had been raped, the Penn State administration simply responded by barring Sandusky from bringing young boys onto the university campus. At the end of the day, neither Paterno nor any of the highly positioned university administrators reported the alleged assault of a minor to the police and other proper authorities. Within a week after the story broke in the national media eight years later, Paterno, Schultz, Curley, and Spanier had all been fired. Sandusky was initially charged with "more than 50 charges stemming from accusations that he molested boys for years on Penn State property, in his home and elsewhere."[14] The charges included involuntary sexual intercourse, indecent assault, unlawful contact with a minor, corruption of minors, and endangering the welfare of a minor.

In the most shameful of ironies, the national response to the story has similarly engaged in a covering-up of the violent victimization of children that lies at its core. The young boys who were sexually abused have been relegated to a footnote in a larger and more glamorous story about the rise and sudden fall and eventual death of the legendary Joe Paterno, a larger-than-life athletic icon. Their erasure is also evident in the equally sensational narrative about how the university attempted to hide the horrific details of Sandusky's history of sexual abuse by perpetuating a culture of silence in order to protect the privilege and power of the football and academic elite at Penn State. If any attention was paid at all to distraught and disillusioned youth, it was to focus on the Penn State students who rallied around "Joe-Pa," not on the youth who bore the weight into their adulthood of the egregious crimes of rape, molestation, and abuse. As many critics have pointed out, both dominant media narratives fail to register just how deeply this tragedy descends in terms of what it reveals about our nation's priorities about youth and our increasing unwillingness to shoulder the responsibility—as much moral and intellectual as financial—for their care and development as human beings.

Michael Bérubé rightly asserts that the scandal at Penn State and the ensuing "student riots on behalf of a disgraced football coach" should not be used to condemn the vast majority of teachers, researchers, and students at Penn State, "none of whom had anything to do with this mess."[15] Equally pertinent is his observation that Penn State has a long history of rejecting any viable notion of shared governance and that "decisions, even about academic programs, are made by the central administration, and faculty members are 'consulted' afterward."[16] The American Association of University Professors (AAUP) extended Bérubé's argument, insisting that the lack of faculty governance has to be understood as a consequence of a university system that favors the needs of a sports empire over the educational needs of students, the working conditions of faculty, and health and safety of vulnerable children. As Cary Nelson and Donna Potts point out,

> Recent accounts of the systemic cover-up of allegations of sexual assaults on young boys at Penn State indicate that the unchecked growth of a sports empire held unaccountable to the rest of the university community coincided with the steady erosion of faculty governance. Genuine shared governance, which involves meaningful participation by the faculty in all aspects of an institution, could have resulted in these

alleged crimes being reported to city and state police years ago, and might have spared some of the victims the trauma they endured, and indeed continue to endure, because of the memories that remain, and the legal and judicial processes they still face. The national Council of the American Association of University Professors joins with Penn State faculty member Michael Bérubé in calling on the Penn State administration to begin treating faculty members, and their elected representatives on the Faculty Senate, as equal partners in the institution.[17]

The call for forms of shared governance in which faculty through their elected representatives are treated with respect and exercise power alongside administrators signals an important issue—namely, how many university administrations operate in nontransparent and unaccountable ways that prioritize financial matters over the well-being of students and faculty. At the same time, it is not uncommon for entrepreneurial faculty members to transgress established strategic priorities and circumvent layers of university oversight and adjudication altogether by bringing in earmarked funding for a pet project (through which s/he stands to gain), confident no administrator can refuse cash up front, whatever the Faustian bargain attached to it.

Big money derived from external sources has changed the culture of universities across the United States in other ways as well. For example, in 2010, Penn State made $70,208,584 in total football revenue and $50,427,645 in profits; moreover, it was ranked third among US universities in bringing in football revenue. As part of the huge sports enterprise that is NCAA Division I Football, Penn State and other high-profile "Big Ten" universities not only make big money but also engage in a number of interlocking campus relationships with private-sector corporations. Lucrative deals that generate massive revenue are made through media contracts involving television broadcasts, video games, and Internet programming. Substantial profits flow in from merchandizing football goods, signing advertising contracts, and selling an endless number of commodities from toys to alcoholic beverages and fast food at the stadium, tailgating parties, and sports bars. Yet the flow of capital is not unidirectional. Universities also pay out impressive amounts of money to support such enterprises and to attract star athletes; they hire support staffing from janitorial positions to top physicians in sports medicine and celebrity coaches; they pay to maintain equipment, grounds, stadia, and myriad other associated services. Consider Beaver Stadium—the outdoor college football monument to misplaced academic priorities—which has a seating capacity of 106,572 seats that require cleaning and maintenance. The stadium holds as many people as the entire population of State College, including Penn State students, all of whom require armies of staff to accommodate their needs. In this instance, the circulation of money and power on university campuses mimics its circulation in the corporate world, saturating public spaces and the forms of sociality they encourage with the imperatives of the market. Money from big sports programs also has an enormous influence on shaping agendas *within* the university that play to their advantage, from the neoliberalized, corporatized commitments of an increasingly ideologically incestuous central administration to the allocation of university funds to support the athletic complex and the transfer of scholarship money to athletes rather than academically qualified but financially disadvantaged students. As *Slate* writer J. Bryan Lowder puts it, big sports "wield too much influence over college life. In an institution that is meant to instill the liberal values of critical thinking and an egalitarian sense of equality in its students, having special dining rooms or living quarters for athletes . . . is a bad idea."[18]

In addition to the enormous distraction from academic mission that college sports have come to represent (for the students no less than the administration), one could also argue that these highly profitable and much celebrated sports programs have consolidated a culture of white masculine privilege, gender illiteracy, and sexual violence—violence that the Penn State scandal reveals has extended to both young women and children. We cannot emphasize enough the fact that young men are not biologically predisposed to any of these attitudes or behaviors; they have learned them. Sexism, misogyny, and violence run through US culture like an electric current; big-money sports only add more juice. What should be deeply unsettling and yet remains unspoken in mainstream media analyses is that the youth have also learned these lessons *at the university*, where they have been immersed in a culture that favors entertainment over education—the more physical and destructive the better—competition over collaboration, a worshipful stance toward iconic sports heroes over thoughtful engagement with academic leaders who should inspire by virtue of their intellectual prowess and moral courage, and herd-like adhesion to coach and team over and against one's own capacity for informed judgment and critical analysis. The consolidation of masculine privilege in such instances enshrines patriarchal values and exhibits an astonishing indifference to repeated cases of sexual assaults on college campuses.

Sexual assault is a major problem on college campuses across the United States, as revealed in national statistics demonstrating that "one in five women [was] sexually assaulted while in college, and approximately 81 percent of students experienced some form of sexual harassment during their school years."[19] However, in the years we taught at Penn State, it reached alarming proportions. According to the Center for Women Students on the university's main campus, "At Penn State approximately 100 students sought assistance for sexual assault during the 1996–97 academic year."[20] For those familiar with the behavior often exhibited by victims of sexual violence, the fact that one hundred students came forward in a single year is simply shocking, given the overwhelming reticence most victims feel about reporting attacks. In addition to feeling fear and shame, the reluctance to report an assault is reinforced when the victim believes that it will seldom result in arrest or conviction. Put simply, this means that the extent of cases and many of the consequences of sexual assault, physical abuse, hazing, and violence on college campuses are probably much greater than what is actually known.

The Penn State scandal clearly revealed that women are not the only victims of rising masculinist aggression and sometimes lethal violence, as did a number of stories released in subsequent weeks about sexual abuse at Syracuse University and the death of Robert Champion from hazing by other band members at Florida A&M University. Julian White, the band director, said he had notified the university administration repeatedly about the hazing, but that nothing was done about it. He also claimed that there has been a long history of hazing among college marching bands.[21] With respect to the ritual hazing associated with athletic teams, *New York Times* columnist Joe Nocera argues that at the heart of such violence is the refusal of big sports schools either to acknowledge such behavior or to punish those who engage in it. In the end, Nocera offers the rather anemic proposal that universities should "treat players and coaches the same way everyone else is treated," and in doing so can impart the right lessons.[22] This suggestion may be sincere, but it ignores the larger governmental and institutional forces that make the postsecondary sector so vulnerable and so attractive to sources of external funding.

Perhaps equally alarming is that such banal solutions overlook the dramatic cultural shifts that big-money sports—at the professional no less than the collegiate level—have introduced to both campus life and the mainstream culture, the essence of which can be summed up in the title of a December 2011 opinion column in the *New York Times*: "Are We Not Man Enough?" The thrust (so to speak) of the argument by author Steve Kettmann is that through the influence of sports culture, more and more men have become attracted to steroid use, seeking to feel younger, more powerful, more aggressive, more virile, and more "sexy." In fact, serial steroid abuse scandals in professional baseball in recent years have proven a perverse boon to the "juicing" industry. Kettmann notes:

> Total testosterone prescriptions have skyrocketed, from 1.75 million in 2002 to 4.5 million last year. The demand, said John Hoberman, author of "Testosterone Dreams," isn't limited to would-be pro athletes; it extends to "police officers, bouncers, biker gangs and the 'anti-aging' industry that provides legal prescriptions to millions of older males."[23]

The illegal, illicit, and dangerous dimensions of steroid use notwithstanding, the shift in cultural norms relating to gender and sexuality raises some troubling questions. What Kettmann pointedly asks of a corporate culture that pushes "juicing" like a new line of soft drinks, we would do well to pose to colleges and universities: "Do we really want to feed a business culture that increasingly elevates cocksure confidence and pushiness above all else, especially if it filters into everyday life? In an era marked by the dangerous decisions of an entire industry full of gung-ho alpha males, shouldn't we be wary of a culture that pushes us even further in that direction?"[24]

To be sure, recent events on a number of college campuses reveal that business culture is not the only culprit in perpetuating the abuses of masculinist power and privilege. Claire Potter, writing in the *Chronicle of Higher Education,* argues that Penn State and universities in general have a vested interest in safeguarding their reputations by covering up acts of sexual violence. For Potter, "Universities substitute private hearings, counseling and mediation for legal proceedings: while women often choose this route, rather than filing felony charges against their assailants, it doesn't always serve their interest to do so. But it always serves the interests of the institution not to have such cases go to court."[25] Given how events have unfolded at the university, Potter's withering charge that Penn State has a greater interest in protecting its brand name than in protecting students—who are reduced to revenue-producing entities rather than seen as young people to whom it has the responsibility intellectually and ethically to shape and inspire—gains considerable force. For Potter, social power at universities dominated by a big sports culture often expresses itself not just in the glory of the game, the reputation of the coaches, or the herd-like devotion to a team, but also in forms of sexual power aimed at abusing female students. Potter wants to move these incidents away from the sports pages and popular media into classrooms where they can be understood within a larger set of economic, social, and political contexts and appropriately challenged.

In writing about Penn State's patriarchal culture and its relationship to big sports programs, Katha Pollitt contributes an insightful analysis about what she calls "the patriarchal aspect of the Penn State scandal." Pollitt writes:

> I know it's predictable and boring, but come on, people! There really is a message here about masculine privilege: the deification of a powerful old man who can do no wrong, an all-male hierarchy protecting itself (hello, pedophile priests), a culture of entitlement and a truly astonishing lack of concern about sexual violence. This last is old news, unfortunately: sexual assaults by athletes are regularly covered up or lightly punished by administrations, even in high school, and society really doesn't care all that much . . . According to *USA Today*, an athlete accused of a sex crime has a very good chance of getting away with it. If Sandusky had abused little girls, let alone teenage or adult women, would he be in trouble today? Or would we say, like the neighbors of an 11-year-old gang-raped in Cleveland, Texas, that she was asking for it?[26]

Pollitt argues that college sports distort academic programs and promote a culture of violence. Her answer to such problems is to close down college sports that make money and simply transform all athletic programs into nonprofit entities, hence removing them from the money, power, and profit-oriented influence that make them a semi-autonomous force on so many college campuses. Sophia McClennen, a professor at Penn State, argues that the fact that all of the people involved in the Penn

State scandal were men not only tarnishes the entire campus but offers no understanding of what alternative models of masculinity might look like, models based on what she calls an "ethical masculinity."[27]

The hardened culture of masculine privilege, big money, and sports at Penn State is reinforced as much through a corporate culture that makes a killing off the entire enterprise as it is through a retrograde culture of illiteracy—defined less in terms of an absence of knowledge about alternatives to normative gender behavior and more in terms of a wilfully embraced ignorance—that is deeply woven into the fabric of campus life. Even and especially in higher education, one cannot escape the visual and visceral triumph of consumer culture, given how campuses have come to look like shopping malls, treat students as customers, confuse education with training, and hawk entertainment and commodification rather than higher learning as the organizing principles of student life. Across universities, the ascendancy of corporate values has resulted in a general decline in student investment in public service, a weakening of social bonds in favor of a survival-of-the-fittest atmosphere, and a pervasive undercutting of the traditional commitments of a liberal arts education: critical and autonomous thinking, a concern for social justice, and a robust sense of community and global citizenship.

As academic labor is linked increasingly to securing financial grants or downsized altogether, students often have little other option than to take courses that have a narrow instrumental purpose, and those who hold powerful administrative positions increasingly spend much of their time raising money from private donors. The notion that the purpose of higher education might be tied to the cultivation of an informed, critical citizenry capable of actively participating and governing in a democratic society has become cheap sloganeering on college advertising copy, losing all credibility in the age of big money, big sports, and corporate influence. Educating students to resist injustice, refuse antidemocratic pressures, or learn how to make authority and power accountable remains at best a receding horizon—in spite of the fact that such values are precisely why universities are pilloried by moneyed Republicans as hotbeds of Marxist radicals.

The displacement of academic mission by a host of external corporate and military forces surely helps to explain the spontaneous outbreak of rioting by a segment of Penn State students once the university announced that Joe Paterno had been fired as the coach of the storied football team. Rather than holding a vigil for the minors who had been repeatedly sexually abused, students ran through State College wrecking cars, flipping a news truck, throwing toilet paper into trees, and destroying public property. J. Bryan Lowder understands this type of behavior as part of a formative culture of social indifference and illiteracy reinforced by the kind of frat-house insularity produced on college campuses where sports programs and iconic coaches wield too much influence. He writes:

> Building monuments to a man whose job is, at the end of the day, to teach guys how to move a ball from one place to another, is . . . inappropriate. And, worst of all, allowing the idea that anyone is infallible—be it coach, professor or cleric—to fester and infect a student body to the point that they'd sooner disrupt public order than face the truth is downright toxic to the goals of the university. . . . Blind, herd-like dedication to a coach or team or school is pernicious. Not only does it encourage the kind of wild, unthinking behavior displayed in the riot, but it also fertilizes the lurid collusion and willful ignorance that facilitated these sex crimes in the first place. But what to do? As David Haugh asked in the *Chicago Tribune*: "When will [the students] realize, after the buzz wears off and sobering reality sinks in, that they were defending the right to cover up pedophilia?"[28]

A number of critics have used the Penn State scandal to call attention to the crisis of moral leadership that characterizes the neoliberal managerial models that now exert a powerful influence over how university administrations function. As democratic culture and values are replaced by market mentalities and moralities, once laudable commitments to socially ameliorative reform are replaced by a narrow focus on individual achievement. Collective responsibility and agency have given way to individual self-interest and the privatization of rights discourse, such that students' "rights" to freely express sexist or racist views are routinely upheld at the expense of an entire social group's right to a respectful learning environment free of insult and harassment. The results of such cultural shifts at institutions like Penn State and Florida A&M have been nothing short of abhorrent and appalling. As the investment in the public good collapses, leadership cedes to reductive forms of management, concerned less with big ideas than with appealing to the pragmatic demands of the market, such as raising capital, streamlining resources, and separating learning from any viable understanding of social change. Anything that impedes profit margins and the imperatives of instrumental rationality with its cult of measurements and efficiencies is seen as useless. Within the logic of the new managerialism, there is little concern for matters of justice, fairness, equity, and the general improvement of the human condition insofar as these relate to expanding and deepening the imperatives and ideals of a substantive democracy. Discourses about austerity, budget shortfalls, managing deficits, restructuring, and accountability so popular among college administrators serve largely as a cover "for a recognisably ideological assault on all forms of public provision."[29]

Critics of a now dominant managerial approach to higher education, such as Cathy Davidson, an English professor and former vice-provost at Duke University, point to the recent attacks by campus police on students—highlighting in particular the aggressive pepper-spraying of peacefully demonstrating students at the University of California at Davis in particular—as egregious examples of the failure of university leadership.[30] And so it would appear that too many administrators are incapable of engaging students as students, rather than as consumers or even criminals. Penn State and UC Davis are only two of the latest examples that bespeak an absence of intellectual leadership and moral authority in the postsecondary sector, precisely in that vaunted space essential for the articulation of new ideas and visions that speak to the profound economic, social, and political problems that students confront at this time in history. Goldie Blumenstyk and Jack Stripling argue that ethically challenged leadership at universities such as Penn State suggests broader questions about the moral credibility of postsecondary administrators. They rightfully argue that such scandals send the message that university leaders are more concerned about big money and protecting corporate interests than they are about educating and protecting students.[31] For instance, consider the fate of Graham B. Spanier, who was not only fired as president of Penn State in 2011 but also has been indicted on eight counts, five of which are felonies, that include perjury, obstruction of justice, endangering the welfare of children, and failure to properly report suspected abuse. Nevertheless, Spanier's legal fees are covered by Penn

State and the university, in terminating him "without cause," offered him "$1.2 million in severance pay, $1.2 million in deferred compensation, and $700,000 for a one-year sabbatical that began when he was fired," making him the highest paid "leader of any other major public college" for 2011–2012.[32] It appears that the culture of secrecy has its privileges, at least at Penn State University, even after it was exposed for the corrupt role it played in covering up the horrendous sexual assaults committed against a number of young boys.

One consequence of this failure of leadership is that it continues to feed the negative press that universities have increasingly been saddled with because they are no longer understood to serve the greater good; they are instead seen by many as insular and ineffectual in educating the next generation of critical thinkers and responsible citizens. Not only do they increasingly appear to be the preserve of private and commercial interests, but they have become symbols of bad faith. What is the public to think when university leaders, such as UC Davis's Linda P. Katehi, call in police in riot gear to deal with students setting up tents? Or when university leaders allow billionaires such as the Koch brothers to pledge $1.5 million to Florida State University in exchange for allowing their representatives to "screen and sign off on" faculty hired in the economics department?[33] What happens to the moral high ground and public trust once invested in university leaders when they become complicit with policies that underfund universities and strip students of needed social provisions, while at the same time supporting state budgets that increase prison construction and cut taxes for the rich?

If university presidents cannot defend the university as a public good, but instead, as in the case of Penn State, align themselves with big money, big sports, and the instrumentalist values of finance capital, they will not be able to mobilize the support of the broader public and will have no way to defend themselves against the neoliberal and conservative attempts by state governments to continually defund higher education. In recent years, universities have not thought twice about placing the burden of financial shortfalls on the backs of students—even as that burden grows apace, wrought by austerity measures, or by internal demands for new resources and space to keep up with record growth, or by new competition with international and online educational institutions. All this amounts to a poisonous student tax, one that has the consequence of creating an enormous debt for many students. Penn State has one of the highest tuition rates of any public college—amounting to $14,416 per year. But it is hardly alone in what has become a pitched competition to raise fees. Some public colleges, such as Florida State College, have increased tuition by 49 percent in two years! The lesson here is that abuse of young people comes in many forms, extending from egregious acts of child rape and sexual violence against women to the creation of a generation of students burdened by massive debt and a bleak, if not quite hopeless, jobless future.

The Penn State scandal is indicative of both the ongoing war on youth and the increase in the devaluation of higher education as a democratic public sphere. This is a scandal that has wrought destruction on all levels of schooling and leaves its brutalizing imprint on the social practices and rituals of exchange that shape daily life. Students are no longer seen as harbingers of our dreams. They are no longer treated with the care and concern one would extend to a unique and precious resource; they are no longer the most important symbols of the health and future of a democratic society. Instead, as Jean Comaroff and John Comaroff have insisted, youth have become "creatures of our nightmares, of our social impossibilities and our existential angst."[34] In universities, they are now viewed as revenue streams, potential recruits for the military, or workers to fill proliferating low-wage jobs in the global marketplace. Students are locked into, once again, what has been called "an abyss of failed sociality."[35] They are forced to witness years of a systemic and debilitating disinvestment in their future. They have watched as politicians and state governments have defunded higher education, wasted economic resources on ruinous military adventures, devalued any notion of critical learning in their obsession with high-stakes testing and accountability schemes, and made it impossible for many working- and middle-class students to afford a college education. Instead of entering a world in which they are offered dignity and a good life, young people are aggressively recruited to serve in military death machines, forced to live with their parents because they lack decent employment, and confronted with a future that offers them diminishing resources and even less hope. Surely, they have every right to revolt, not just in London, Montreal, Paris,

Tehran, Toronto, and Damascus but also in Boston, Oakland, and New York City.

All of the aforementioned responses to the scandal at Penn State offer valuable insights into the conditions of its unfolding, and to these we wanted to bring a larger and more historicized conceptual framework. In so doing, we have attempted to connect particularized criticisms with those systemic forces at work nationally and internationally in the transformation of higher education in North America. The Penn State scandal is symptomatic of a much larger set of challenges—and the abuses they almost invariably invite—that are deeply interconnected and mutually informing. On the one hand, Penn State symbolizes the corruption of higher education by big sports, governmental agencies, and corporate power with vested interests and deep pockets. On the other hand, the tragedy can surely be seen as a part of what we have been calling the war on youth. The media emphasis on the fall of Joe Paterno, the indictments and firing of high-ranking university administrators, and the alleged failure of a chain of command, while not incidental to the ongoing abuse, serves ironically to deflect attention from the egregious sexual assault of more than a dozen young boys who have carried this grievous burden into their adulthood. Students, faculty, and administrators also pay a terrible price when a university loses its moral compass and refashions itself in the values, principles, and managerial dictates of a corporate culture.

Neither the media accounts of the rise and fall of a celebrity coach nor what many insiders would like to characterize as a woeful series of administrative miscommunications tell us much about how Penn State is symptomatic of what has happened to a number of universities since at least the mid-1940s, and at a quickened pace since the 1980s. Penn State, like many of its institutional peers, has become a corporate university caught in the grip of the military-industrial complex rather than existing as a semi-autonomous institution driven by an academic mission, public values, and ethical considerations.[36] It is a paradigmatic example of mission drift, one marked by a fundamental shift of the university away from its role as a vital democratic public sphere toward an institutional willingness to subordinate educational values to market values. As Peter Seybold has suggested, the Penn State scandal is indicative of the ongoing corruption of teaching, research, and pedagogy that has taken place in higher education.[37] Beyond the classroom and the lab, evidence of ongoing corporatization abounds: bookstores and food services are franchised; part-time labor replaces full-time faculty; classes are oversold; and online education replaces face-to-face teaching, less as a pedagogical innovation and more as a means to deal with the capacity issues now confronting those universities that pursued financial sustainability through aggressive growth.[38]

The corporate university is descending more and more into what has been called "an output fundamentalism," prioritizing market mechanisms that emphasize productivity and performance measures that make a mockery of quality scholarship and diminish effective teaching—scholarly commitments are increasingly subordinated to bringing in bigger grants to supplement operational budgets negatively impacted by the withdrawal of governmental funding.[39] In the face of such pressures, faculty have experienced unprovoked employer militancy in the name of austerity at universities across the country and the world over in Egypt, Venezuela, Chile, Madagascar, New Zealand, the United Kingdom, and Australia. Higher education no longer makes a claim to those principles or goals grounded in a belief that the health and sustainability of democratic nations depend on the informed judgments, ethical standards, and modes of critical engagement exercised by citizens within the societies they inhabit.

In addition, the student experience has hardly been untouched by these shock waves, which have further undermined the genuinely intellectual, financial, social, and democratic needs of undergraduate and graduate students alike. Young people are increasingly devalued as knowledgeable, competent, and socially responsible, in spite of the fact that their generation will inevitably be the leaders of tomorrow. Put bluntly, many university administrators demonstrate a notable lack of imagination, conceiving of students primarily in market terms and showing few qualms about subjecting young people to forms of education as outmoded as the factory assembly lines they emulate. Campus extracurricular activities unfold in student commons designed in the image of shopping centers and high-end entertainment complexes. Clearly, students are not perceived as worthy of the kinds of financial, intellectual, and cultural investments necessary to enhance their capacities to be critical and informed individual and social agents. Nor are they provided with the knowledge and skills necessary to understand and negotiate the complex political, economic, and social worlds in which they live and the many challenges they face now and will face in the future. Instead of being institutions that foster democracy, public engagement, and civic literacy, universities and colleges now seduce and entertain students as prospective clients, or, worse yet, act as recruitment offices for the armed forces.[40] Put simply, students are being sold on a certain type of collegial experience that often has very little to do with the quality of education they might receive, while university leaders appear content to have faculty provide entertainment and distraction for students in between football games.

Whereas US universities are caught in the iron grip of the "age of austerity," just beyond its so-called ivory towers, citizens are witnessing the mega-prosperity of a rich elite reminiscent of the Gilded Age.[41] Despite their deeply entwined relation with consumer culture, today's youth are well acquainted with austerity, given the disproportionate impact such measures have on their lives, and know very little about prosperity, with the exception of what they see on the screen. The return to an age of greed and corporate monopolies, accompanied by a brutal survival-of-the-fittest ethic, is made obvious by the dreamworlds of consumption circulated by the mass media, and it is also evident in the actions of right-wing politicians who want to initiate policies that take the country back to the late nineteenth century—a time in which the reforms of the New Deal, the Great Society, and the Progressive Era did not exist.

This Gilded Age was a period in which robber barons, big oil, railroad magnates, and others among the superrich spread their corrupting influence throughout the political, economic, and cultural landscapes— without having to deal with irritating social reforms such as Social Security, Medicare, Medicaid, child labor laws, environmental protections, affirmative action, civil rights, union rights, antitrust laws, a progressive income tax, and a host of others. This was a period when money flowed and privilege for the very few shaped practically all aspects of American life, making a mockery out of democracy and imposing massive amounts of human suffering on the vast majority of Americans. Women could not vote and were seen as second-class citizens, Blacks were treated harshly under Jim Crow policies, young people were exploited through brutal labor conditions, education was limited to the moneyed classes, inequality in wealth and income reached extreme disparities, slums festered, and politicians were in the pocket of the rich.

In time, protest movements emerged among students, workers, unions, women, people of color, and others to address these injustices. Labor became a potent force in the first half of the twentieth century. Then Blacks mobilized a formidable civil rights movement, and women's groups organized to address a range of injustices. Students were involved in these as well and advanced the cause of the antiwar movement, thereby infusing new life into the drive for participatory democracy both within and outside of higher education. By the early 1970s, gay, lesbian, and transgender groups were also visibly fighting to gain basic civil rights. These movements produced notable victories in deepening and expanding the promise and possibilities of a substantive democracy. Yet they quickly became the focus of a powerfully organized backlash on the part of conservatives, who organized a right-wing cultural revolution that successfully rolled back many of the progressive gains that had emerged in the decades of struggle that came to define much of the twentieth century.

The attack on higher education has gained considerable momentum since the 1980s and must be understood as part of a much larger assault on all aspects of the welfare state, social provisions, public goods, and democracy itself. Under a regime of neoliberal capitalism with its savage assaults on the public waged through deregulation, privatization, and commodification, all those public spheres that provide the values, social relations, knowledge, and skills to participate meaningfully in the democratic life of the nation are disappearing. And with these, we are losing opportunities to learn how to translate personal troubles to public issues, show respect and care for the rights of others, and recognize those antidemocratic pressures that make a mockery out of freedom and smother the discourses of justice, equality, and social rights. As big money, big sports, and the culture of illiteracy, violence, and corruption they inspire make clear, schooling is no longer about educating students. Rather, it is about exploiting them when not infantilizing them in the name of entertainment. Matters of politics, ethics, and social responsibility are increasingly being replaced with individual self-interest motivated by the imperatives of gaining a competitive edge and instant gratification. What the Penn State scandal reveals is the urgency with which universities must resist all attempts to be harnessed to the commercial demands of big sports, the financial needs of corporations, or the violence of the national security state.

In the aftermath of the Penn State scandal, the university's Board of Trustees commissioned former federal judge and FBI director Louis J. Freeh to investigate how the university handled the Sandusky affair. The Freeh Report makes clear that there was a concerted attempt to cover up the acts of a serial predator, Jerry Sandusky, while willfully disregarding the welfare of the children he abused. In damning fashion, the report stated:

> Our most saddening and sobering finding is the total disregard for the safety and welfare of Sandusky's child victims by the most senior leaders at Penn State. The most powerful men at Penn State failed to take any steps for 14 years to protect the children who Sandusky victimized. Messrs. Spanier, Schultz, Paterno and Curley never demonstrated, through actions or words, any concern for the safety and well-being of Sandusky's victims until after Sandusky's arrest. . . . Taking into account the available witness statements and evidence, it is more reasonable to conclude that, in order to avoid the consequences of bad publicity, the most powerful leaders at Penn State University—Messrs. Spanier, Schultz, Paterno and Curley—repeatedly concealed critical facts relating to Sandusky's child abuse from the authorities, the Board of Trustees, Penn State community, and the public at large. Although concern to treat the child abuser humanely was expressly stated, no such sentiments were ever expressed by them for Sandusky's victims.[42]

Given the reporting that took place as the scandal unfolded, much of this is not news, though the report makes clear the nature and depth of the cover-up and provides some important new details. While the Freeh Report reveals that the cover-up at the top of the Penn State administration "was an active agreement to conceal," it raises further questions about how the justice system works in this country when it comes to prosecuting the rich and powerful, who engage increasingly in a bottomless pit of corruption and moral irresponsibility. At his press conference, Freeh, when asked if criminal charges should be brought against a number of people, including former President Spanier, replied that "it's up to others to decide whether that's criminal." Freeh's reply suggests he was acting cautiously, given that some of the people who hired him might be indicted, but he unknowingly touched on another related and important issue. That is, justice in America works primarily for the rich and powerful and against the poor and marginalized. Freeh's response or equivocation reveals what is well known—the rich and powerful rarely get prosecuted for their crimes or what the *Economist* has called "the rotten heart of finance."[43] Just ask the CEOs who run Barclays, JPMorgan Chase, Citibank, GlaxoSmithKline, and so on.

Soon after the release of the Freeh Report, the NCAA, the governing body of US college sports, announced a series of unprecedented sanctions against Penn State University. These included a record $60 million fine, a reduction in football scholarships, the banning of Penn State from participating in bowl games and any other post-season play for four years, and the nullification of all wins by the Penn State football team from 1998 to 2011. What is unprecedented in this judgment is that the NCAA involved themselves in a case that should have best been resolved as a civil and criminal matter. Not only is the verdict overly harsh, draining money from university academic programs that could benefit disadvantaged students, but it is also hypocritical. As Dave Zirin points out, the NCAA is a "multi-billion dollar entity that builds its money on the idea of turning coaches into deities, turning football programs into too-big-to fail operations, and turning players into basically unpaid campus workers as opposed to student athletes. That's the root of the problem here."[44]

What we have here are echoes of the big banks, corporations, and financial services regulating themselves and "acting without oversight and with the kind of heavy hand that precludes any semblance of democratic oversight."[45] There is no moral high ground to be found in the NCAA's actions, for, as Zirin reminds us, the NCAA has "morphed into this kind of operation where they negotiate $10.8 billion television deals, where they sell the likenesses of players to video games, where they sell the likenesses of players on credit cards for well-heeled boosters. This is what the NCAA has become."[46] It is no wonder that the *Chronicle of Higher Education* published a story, without critical commentary, shamelessly suggesting that faculty and students were the real victims of the Penn State scandal. As Robin Wilson reports in the story, without irony, "Penn State professors and students say they sometimes feel like victims themselves, as they are confronted by outsiders who want to blame them, and the entire university for what Mr. Sandusky did. They wonder how they will ever move on."[47]

One indication of what it would take for Penn State to move on can be gleaned from the decision on the part of the university to pay $59.7 million to twenty-six young men who were victims of sexual abuse. The current university president of Penn State, Rodney Erickson, called the settlement "another step forward in the healing process for those hurt by Mr. Sandusky, and another step forward for Penn State."[48] Settling with the victims of such abuse is no small matter, but if the university truly wants to move forward it must also address with due diligence the elimination of those economic, political, and cultural forces that gave rise to a culture of hypermasculinity and sexual violence—a culture that saturates the larger society and one that Penn State willingly inhabited and celebrated with impunity. Clearly, it will take a great deal more than a much-publicized financial settlement and the punishment of those responsible for the sexual crimes committed against so many young boys for Penn State to come to grips with its sordid history and embrace of a business-oriented sports culture that refused to recognize the damage it did both to its own mission and to the victims of its concentrated bureaucratic power and moral turpitude.

Let's be clear, what is on trial here is not simply those who colluded to protect the reputation of a storied football program and the reputation of Penn State University but a society governed by large corporate entities, radicalized market-driven values, a survival-of-the-fittest ethic, and an unregulated drive for profit-making regardless of the human and social costs. This is an ethic that views many children and young people as disposable, refusing to acknowledge its responsibility to future generations while creating the social, economic, and political conditions in which the pain and suffering of young people simply disappear. As a number of recent banking scandals reveal, big money and the institutions it creates now engage unapologetically in massive criminal behavior and corruption, but the individuals who head these corporations, extending from JPMorgan Chase Bank to Barclays, are rarely prosecuted. The message is clear. Once again, crime pays for the rich and powerful. We can only understand what happened to the young victims at Penn State if we also acknowledge what recently was revealed about the criminal actions against children perpetrated by pharmaceutical giant GlaxoSmith-Kline. In this instance, Glaxo illegally marketed Paxil to children, gave kickbacks to doctors, and made false claims about the drug, even though one major clinical trial found "that teens who took the drug for depression were more likely to attempt suicide than those receiving placebo pills."[49] Penn State and Glaxo are symptomatic of a much larger shift in the culture and the relations of power that shape it.

Rather than representing a society's dreams and hope for the future, young people, especially poor white and minority children, have become a nightmare, an excess, and disposable in the age of casino capitalism and big money. It is crucial that the American public connect the kind of institutional abuse we see from Penn State, GlaxoSmithKline, and Barclays with the values and relations of power that are responsible for a society in which 53 percent of college graduates are jobless, social provisions for young people are being slashed, corporations get tax deductions while state governments eliminate vital public services, and students assume a massive debt because it is easier for the federal government to fund wars and invest in prisons than in public and higher education. Connect these dots and Penn State becomes only one shameful and corrupt marker in a much larger scandal that reveals an ongoing and aggressive war on youth. Everywhere we look, young people are under siege. Twenty percent of young people live in poverty and over 42 percent live in low-income homes. Young people now find themselves in debt, jobless, incarcerated, or unemployed. Stories about young people being denied the right to vote, being abused in juvenile detention centers, taking on jobs that pay the minimum wage or worse, living at home with their parents while unemployed, and facing a bleak future rarely seem to arouse the concerns of the American public or its governing politicians. All the while, the ruling corporate and financial elite use their power to punish those marginalized by class, race, and ethnicity—slashing social benefits, increasing tuition, refusing to abolish punitive bankruptcy laws, denigrating young people as lazy, and refusing to invest in their future.

Against the notion that the neoliberal market should organize and mediate every human activity, including how young people are educated, we need a vision for democratic politics and institutions that guides the creation of a formative culture that teaches students and others that "they are not fated to accept the given regime of educational degradation" and the eclipse of civic and intellectual culture in the academy.[50] What is crucial to recognize is that higher education may be the most viable public sphere left in which democratic principles, modes of knowledge, and values can be taught, defended, and exercised. Surely, public higher education remains one of the most important institutions in which a country's commitment to young people can be made visible and concrete. The scandal at Penn State illuminates a profound crisis in American life, one that demands critical reflection—for those inside and outside the academy—on the urgent challenges facing higher education as part of the larger interconnecting crisis of youth and democracy. It demands that we connect the dots between the degradation of higher education and those larger economic, political, cultural, and social forces that benefit from such an unjust and unethical state of affairs—and which, in the end, young people will pay for with their sense of possibility and their hope for the future.

Learning from the Penn State scandal requires that faculty, parents, artists, cultural workers, and others listen to students who are mobilizing all across the country and around the world as part of a broader effort to reclaim a democratic language and political vision. These insightful and motivated youth are rejecting the narrow prescriptions and heavy burdens that would be foisted upon them, and choosing instead to invent a new understanding of what it means to make substantive democracy possible (see chapter 6). Until we understand how the larger culture of political, institutional, and economic corruption abuses young people, rewards the rich, and destroys democracy, Penn State will remain a sideshow that simply distracts from the real issue of what constitutes child abuse: the scandal of Penn State represents the scandal of America.

CHAPTER FIVE

On the Urgency for Public Intellectuals in the Academy

"The university is a critical institution or it is nothing."
—Stuart Hall

I want to begin with the words of the late African American poet, Audre Lorde, a formidable writer, educator, feminist, gay rights activist, and public intellectual, who displayed a relentless courage in addressing the injustices she witnessed all around her. She writes:

> Poetry is not a luxury. It is a vital necessity of our existence. It forms the quality of the light within which we predicate our hopes and dreams toward survival and change, first made into language, then into idea, then into more tangible action. Poetry is the way we help give name to the nameless so it can be thought. The farthest horizons of our hopes and fears are cobbled by our poems, carved from the rock experiences of our daily lives.[1]

And although Lorde refers to poetry here, I think a strong case can be made that the attributes she ascribes to poetry can also be attributed to higher education—a genuine higher education.[2] In this case, an education that includes history, philosophy, all of the arts and humanities, the criticality of the social sciences, the world of discovery made manifest by natural science, and the transformations in health and in law wrought by the professions that are at the heart of what it means to know something about the human condition. Lorde's defense of poetry as a mode of education is especially crucial for those of us who believe that the university is nothing if it is not a public trust and social good: that is, a critical institution infused with the promise of cultivating intellectual insight, the imagination, inquisitiveness, risk-taking, social responsibility, and the struggle for justice. At best, universities should be at the "heart of intense public discourse, passionate learning, and vocal citizen involvement in the issues of the times."[3] It is in the spirit of such an ideal that I first want to address those larger economic, social, and cultural interests that threaten this notion of education, especially higher education.

As I have stated throughout this book, in spite of being discredited by the economic recession of 2008, market fundamentalism or unfettered free-market capitalism has once again become a dominant force for producing a corrupt financial service sector, runaway environmental devastation, egregious amounts of human suffering, and the rise of what has been called the emergence of "finance as a criminalized, rogue industry."[4] The Gilded Age is back with huge profits for the ultra-rich, banks, and other large financial service institutions while at the same time increasing impoverishment and misery for the middle and working classes. The American dream, celebrating economic and social mobility, has been transformed into not just an influential myth but also a poisonous piece of propaganda. One indication of the undoing of the American dream into an American nightmare can be seen in the fact that "the most striking change in American society in the past generation—roughly since Ronald Reagan was elected President—has been the increase in the inequality of income and wealth" and the concentration of wealth into fewer and fewer hands.[5]

I want to revisit the state of inequality in America because any discourse about the purpose of higher education and the responsibility of academics as public intellectuals has to begin with how matters of wealth and power are changing the purpose and meaning of education, teaching, and the conditions under which academics now labor. The current assaults on higher education cannot be removed from the war on youth, unions, students, public servants, and the public good. Moreover, the financial crisis of the last few years has become a cover for advancing the neoliberal revolution and assault on higher education. For example, when University of Texas at Austin president Bill Powers argues for what he calls a "business productivity initiative" to save money, he is not simply responding to a projected budget shortfall. Under the dictates of neoliberal austerity policies, he is changing the nature of education at UT by arguing that the research initiatives will be evaluated and deemed most profitable in terms of their benefits to various industries. Those academic courses and departments that are aligned with and provide potential profits for industry will receive the most funding. As Reihaneh Hajibeigi points out, "this means liberal arts majors and departments will be given minimal funding if the benefits of those studies aren't seen as being profitable to UT."[6]

The figures listed below point to a different kind of crisis, one that puts in peril the most basic and crucial institutions that make a democracy possible along with the formative culture and critical agents that support and protect it. We need to be reminded as part of the pedagogy of public memory that these figures matter, given their role as both flashpoints that signal a rupture from the increasingly lost promises of a democracy to come and a call to conscience in addressing the horrors of the growing antidemocratic tendencies that make clear the presence of an emerging authoritarianism in the United States. We live at a time of immense contradictions, problems, and antagonisms, and such figures offer us a way to both make visible disparities in power relations and to address the necessity of combining moral outrage with ongoing political struggles. If democracy needs a keen sense of the common good and a robust understanding of education as a public good, these statistics signify the death of both—a vanishing point at which the ideas, policies, and institutions that sustain democratic public life and civic education dissolve into the highest reaches of power, avarice, and wealth.

The United States now "has the highest level of inequality of any of the advanced countries."[7] One measure of the upward shift in wealth is evident in Joseph E. Stiglitz's claim that "in the 'recovery' of 2009–2010, the top 1% of US income earners captured 93% of the income growth."[8] The vast inequities and economic injustice at the heart of the mammoth gap in income and wealth become even more evident in a number of revealing statistics. For example, "the average pay for people working in U.S. investment banks is over $375,000 while senior officers at Goldman Sachs averaged $61 million each in compensation for 2007."[9] In addition, the United States beats out every other developed nation in producing extreme income and wealth inequalities for 2012. The top 1 percent now owns "about a third of the American people's total net worth, over 40 percent of America' total financial wealth . . . and half of the nation's total income growth."[10] Andrew Gavin Marshall provides even more granular figures. He writes:

> Looking specifically at the United States, the top 1% own more than 36% of the national wealth and more than the combined wealth of the bottom 95%. Almost all of the wealth gains over the previous decade went to the top 1%. In the mid-1970s, the top 1% earned 8% of all national income; this number rose to 21% by 2010.[11]

In this instance, the absolute acceleration of the gap in income and especially wealth results in the quickening of misery, impoverishment, and hardship for many Americans while furthering what might be called a thin and failed conception of democracy. At the same time, political illiteracy and religious fundamentalism have cornered the market on populist rage, providing support for an escalating political and economic crisis.[12] Pointing to some of the ugly extremes produced by such inequality, Paul Buchheit includes the following: each of the right-wing, union-busting Koch brothers made $3 billion per hour from their investments; the difference in hourly wages between CEOs and minimum-wage workers was "$5,000.00 per hour vs. $7.25 per hour," "The poorest 47% of Americans have no wealth," and "the 400 wealthiest Americans own as much wealth as 80 million families—62% of America."[13]

At the risk of being repetitious, I want to stress a range of statistics that may say little about cause and effect but that do, as Bauman notes, "challenge our all-too-common ethical apathy and moral indifference . . . they also show, and beyond reasonable doubt, that the idea of the pursuit of a good life and happiness being a self-referential business for each individual to pursue and perform on his or her own is an idea that is grossly misconceived."[14] While wealth and income are redistributed to the top 1 percent, the United States fails to provide adequate health and safety for its children and citizens. Both a 2007 UNICEF report and a 2009

OECD study ranked the United States near the bottom of the advanced industrial countries for children's health and safety and twenty-seventh out of thirty for child poverty. Median wealth for Hispanic and Black households has been reduced to almost zero as a result of the recession; young people are increasing unable to attend college because of soaring tuition rates, and those that do attend are increasingly strapped with unmanageable debts and few jobs that will enable them to pay off their loans. More than 50 million Americans lack health care and many will die as a result of state cutbacks in Medicaid programs. The justice system is racially and class bound and increasingly incarcerates large numbers of poor minorities of class and color while refusing to prosecute hundreds of executives responsible for billions of dollars lost due to fraud and corruption.[15]

It is important to note that the violence of unnecessary hardship and suffering produced by neoliberal ideology and values is not restricted to the economic realm. Neoliberal violence also wages war against the modernist legacy of "questioning the givens, in philosophy as well as in politics and art."[16] Ignorance is no longer a liability in neoliberal societies but a political asset endlessly mediated through a capitalist imaginary that thrives on the interrelated registers of consumption, privatization, and depoliticization. Manufactured ignorance is the new reigning mode of dystopian violence, spurred on by a market-driven system that celebrates a passion for consumer goods over a passionate desire for community affairs, the well-being of the other, and the principles of a democratic society.[17] As the late Cornelius Castoriadis brilliantly argues, under neoliberalism, the thoughtless celebration of economic progress becomes the primary legitimating principle to transform "human beings into machines for producing and consuming."[18]

Under such circumstances, to cite C. W. Mills, we are seeing the breakdown of democracy, the disappearance of critical intellectuals, and "the collapse of those public spheres which offer a sense of critical agency and social imagination."[19] In the last few decades, we have seen the forces of market fundamentalism attempt to strip education of its public values, critical content, and civic responsibilities as part of its broader goal of creating new subjects wedded to consumerism, risk-free relationships, and the destruction of the social state. Tied largely to instrumental ideologies and measurable paradigms, many institutions of higher education are now committed almost exclusively to economic goals, such as preparing students for the workforce and transforming faculty into an army of temporary subaltern labor—all done as part of an appeal to rationality, one that eschews matters of inequality, power, and ethical grammars of suffering.[20] Universities have not only strayed from their democratic mission, they also seem immune to the plight of students who have to face a harsh new world of high unemployment, the prospect of downward mobility, debilitating debt, and a future that mimics the failures of the past.

The question of what kind of education is needed for students to be informed and active citizens is rarely asked.[21] In the absence of a democratic vision of schooling, it is not surprising that some colleges and universities are not only increasingly opening their classrooms to the Defense Department and national intelligence agencies but also aligning themselves with those commanding apparatuses that make up the punishing state.[22] In the first instance, one cannot but be puzzled by Yale University's decision to allow the Department of Defense to fund the US Special Operations Command Center of Excellence for Operational Neuroscience—a program designed to "teach special operations personnel the art of 'conversational,' and 'cross cultural intelligence gathering, and pay volunteers from the community's vast immigrant population (mainly poor Hispanics, Moroccans and Iraqis) to serve as test subjects."[23] In other words, Yale would invite "military intelligence to campus to hone their wartime interrogation techniques on the local nonwhite population."[24] In another symptomatic instance of mission drift, Florida Atlantic University in Boca Raton attempted to put together a deal to rename its football stadium after the GEO Group, a private prison corporation "whose record is marred by human rights abuses, by lawsuits, by unnecessary deaths of people in their custody and a whole series of incidents."[25] One Mississippi judge called GEO "an inhuman cesspool."[26] And as Dave Zirin points out, GEO's efforts to spend $6 million "to rename the home of the FAU Owls was an effort to normalize their name: GEO Group, just another corporation you can trust, the Xerox of private prisons."[27] As a result of numerous protests by FAU students, faculty, and outside civil rights groups, the company withdrew its $6 million donation.[28] The "Stop Owlcatraz" campaign exposed not only the often poisonous links between corporations and universities but also the workings of a "deeply racist system of mass incarceration" that should be high on the list of issues faculty and students should be addressing as part of a broader campaign to connect the academy to public life.[29]

The antidemocratic values that drive free-market fundamentalism are embodied in policies now attempting to shape diverse levels of higher education all over the globe. The script has now become overly familiar and increasingly taken for granted, especially in the United States. As I have mentioned throughout this book, shaping the neoliberal framing of public and higher education is a corporate-based ideology that embraces standardizing the curriculum, top-down governing structures, courses that promote entrepreneurial values, and the reduction of all levels of education to job training sites. For example, one university is offering a master's degree to students who commit to starting a high-tech company while another allows career advisers to teach capstone research seminars in the humanities. In one of these classes, the students were asked to "develop a 30-second commercial on their 'personal brand.'"[30]

Central to this neoliberal view of higher education is a market-driven paradigm that wants to eliminate tenure, turn the humanities into a job preparation service, and reduce most faculty to the status of part-time and temporary workers, if not simply a new subordinate class of disempowered educators. The indentured service status of such faculty is put on full display as some colleges have resorted to using "temporary service agencies to do their formal hiring."[31] Faculty in this view are regarded as simply another cheap army of reserve labor, a powerless group that universities are eager to exploit in order to increase the bottom line while disregarding the needs and rights of academic laborers and the quality of education that students deserve.

There is little talk in this view of higher education about shared governance between faculty and administrators, nor of educating students as critical citizens rather than potential employees of Walmart. There are few attempts to affirm faculty as scholars and public intellectuals who have both a measure of autonomy and power. Instead, faculty members are increasingly defined less as intellectuals than as technicians and grant writers. Students fare no better in this debased form of education and are treated either as consumers or as restless children in need of high-energy entertainment—as was made clear in the 2012 Penn State scandal, as mentioned in chapter 4. Nor is there any attempt to legitimate higher education as a fundamental sphere for creating the agents necessary for an aspiring democracy. This neoliberal, corporatized model of higher education exhibits a deep disdain for critical ideals, public spheres, knowledge, and practices that are not directly linked to market values, business culture, the economy, or the production of short-term financial gains. In fact, the commitment to democracy is beleaguered, viewed less as a crucial educational investment than as a distraction that gets in the way of connecting knowledge and pedagogy to the production of material and human capital. Such modes of education do not foster a sense of organized responsibility central to a democracy. Instead, they foster what might be called a sense of organized irresponsibility—a practice that underlies the economic Darwinism and civic corruption at the heart of American politics.

Higher Education and the Crisis of Legitimacy

In the United States, many of the problems in higher education can be linked to low funding, the domination of universities by market mechanisms, the rise of for-profit colleges, the intrusion of the national security state, and the lack of faculty self-governance, all of which not only contradicts the culture and democratic value of higher education but also makes a mockery of the very meaning and mission of the university as a democratic public sphere. Decreased financial support for higher education stands in sharp contrast to increased support for tax benefits for the rich, big banks, the defense budget, and megacorporations. Rather than enlarge the moral imagination and critical capacities of students, too many universities are now wedded to producing would-be hedge fund managers, depoliticized students, and creating modes of education that promote a "technically trained docility."[32] Strapped for money and increasingly defined in the language of corporate culture, many universities are now "pulled or driven principally by vocational, [military], and economic considerations while increasingly removing academic knowledge production from democratic values and projects."[33] While there has never been a golden age when higher education was truly liberal and democratic, the current attack on higher education by religious fundamentalists, corporate power, and the apostles of neoliberal capitalism appears unprecedented in terms of both its scope and intensity. The issue here is not to idealize a past that has been lost but to reclaim elements of a history in which the discourses of critique and possibility offered an alternative vision of what form higher education might take in a substantive democratic society.

Universities are losing their sense of public mission, just as leadership in higher education is being banalized and stripped of any viable democratic vision. College presidents are now called CEOs and move without apology between interlocking corporate and academic boards. With few exceptions, they are praised as fundraisers but rarely acknowledged for the force of their ideas. In this new Gilded Age of money and profit, academic subjects gain stature almost exclusively through their exchange value on the market. It gets worse. In one egregious recent example, BB&T Corporation, a financial holdings company, gave a $1 million gift to Marshall University's business school on the condition that *Atlas Shrugged* by Ayn Rand (Paul Ryan's favorite book) be taught in a course. What are we to make of the integrity of a university when it accepts a monetary gift from a corporation or rich patron demanding as part of the agreement the power to specify what is to be taught in a course or how a curriculum should be shaped? Some corporations and universities now believe that what is taught in a course is not an academic decision but a market consideration.

Questions regarding how education might enable students to develop a keen sense of prophetic justice, utilize critical analytical skills, and cultivate an ethical sensibility through which they learn to respect the rights of others are becoming increasingly irrelevant in a market-driven and militarized university. As the humanities and liberal arts are downsized, privatized, and commodified, higher education finds itself caught in the paradox of claiming to invest in the future of young people while offering them few intellectual, civic, and moral supports.[34]

If the commercialization, commodification, and militarization of the university continue unabated, higher education will become yet another of a number of institutions incapable of fostering critical inquiry, public debate, acts of justice, and public values.[35] But the calculating logic of the corporate university does more than diminish the moral and political vision and practices necessary to sustain a vibrant democracy and an engaged notion of social agency. It also undermines the development of public spaces where critical dialogue, social responsibility, and social justice are pedagogically valued—viewed as fundamental to providing students with the knowledge and skills necessary to address the problems facing the nation and the globe. Such democratic public spheres are especially important at a time when any space that produces "critical thinkers capable of putting existing institutions into question" is under siege by powerful economic and political interests.[36]

Higher education has a responsibility not only to search for the truth regardless of where it may lead but also to educate students to be capable of holding authority and power politically and morally accountable, while at the same time sustaining "the idea and hope of a public culture."[37] Though questions regarding whether the university should serve *strictly* public rather than private interests no longer carry the weight of forceful criticism they did in the past, such questions are still crucial in addressing the purpose of higher education and what it might mean to imagine the university's full participation in public life as the protector and promoter of democratic values. Toni Morrison is instructive in her comment that "if the university does not take seriously and rigorously its role as a guardian of wider civic freedoms, as interrogator of more and more complex ethical problems, as servant and preserver of deeper democratic practices, then some other regime or ménage of regimes will do it for us, in spite of us, and without us."[38]

What needs to be understood is that higher education may be one of the few public spheres left where knowledge, values, and learning offer a glimpse of the promise of education for nurturing public values, critical hope, and a substantive democracy. It may be the case that everyday life is increasingly organized around market principles, but confusing a market-determined society with democracy hollows out the legacy of higher education, whose deepest roots are moral, not commercial. This is a particularly important insight in a society where not only is the free circulation of ideas being replaced by ideas managed by the dominant media, but also where critical ideas are increasingly viewed or dismissed as banal, if not reactionary. Celebrity worship and the commodification of culture now constitute a powerful form of mass illiteracy and increasingly permeate all aspects of the educational force of the wider cultural apparatus. But mass illiteracy does more than depoliticize the public; it also becomes complicit with the suppression of dissent. Intellectuals who engage in dissent and "keep the idea and hope of a public culture alive,"[39] are often dismissed as irrelevant, extremist, elitist, or un-American. We now live in a world in which the politics of dis-imagination dominates, such that any writing or public discourse that bears witness to a critical and alternative sense of the world is dismissed as having nothing to do with the bottom line. Imagine how this quote from the late and great public intellectual James Baldwin would be received today.

> You write in order to change the world knowing perfectly well that you probably can't, but also knowing that [writing] is indispensable to the world. The world changes according to the way people see it, and if you alter even by a millimeter the way people look at reality, then you can change it.[40]

In a dystopian society, utopian thought becomes sterile and even Baldwin's prophetic words are out of place, though more important than ever. In spite of the legacy and existence of public intellectuals that extend from Baldwin and C. Wright Mills to Naomi Klein and Barbara Ehrenreich, we live in a new and more dangerous historical conjuncture. Anti-public intellectuals now dominate the larger cultural landscape, all too willing to flaunt co-option and reap the rewards of venting insults at their assigned opponents while being reduced to the status of paid servants of powerful economic interests. But the problem is not simply with the rise of a right-wing cultural apparatus dedicated to preserving the power and wealth of the rich and corporate elite. As Stuart Hall recently remarked, the state of the Left is also problematic in that, as he puts it, "The left is in trouble. It's not got any ideas, it's not got any independent analysis of its own, and therefore it's got no vision. It just takes the temperature. . . . It has no sense of politics being educative, of politics changing the way people see things."[41]

The issue of politics being educative, of recognizing that matters of pedagogy, subjectivity, and consciousness are at the heart of political and moral concerns should not be lost on either academics or those concerned about not only what might be called writing in public but also the purpose and meaning of higher education itself. Democracy places civic demands upon its citizens, and such demands point to the necessity of an education that is broad-based, critical, and supportive of meaningful civic values, participation in self-governance, and democratic leadership. Only through such a formative and critical educational culture can students learn how to become individual and social agents, rather than merely disengaged spectators, able both to think otherwise and to act upon civic commitments that "necessitate a reordering of basic power arrangements" fundamental to promoting the common good and producing a meaningful democracy.[42] This is not a matter of imposing values on education and in our classrooms. The university and the classroom are already defined through power-laden discourses and a myriad of values that are often part of the hidden structures of educational politics and pedagogy. A more accurate position would be, as Toni Morrison notes, to take up our responsibility "as citizen/scholars in the university to accept the consequences of our own value-redolent roles." She continues: "Like it or not, we are paradigms of our own values, advertisements of our own ethics—especially noticeable when we presume to foster ethics-free, value-lite education."[43]

Dreaming the Impossible

Reclaiming higher education as a democratic public sphere begins with the crucial project of challenging, among other things, those market fundamentalists, religious extremists, and rigid ideologues who harbor a deep disdain for critical thought and healthy skepticism, and who look with displeasure upon any form of education that teaches students to read the word and the world critically. The radical imagination in this discourse is considered dangerous and a dire threat to political authorities. Needless to say, education is not only about issues of work and economics, but also about questions of justice, social freedom, and the capacity for democratic agency, action, and change, as well as the related issues of power, inclusion, and social responsibility.[44] These are educational and political issues, and they should be addressed as part of a broader effort to reenergize the global struggle for social justice and democracy.

Martin Luther King Jr. is instructive here because he recognized clearly that when matters of social responsibility are removed from matters of agency, the content of politics and democracy are deflated. He writes:

> When an individual is no longer a true participant, when he no longer feels a sense of responsibility to his society, the content of democracy is emptied. When culture is degraded and vulgarity enthroned, when the social system does not build security but induces peril, inexorably the individual is impelled to pull away from a soulless society.[45]

If young people are to develop a respect for others, social responsibility, and keen sense of civic engagement, pedagogy must be viewed as the cultural, political, and moral force that provides the knowledge, values, and social relations to make such democratic practices possible. If higher education is to characterize itself as a site of critical thinking, collective work, and public service, educators and students will have to redefine the knowledge, skills, research, and intellectual practices currently favored in the university. Central to such a challenge is the need to position intellectual practice "as part of an intricate web of morality, rigor and responsibility"[46] that enables academics to speak with conviction, use the public sphere to address important social problems, and demonstrate alternative models for bridging the gap between higher education and the broader society. Connective practices are crucial in that it is essential to develop intellectual practices that are collegial rather than competitive, refuse the instrumentality and privileged isolation of the academy, link critical thought to a profound impatience with the status quo, and connect human agency to the idea of social responsibility and the politics of possibility.

Connection also means being openly and deliberately critical and worldly in one's intellectual work. Increasingly, as universities are shaped by a culture of fear in which dissent is equated with treason, the call to be objective and impartial, whatever one's intentions, can easily echo what George Orwell called the official truth or the establishment point of view. Lacking a self-consciously democratic political focus, teachers are often reduced to the role of a technician or functionary engaged in formalistic rituals, unconcerned with the disturbing and urgent problems that confront the larger society or the consequences of one's pedagogical practices and research undertakings. In opposition to this model, with its claims to and conceit of political neutrality, I argue that academics should combine the mutually interdependent roles of critical educator and active citizen. This requires finding ways to connect the practice of classroom teaching with the operation of power in the larger society and to provide the conditions for students to view themselves as critical agents capable of making those who exercise authority and power answerable for their actions. Such an intellectual does not train students solely for jobs but also educates them to question critically the institutions, policies, and values that shape their lives, relationships to others, and connections to the larger world.

I think Stuart Hall is on target here when he insists that educators also have a responsibility to provide students with "critical knowledge that has to be ahead of traditional knowledge: it has to be better than anything that traditional knowledge can produce, because only serious ideas are going to stand up."[47] At the same time, he insists on the need for educators to "actually engage, contest, and learn from the best that is locked up in other traditions," especially those attached to traditional academic paradigms.[48] Students must be made aware of the ideological and structural forces that promote needless human suffering while also recognizing that it takes more than awareness to resolve them. This is the kind of intellectual practice that Zygmunt Bauman calls "taking responsibility for our responsibility,"[49] one that is attentive to the suffering and needs of others. At the very least, such responsibility means rejecting what Irving Howe calls the honored place that capitalism has found for intellectuals who now speak for power rather than for the truth and consider themselves noble guardians of the status quo.[50]

Education cannot be decoupled from what Jacques Derrida calls a democracy to come, that is, a democracy that must always "be open to the possibility of being contested, of contesting itself, of criticizing and indefinitely improving itself."[51] Within this project of possibility and impossibility, education must be understood as a deliberately informed and purposeful political and moral practice, as opposed to one that is either doctrinaire, instrumentalized, or both. Moreover, a critical pedagogy should be engaged at all levels of schooling. Similarly, it must gain part of its momentum in higher education among students who will go back to the schools, churches, synagogues, and workplaces in order to produce new ideas, concepts, and critical ways of understanding the world in which they live. This is a notion of intellectual practice and responsibility that refuses the insular, overly pragmatic, and privileged isolation of the academy. It also affirms a broader vision of learning that links knowledge to the power of self-definition and to the capacities of students to expand the scope of democratic freedoms, particularly those that address the crisis of education, politics, and the social as part and parcel of the crisis of democracy itself.

In order for critical pedagogy, dialogue, and thought to have real effects, they must advocate the message that all citizens, old and young, are equally entitled, if not equally empowered, to shape the society in which they live. This is a message we heard from the brave students fighting tuition hikes and the destruction of civil liberties and social provisions in Quebec and to a lesser degree in the Occupy Wall Street movement. These young people who are protesting against the 1 percent recognize that they have been written out of the discourses of justice, equality, and democracy and are not only resisting how neoliberalism has made them expendable, they are also arguing for a collective future very different from the one on display in the current political and economic systems in which they feel trapped. These brave youth are insisting that the relationship between knowledge and power can be emancipatory, that their histories and experiences matter, and that what they say and do counts in their struggle to unlearn dominating privileges, productively reconstruct their relations with others, and transform, when necessary, the world around them.

If educators are to function as public intellectuals, they need to listen to young people who are producing a new language in order to talk about inequality and power relations, attempting to create alternative democratic public spaces, rethinking the very nature of politics, and asking serious questions about what democracy is and why it no longer exists in the United States. Simply put, educators need to argue for forms of pedagogy that close the gap between the university and everyday life. Their curricula need to be organized around knowledge of those communities, cultures, and traditions that give students a sense of history, identity, place, and possibility. More importantly, they need to join students in engaging in a practice of freedom that points to new and radical forms of pedagogies that have a direct link to building social movements in and out of the colleges and universities.

Although there are still a number of academics such as Noam Chomsky, Angela Davis, John Ralston Saul, Bill McKibben, Germaine Greer, and Cornel West who function as public intellectuals, they are often shut out of the mainstream media or characterized as marginal, unintelligible, and sometimes unpatriotic figures. At the same time, many academics find themselves laboring under horrendous working conditions that either don't allow for them to write in a theoretically rigorous and accessible manner for the public because they do not have time—given the often intensive teaching demands of part-time academics and increasingly of full-time, nontenured academics as well. Or they retreat into a kind of theoreticism in which theory becomes lifeless, detatched from any larger project or the realm of worldly issues. In this instance, the notion of theory as a resource—if not theoretical rigor itself—is reduced to a badge of academic cleverness, shorn of the potential to advance thought within the academy or to reach a larger audience outside their academic disciplines.

Consequently, such intellectuals often exist in hermetic academic bubbles cut off from both the larger public and the important issues that impact society. To no small degree, they have been complicit in the transformation of the university into an adjunct of corporate and military power. Such academics have become incapable of defending higher education as a vital public sphere and unwilling to challenge those spheres of induced mass cultural illiteracy and firewalls of jargon that doom to extinction critically engaged thought, complex ideas, and serious writing for the public. Without their intervention as public intellectuals, the university defaults on its role as a democratic public sphere capable of educating an informed public, a culture of questioning, and the development of a critical formative culture connected to the need, as Cornelius Castoriadis puts it, "to create citizens who are critical thinkers capable of putting existing institutions into question so that democracy again becomes society's movement."[52]

Before his untimely death, Edward Said, himself an exemplary public intellectual, urged his colleagues in the academy to directly confront those social hardships that disfigure contemporary society and pose a serious threat to the promise of democracy. He urged them to assume the role of public intellectuals, wakeful and mindful of their responsibilities to bear testimony to human suffering and the pedagogical possibilities at work in educating students to be autonomous, self-reflective, and socially responsible. Said rejected the notion of a market-driven pedagogy, one that created cheerful robots and legitimated organized recklessness and illegal legalities. In opposition to such a pedagogy, Said argued for what he called a pedagogy of wakefulness and its related concern with a politics of critical engagement. In commenting on Said's public pedagogy of wakefulness, and how it shaped his important consideration of academics as public intellectuals, I begin with a passage that I think offers a key to the ethical and political force of much of his writing. This selection is taken from his memoir, *Out of Place*, which describes the last few months of his mother's life in a New York hospital and the difficult time she had falling to sleep because of the cancer that was ravaging her body. Recalling this traumatic and pivotal life experience, Said's meditation moves between the existential and the insurgent, between private pain and worldly commitment, between the seductions of a "solid self" and the reality of a contradictory, questioning, restless, and at times, uneasy sense of identity. He writes:

> "Help me to sleep, Edward," she once said to me with a piteous trembling in her voice that I can still hear as I write. But then the disease spread into her brain—and for the last six weeks she slept all the time—my own inability to sleep may be her last legacy to me, a counter to her struggle for sleep. For me sleep is something to be gotten over as quickly as possible. I can only go to bed very late, but I am literally up at dawn. Like her I don't possess the secret of long sleep, though unlike her I have reached the point where I do not want it. For me, sleep is death, as is any diminishment in awareness. . . . Sleeplessness for me is a cherished state to be desired at almost any cost; there is nothing for me as invigorating as immediately shedding the shadowy half-consciousness of a night's loss than the early morning, reacquainting myself with or resuming what I might have lost completely a few hours earlier. I occasionally experience myself as a cluster of flowing currents. I prefer this to the idea of a solid self, the identity to which so many attach so much significance. These currents like the themes of one's life, flow along during the waking hours, and at their best, they require no reconciling, no harmonizing. They are "off" and may be out of place, but at least they are always in motion, in time, in place, in the form of all kinds of strange combinations moving about, not necessarily forward, sometimes against each other, contrapuntally

yet without one central theme. A form of freedom, I like to think, even if I am far from being totally convinced that it is. That skepticism too is one of the themes I particularly want to hold on to. With so many dissonances in my life I have learned actually to prefer being not quite right and out of place.[53]

Said posits here an antidote to the seductions of conformity, a disciplinarily induced moral coma, and the lure of corporate money. For Said, it is a sense of being awake, displaced, caught in a combination of diverse circumstances that suggests a pedagogy that is cosmopolitan and imaginative—a public-affirming pedagogy that demands a critical and engaged interaction with the world we live in, mediated by a responsibility for challenging structures of domination and for alleviating human suffering. That is, a pedagogy that writes the public. As an ethical and political practice, a public pedagogy of wakefulness rejects modes of education removed from political or social concerns, divorced from history and matters of injury and injustice. Said's notion of a pedagogy of wakefulness includes "lifting complex ideas into the public space," recognizing human injury inside and outside of the academy, and acting on the assumption that there is more hope in the world when we can use theory to question what is taken for granted and change things.[54] This is a pedagogy in which academics are neither afraid of controversy or the willingness to make connections that are otherwise hidden, nor are they afraid of making clear the connection between private issues and broader elements of society's problems.

For Said, being awake becomes a central metaphor for defining the role of academics as public intellectuals, defending the university as a crucial public sphere, engaging how culture deploys power, and taking seriously the idea of human interdependence while at the same time always living on the border—one foot in and one foot out, an exile and an insider for whom home was always a form of homelessness. As a relentless border-crosser, Said embraced the idea of the "traveler" as an important metaphor for engaged intellectuals. As Stephen Howe, referencing Said, points out, "It was an image which depended not on power, but on motion, on daring to go into different worlds, use different languages, and 'understand a multiplicity of disguises, masks, and rhetorics. Travelers must suspend the claim of customary routine in order to live in new rhythms and rituals . . . the traveler crosses over, traverses territory, and abandons fixed positions all the time.'"[55] And as a border intellectual and traveler, Said embodied the notion of always "being quite not right," evidenced by his principled critique of all forms of certainties and dogmas and his refusal to be silent in the face of human suffering at home and abroad.

Being awake meant refusing the now popular sport of academic-bashing or embracing a crude call for action at the expense of rigorous intellectual and theoretical work. On the contrary, it meant combining rigor and clarity, on the one hand, and civic courage and political commitment, on the other. A pedagogy of wakefulness meant using theory as a resource, recognizing the worldly space of criticism as the democratic underpinning of public-ness, defining critical literacy not merely as a competency but as an act of interpretation linked to the possibility of intervention in the world. It pointed to a kind of border literacy in the plural, in which people learned to read and write from multiple positions of agency; it also was indebted to the recognition forcibly stated by Hannah Arendt that "Without a politically guaranteed public realm, freedom lacks the worldly space to make its appearance."[56]

For those brave academics such as Said, Pierre Bourdieu, Ellen Willis, and others, public intellectuals have a responsibility to unsettle power, trouble consensus, and challenge common sense. The very notion of being an engaged public intellectual is neither foreign to nor a violation of what it means to be an academic scholar but central to its very definition. According to Said, academics have a duty to enter into the public sphere unafraid to take positions and generate controversy, functioning as moral witnesses, raising political awareness, making connections to those elements of power and politics often hidden from public view, and reminding "the audience of the moral questions that may be hidden in the clamor and din of the public debate."[57] At the same time, Said criticized those academics who retreated into a new dogmatism of the disinterested specialist that separates them "not only from the public sphere but from other professionals who don't use the same jargon."[58] This was especially unsettling to him at a time when complex language and critical thought remain under assault in the larger society by all manner of antidemocratic forces. But there is more at stake here than a retreat into convoluted discourses that turn theory into a mechanical act of academic referencing and a deadly obscurantism, there is also the retreat of intellectuals from being able to defend the public values and democratic mission of higher education. Or, as Irving Howe put it, "intellectuals have, by and large, shown a painful lack of militancy in defending the rights which are a precondition of their existence."[59]

The view of higher education as a democratic public sphere committed to producing young people capable and willing to expand and deepen their sense of themselves, to think about the world critically, "to imagine something other than their own well-being," to serve the public good, and to struggle for a substantive democracy has been in a state of acute crisis for the last thirty years.[60] When faculty assume, in this context, their civic responsibility to educate students to think critically, act with conviction, and connect what they learn in classrooms to important social issues in the larger society, they are often denounced for politicizing their classrooms and for violating professional codes of conduct, or, worse, labeled as unpatriotic.[61] In some cases, the risk of connecting what they teach to the imperative to expand the capacities of students to be both critical and socially engaged may cost academics their jobs, especially when they make visible the workings of power, injustice, human misery, and the alterable nature of the social order. What do the liberal arts and humanities amount to if they do not teach the practice of freedom, especially at a time when training is substituted for education? Gayatri Spivak provides a context for this question with her comment: "Can one insist on the importance of training in the humanities in [a] time of legitimized violence?"[62]

In a society that remains troublingly resistant to or incapable of questioning itself, one that celebrates the consumer over the citizen and all too willingly endorses the narrow values and interests of corporate power, the importance of the university as a place of critical learning, dialogue, and social justice advocacy becomes all the more imperative. Moreover, the distinctive role that faculty play in this ongoing pedagogical project of democratization and learning, along with support for the institutional conditions and relations of power that make it possible, must be defended as part of a broader discourse of excellence, equity, and democracy.

Despite the growing public recognition that market fundamentalism has fostered a destructive alignment among the state, corporate capital, and transnational corporations, there is little understanding that such an alignment has been constructed and solidified through a ne-oliberal disciplinary apparatus and corporate pedagogy produced in part in the halls of higher education and through the educational force of the larger media culture. The economic Darwinism of the last thirty years has done more than throw the financial and credit systems into crisis; it has also waged an attack on all those social institutions that support critical modes of agency, reason, and meaningful dissent. And yet, the financial meltdown most of the world is experiencing is rarely seen as part of an educational crisis in which the institutions of public and higher education have been conscripted into a war on democratic values. Such institutions have played a formidable, if not shameless, role in reproducing market-driven beliefs, social relations, identities, and modes of understanding that legitimate the institutional arrangements of cut-throat capitalism. William Black calls such institutions purveyors of a "criminogenic environment"—one that promotes and legitimates market-driven practices that include fraud, deregulation, and other perverse practices.[63] Black claims that the most extreme pedagogical expression of such an environment can be found in business schools, which he calls "fraud factories" for the elite.[64]

There seems to be an enormous disconnect between the economic conditions that led to the devastating financial meltdown and the current call to action by a generation of young people and adults who have been educated for the last several decades in the knowledge, values, and identities of a market-driven society. Clearly, this generation will not solve this crisis if they do not connect it to the assault on an educational system that has been reduced to a lowly adjunct of corporate interests and the bidding of the warfare state.

Higher education represents one of the most important sites over which the battle for democracy is being waged. It is the site where the promise of a better future emerges out of those visions and pedagogical practices that combine hope, agency, politics, and moral responsibility as part of a broader emancipatory discourse. Academics have a distinct and unique obligation, if not political and ethical responsibility, to make learning relevant to the imperatives of a discipline, scholarly method, or research specialization. If democracy is a way of life that demands a formative culture, educators can play a pivotal role in creating forms of pedagogy and research that enable young people to think critically, exercise judgment, engage in spirited debate, and create those public spaces that constitute "the very essence of political life."[65]

Finally, I want to suggest that while it has become more difficult to imagine a democratic future, we have entered a period in which young people all over the world are protesting against neoliberalism and its pedagogy and politics of disposability. Refusing to remain voiceless and powerless in determining their future, these young people are organizing collectively in order to create the conditions for societies that refuse to use politics as an act of war and markets as the measure of democracy. They are taking seriously the words of the great abolitionist Frederick Douglass, who bravely argued that freedom is an empty abstraction if people fail to act, and "if there is no struggle, there is no progress."[66] Their struggles are not simply aimed at the 1 percent but also at the 99 percent as part of a broader effort to get them to connect the dots, educate themselves, and develop and join social movements that can rewrite the language of democracy and put into place the institutions and formative cultures that make it possible. Stanley Aronowitz is right in arguing that

> The system survives on the eclipse of the radical imagination, the absence of a viable political opposition with roots in the general population, and the conformity of its intellectuals who, to a large extent, are subjugated by their secure berths in the academy. [At the same time,] it would be premature to predict that decades of retreat, defeat and silence can be reversed overnight without a commitment to what may be termed "a long march" though the institutions, the workplaces and the streets of the capitalist metropoles.[67]

The protests that began in 2011 in the United States, Canada, Greece, and Spain make clear that this is not—indeed, *cannot be*—only a short-term project for reform but a political movement that needs to intensify, accompanied by the reclaiming of public spaces, the progressive use of digital technologies, the development of public spheres, the production of new modes of education, and the safeguarding of places where democratic expression, new identities, and collective hope can be nurtured and mobilized. A formative culture must be put in place pedagogically and institutionally in a variety of spheres extending from churches and public and higher education to all those cultural apparatuses engaged in the production and circulation of knowledge, desire, identities, and values.

Clearly, such efforts need to address the language of democratic revolution rather than the seductive incremental adjustments of liberal reform. This suggests calling for a living wage, jobs programs (especially for the young), the democratization of power, economic equality, and a massive shift in funds away from the machinery of war and big banks, as well as building a social movement that not only engages in critique but also makes hope a real possibility by organizing in order to seize power. We need collective narratives that inform collective struggles. In this instance, public intellectuals can play a crucial role in providing theoretical resources and modes of analyses that can help to shape such narratives along with broader social movements and collective struggles. There is no room for failure here because failure would cast us back into the clutches of authoritarianism—which, while different from previous historical periods, shares nonetheless the imperative to proliferate violent social formations and a death-dealing blow to the promise of a democracy to come.

Given the urgency of the problems faced by those marginalized by class, race, age, and sexual orientation, I think it is all the more crucial to take seriously the challenge of Derrida's provocation that "We must do and think the impossible. If only the possible happened, nothing more would happen. If I only I did what I can do, I wouldn't do anything."[68] We may live in dark times, as Hannah Arendt reminds us, but history is open and the space of the possible is larger than the one on display. Academics in their role as public intellectuals can play a crucial part in raising critical questions, connecting critical modes of education to social change, and making clear that the banner of critical independence and civic engagement, "ragged and torn though it may be, is still worth fighting for."[69]

CHAPTER SIX

Days of Rage:
The Quebec Student Protest Movement and the New Social Awakening[1]

> *This isn't a student strike, it's the awakening of society.*
> —**Quebec protest banner**

I n many countries throughout the world, young people are speaking out.[2] They are using their voices and bodies to redefine the boundaries of the possible and to protest the crushing currents of neoliberal regimes that ruthlessly assert their power and policies through appeals to destiny, political theology, and the unabashed certainty bred of fundamentalist faith. From Paris, Athens, and London to Montreal and New York City, young people are challenging the current repressive historical conjuncture by rejecting its dominant premises and practices. Many young people are protesting to create a future inclusive of their dreams in which the principles of justice and equality become key elements of a radicalized democratic and social project. Their efforts importantly involve protests against tuition hikes, austerity measures, joblessness, and deep cuts in public spending. Such protests also signal the awakening of a revolutionary ideal in the service of a new society. In the aftermath of the mass mobilizations spurred by Occupy Wall Street in 2011–12 and

155

the Quebec student strike in 2012, a number of student groups across the United States are now working in a less spectacular fashion to develop democratically based student unions that are capable of advocating for sustainable transformations of higher education and society at large. Through such measures, youth have dared to call for a different world and, in doing so, have exhibited great courage in taking up a wager about the future made from the standpoint of an embattled present. To understand the shared concerns of these youthful protesters and the global nature of the forces they are fighting, it is crucial to situate these diverse student protests within a broader analysis of global capital and the changing nature of its assaults on young people.

The Tyranny of Neoliberalism

Unapologetic in its implementation of austerity measures that cause massive amounts of human hardship and suffering, neoliberal capitalism consolidates class power on the backs of young people, workers, and others marginalized by class, race, and ethnicity.[3] And it appears to no longer need the legitimacy garnered through its false claim to democratic ideals such as free speech, individual liberty, or justice—however tepid these appeals have always been. In the absence of alternative social visions to market-driven values and the increasing separation of global corporate power from national politics, neoliberalism has wrested itself free of any regulatory controls while at the same time removing economics from any consideration of social costs, ethics, or social responsibility. Since the economic collapse of 2008–2009, it has become increasingly evident that neoliberalism's only imperatives are profits and growing investments in global power structures unmoored from any form of accountable, democratic governance.

The devastating fallout of neoliberal capitalism's reorganization of society—the destruction of communities and impoverishment of individuals and families—now becomes its most embraced mode of expression as it is championed, ironically, as the only viable route to economic stability. In this widely accepted, yet dystopian world view, collective misfortune is no longer interpreted as a sign of failing governance or of the tawdry willingness of politicians to serve corporate interests, but attributed to the character flaws of individuals and defined chiefly as a matter of personal responsibility. In fact, government-provided social protections are viewed as pathological. Matters of life and death are removed from traditional modes of democratic governance and made subject to the sovereignty of the market. In this new age of biocapital or "bioeconomics," as Eric Cazdyn calls it, "all ideals are at the mercy of a larger economic logic"[4]—one that unapologetically generates policies that "trample over millions of people if necessary."[5] Neoliberalism's defining ideologies, values, and policies harness all institutions, social practices, and modes of thought to the demands of corporations and the needs of the warfare state. They are as narrowly self-serving as they are destructive.

As collective responsibility is privatized, politics loses its social and democratic character, and the formative culture necessary for the production of engaged critical agents is gravely undermined. An utterly reduced form of agency is now embodied in the figure of the isolated automaton, who is driven by self-interest and eschews any responsibility for the other. As Stuart J. Murray points out, neoliberalism's totalizing discourse of privatization, commodification, deregulation, and hyper-individualism "co-opts and eviscerates the language of the common good."[6] The ascendancy of neoliberal ideology also manifests in an ongoing assault on democratic public spheres, public goods, and any viable notion of equality and social justice. As corporate power is consolidated into fewer and fewer hands, ideological and structural reforms are implemented to transfer wealth and income into the clutches of a ruling financial and corporate elite. This concentration of power is all the more alarming since both Canada and the United States have experienced unprecedented growth in wealth concentration and income inequality since the 1970s. In Canada, as Bruce Campbell notes,

> The richest Canadian 1% has almost doubled its share of the national income pie—from 7% to almost 14%—over the last three decades. The average top 100 CEO's compensation was $6.6 million in 2009, 155 times the average worker's wage [while] 61 Canadian billionaires have a combined wealth of $162 billion, twice as much as the bottom 17 million Canadians.[7]

The United States holds the shameful honor of being "perched at the very top of the global premier league of inequality,"[8] with 1 percent of Americans holding 40 percent of all wealth and 24 percent of all income.[9] Fraud and corruption run rampant through the financial sectors of many advanced industrial countries, burning everything in their path.[10] As Charles Ferguson observes, "major U.S. and European banks have been caught assisting corporate malfeasance by Enron and others, laundering money for drug cartels and the Iranian military, aiding tax evasion, hiding the assets of corrupt dictators, colluding in order to fix prices, and committing many forms of financial fraud."[11] In light of the recent scandals exposing the predatory practices and criminal acts of financial institutions such as HSBC, JPMorgan Chase, and the banking giant Barclays, it is clear that the financial sector has devolved into a financial oligarchy and a global criminal enterprise.[12]

A dire consequence of growing inequality is that more and more people are facing joblessness and poverty, while many already feel they have been written out of a future that might offer them a decent and dignified life. What many have learned the hard way in North America and across the globe is that the impacts of inequality cannot be adequately captured with empirical measures based in the GNP or median incomes. Inequality has a lived experience in which there is "a fatal attraction between poverty and vulnerability, corruption and the accumulation of dangers, as well as humiliation and the denial of dignity."[13] Young people, particularly those transitioning to independent adulthood, have certainly felt the brunt of the intensification of neoliberal policies and are increasingly unemployed, deprived of the most basic social provisions, denied access to decent health care and affordable housing, and faced with diminished educational opportunities. Zygmunt Bauman argues that today's youth have become "outcasts and outlaws of a novel kind, cast in a condition of liminal drift, with no way of knowing whether it is transitory or permanent."[14] That is, the generation of youth in the early twenty-first century has no way of grasping if they will ever "be free from the gnawing sense of the transience, indefiniteness, and provisional nature of any settlement."[15] And those young people further marginalized by race and class now inhabit a social landscape in which they are increasingly disparaged as flawed consumers with no adequate role to play and are considered disposable, while forced to inhabit "zones of social abandonment" extending from bad schools to bulging detention centers and prisons.[16]

With so many young people globally facing a present whose future promises only to preserve and expand those spaces that have become sites of "terminal exclusion,"[17] youth in North America and Europe have exhibited a growing recognition that the real marker of their generation is an ever-expanding mode of precarity. Increasingly stripped of their dignity as students and workers, young protesters in both the United States and Canada have recognized that "the current mode of production and reproduction has become a mode of *production for elimination*, a reproduction of populations that are not likely to be productively used or exploited but are always already superfluous."[18] By some estimates, "nearly 75 million young people around the world are out of work, an increase of four million since the economic crisis of 2008."[19] Youth unemployment rates in Europe are staggering, reaching as high as 50 percent in both Spain and Greece and over 35 percent in Ireland. In the United States, 53 percent of recent college graduates are either unemployed or underemployed.[20] Regardless of its diminished promise of social and economic mobility, higher education now subsidizes institutional budgets with exorbitant tuition rate hikes that effectively prevent working-class and many middle-class youth from even getting an education.

The security that once came with access to public and higher education, the prospect of a decent job, and a state that provided social protections against unexpected and horrible misfortunes has vanished. In a world marked by what Bauman calls "liquid modernity," social structures that depend on long-term planning and investment have disappeared, just as social problems have been individualized along with the task of resolving them.[21] The era of "fixed addresses," stable communities, and social stability is over. Youth are now condemned to unskilled or temporary jobs, commodified social bonds, transient living conditions, and personal commitments that carry a short expiration date. Identities are now temporary, shifting endlessly amid a glut of consumer choices fed by celebrity culture and the corporate evisceration of all significant cultural institutions. Matters of social and personal security are left to the embattled devices of each individual, even as the means for providing genuine safety are largely monopolized by the rich and powerful.[22] As Bauman points out, casino capitalism's "order of egoism" and obsession with privatization "shifts the task of fighting against and (hopefully) resolving socially produced problems onto the shoulders of individual men and women, in most cases much too weak for the purpose, depending on their mostly inadequate skills and insufficient resources."[23]

Nowhere is the precarity that defines the current state of young people more obvious than in the consequences they face daily as the social state is being dismantled, individual rights are effaced, political freedoms are criminalized, and collective rights are all but obliterated. Young people are now told that freedom is about doing what you want without any impediments, especially from the government. What they are not told is that individualized notions of freedom neither address nor provide the social, economic, and political conditions necessary to ensure access to a meaningful job, quality education, decent health care, clean air, and a life of dignity in a just society. Individual freedom removes any sense of community, social responsibility, and solidarity from the discourse of freedom. Individual freedom has to take a detour through collective endeavors of freedom in order to become meaningful. Individual freedom without robust communities is simply code for a stripped-down notion of humanity as disconnected, self-interested automatons lacking any sense of moral accountability, social responsibility, or civic courage. Within the vocabulary of neoliberalism, too many young people are removed from the discourses of community and collective freedom, pushed to the margins of society, and forced to inhabit zones of terminal uncertainty, despair, and exclusion.

Increasingly unemployed, pushed into poverty, politically disenfranchised, and subject to the discipline of a growing punishing state,[24] young people across the globe face a bleak future marked by uncertainty, vulnerability, insecurity, and the burden of mounting debt.[25] Instead of being viewed as a crucial social investment, many youth—especially protesting students and minorities of race and class—are now the objects of law and order, caught in an expanding web of surveillance, criminalization, and governing-through-crime modes of social control.[26]

Tuition Hikes in the Age of Mounting Debt

It is precisely against this background of expanding policies of neoliberal austerity, precarity, despair, diminishing expectations, and state violence that young people in Quebec have organized a protest movement that may be one of the most "powerful challenges to neoliberalism on the continent."[27] Thousands of students have raised their voices in unprecedented opposition to the ideology, modes of governance, and policies of the neoliberal state. The initial cause of the protest movement began in response to an increase in tuition fees announced by the Quebec provincial government in March 2011. The tuition hike was "part of the government's effort to advance neoliberalism in Quebec by introducing new fees for public services and raising existing ones."[28] The government's proposal included raising tuition by $325 per year over five years with the increased fees going into effect in September 2012. The hike amounted to a 75 percent increase over five years, rising from $2,319 to $3,793 by 2017. In February 2012, after the government refused to negotiate with organizations representing student interests, the student leaders called for a strike. Tens of thousands of students responded immediately by boycotting their classes. Many of the province's colleges and universities were shut down as a result.

Mainstream media consistently sided with the Quebec government, downplaying the significance of the tuition increases—even as they pertained to those students who could least afford them and for whom it would have the greatest impact. Critics of the strike repeatedly drew the public's attention to the fact that, even with the increase, tuition fees in Quebec would remain among the lowest in Canada: "Average undergraduate tuition in Canada for 2011–12 is $5,366, but ranges widely from province to province. Quebec has the lowest fees, followed closely by Newfoundland and Labrador. Ontario has the highest average tuition, at $6,640 a year."[29] However, it soon became apparent that the students viewed the tuition increase as only one symptom of an ailing and unjust social order about which they could no longer be silent. The students preferred to speak for themselves rather than have others speak abstractly for them and about them, especially when it came to the material conditions of their own educations and their own futures. It is telling, and will remain telling, that government officials and newspaper pundits instantly responded with anxious indignation, as if wholly caught off guard by the simple fact that students can speak—and speak intelligently, passionately, and urgently about the most pressing issues facing themselves and their society. In a reversal of roles familiar to anyone who actually works in a classroom, the student can also teach the teacher. The first lesson to be learned from the striking students was that the protests were about much more than fee structures. Yet, the government seemed unwilling to assimilate this pedagogical insight, and its heavy-handedness touched a nerve in the larger social body of Quebec, activating new forms of dissent and solidarity.

The action that began as a protest against increasing tuition fees soon developed into a popular uprising, with tens of thousands of postsecondary students and their supporters marching nightly in the streets of Quebec cities and in solidarity demonstrations across Canada.[30] It became a student strike of unprecedented proportions, involving more than two hundred thousand students and rallying many additional supporters for a mass demonstration on March 22, 2012. As the strike progressed and expanded its base of support, over a quarter of a million people joined the demonstrations on a number of occasions and an estimated half million marched in Montreal on May 25, 2012. By July 2012, the Quebec student strike had emerged as not only "the longest and largest student strike in the history of North America," but also "the biggest act of civil disobedience in Canadian history."[31] Now a major broad-based opposition movement against neoliberal austerity measures, the Quebec student strike initiated one of the most powerful, collectively organized challenges to neoliberal ideology, policy, and governance that has occurred globally in some time.

The initial phase of the movement focused almost exclusively on higher-educational reform. The issues addressed in the early stage of the protests included a rejection of the province's call for a tuition increase, a sustained critique of the underfunding of postsecondary education, a critical interrogation of the perils facing a generation forced to live on credit and tied to the servitude of debt, and the opening up of a new conversation about the meaning and purpose of education—in particular, the kind of educational system that is free and removed from corporate influences, and whose mission is defined by its commitment to justice, equality, and support for the broader public good.

Students rejected the tuition hike by arguing that the increase would not only force many working-class students to drop out but also prevent economically disadvantaged students from gaining access to higher education altogether. Expanding this critique, many young people spoke of the tuition increase as symbolic of repressive neoliberal austerity measures that forced them to pay more for their education while offering them a diminished future of dismal job prospects when they graduated. Situating the protest against tuition hikes within a broader critique of neoliberal austerity measures, students were then able to address the fee hikes as part of the growing burden of suffocating debt, government-funding priorities that favor the financial and corporate elite, Prime Minister Harper's ruinous transfer of public funds into an expanding military-industrial complex, and the imposition of corporate culture and corporate modes of governance on all aspects of daily life.

By stressing a pervasive crisis of debt as an issue rather than focusing exclusively on tuition, students were able to highlight the darker registers of finance capital that increasingly foreclose any possibility of a better life for this generation and generations to come. Andrew Gavin Marshall has provided a theoretical service in highlighting the broader effects and politics of the debt crisis. He writes:

> Total student debt now stands at about $20 billion in Canada ($15 billion from Federal Government loans programs, and the rest from provincial and commercial bank loans). In Quebec, the average student debt is $15,000, whereas Nova Scotia and Newfoundland have an average student debt of $35,000, British Columbia at nearly $30,000 and Ontario at nearly $27,000. Roughly 70% of new jobs in Canada require a post-secondary education. Half of students in their 20s live at home with their parents, including 73 per cent of those aged 20 to 24 and nearly a third of 25- to 29-year-olds. On average, a four-year degree for a student living at home in Canada costs $55,000, and those costs are expected to increase in coming years at a rate faster than inflation. It has been estimated that in 18 years, a four-year degree for Canadian students will cost $102,000. Defaults on government student loans are at roughly 14%. The Chairman of the Canadian Federation of Students warned in June of 2011 that, "We are on the verge of bankrupting a generation before they even enter the workplace." The notion, therefore, that Quebec students should not struggle against a bankrupt future is a bankrupted argument.[32]

Connecting student opposition to the tuition hike with the broader issue of expanding debt and the fact that "the average debt for [Canadian] university graduates is around $27,000" helped shift the focus of the strike—viewed by some critics as a narcissistic, collective temper tantrum by whiny students—to a much more public and broader set of considerations. In this instance, what was being indicated by the students calling for higher educational reforms, as Randy Boyagoda points out, was "a profound crisis of faith in the socioeconomic frameworks that have structured and advanced societies across North America and Europe since World War II [as well as] a rejection of the premise of the postwar liberal state: that large-scale institutions and elected leaders are capable of creating opportunities for individual citizens to flourish."[33]

Defending a Free and Democratic Postsecondary Education System

The Quebec protesters made clear how rising tuition fees could be connected to the savage dictates of a debt machine that increases the profits of banks and other financial institutions. But they also went further and raised broader questions about what kind of university system would support such measures. In doing so, they have called into question the increasing corporatization of the university with its market-oriented view of governance, its valuing of research in instrumentalized market terms, its substitution of training for broad-based education, and its view of higher education as a commercial entity. Writing about the Quebec strike, Malav Kanuga states,

> For the students there has been a growing sense of urgency and a shared recognition that increased tuition means a heavier student debt burden, hundreds of more hours a year spent working instead of studying, less access for working-class students, and a shift in university culture toward the market, the commodification of education, the financialization of student life, and the privatization of the university.[34]

But the student activists have not simply denounced the university's role in the reproduction of neoliberal values, gated communities for the affluent, and the engines of social and economic inequality. Student protesters have also strongly argued for a wholesale transformation of higher education in terms of both its mission and how it is funded. Moving from "the crisis of negation" to a project of transformation, the protesters have argued for higher education to be not only free and accessible to all students but also dedicated to the role of educating students to take intellectual risks, think imaginatively, and assume the social responsibilities of critically engaged citizens.[35]

The Quebec student protesters are correct in their demand that Canadian society needs a wholesale revision of how educational institutions and democracies in general listen to and treat young people in a world in which their voices, needs, desires, and growing hardships have been excluded from a public space of articulation. The students have passionately rejected the neoliberal view of higher education as an economic investment unapologetically designed to turn students into consumers and the university into a profit-making entity. They have been strongly critical of neoliberal modes of governance that impose a top-down business culture on faculty, demanding that they assume the role of entrepreneurs rather than autonomous and critically engaged teachers and scholars. In addition, they have rejected the restructuring of academic departments into revenue production units and classrooms into training grounds that mimic the business culture of call centers and Walmarts. Presenting an alternative to the neoliberal model, Quebec students have argued for higher education as a democratic public sphere that does more than provide private returns for individuals and institute policies that aim to banish forever the "horrors" of teaching students to question authority. They have demanded the kind of education that takes seriously the impending challenges of a global democracy and will enable them to mediate the world in terms of democratic rather than commercial values.

More and more young people are insisting that the real value of higher education lies in its capacity to offer everyone the opportunity to receive a free, quality education and the prospect of living in an educated society, both of which are crucial for creating genuine social security, critical agents, and the formative culture necessary for a democracy to thrive. In developing their critique, the protesters have resurrected "the ideal of free post-secondary education—recommended in the 1960s by a famous state-commissioned inquiry, but long since snuffed out among the economic elite."[36] They have made clear the political and moral fault lines between those who believe that education is a "commodity purchased by 'consumers' for self-advancement, and those who would protect it as a right funded by the state for the collective good"—and, in doing so, they have "sparked a fundamental debate about the entire society's future."[37]

Funding the Neoliberal State

Clearly there is more at stake in the Quebec protest movement than concerns over tuition hikes and skyrocketing student debt. A disquieting narrative about the future of young people entering adult life has been extended to the troubling reality of a broader social system that increasingly places its political allegiances, social investments, and economic support in the service of rich and powerful financial institutions while eviscerating the social state and the public treasury. As Martin Lukacs insists, one achievement of the Quebec protest movement has been

> to clarify for a broad swath of society that a tuition hike is not a matter of isolated accounting, but the goal of a neoliberal austerity agenda the world over. Forcing students to pay more for education is part of a transfer of wealth from the poor and middle class to the rich—as with privatization and the state's withdrawal from service provision, tax breaks for corporations, and deep cuts to social programs.[38]

The hidden order of politics at the center of neoliberal austerity measures is difficult to miss and helps explain the misplaced priorities of a Quebec government that in 2006–07 provided $437 million for funding private schools—funds that, as Erika Shaker points out, "would pay for a fee freeze at Quebec universities and have money left over for bursaries for low-income students [while] the remainder could be redirected towards public schools."[39] Shaker suggests that this transfer of funds to private schools "demonstrate[s] that when public money is used to facilitate private access, it's the public infrastructure and the people accessing it who pay the price."[40] The defunding of the social state and higher education and the increasing attack on the social contract are also evident in the Canadian state's willingness in the latter half of the 1990s "to reduce by 50% the federal transfers to the provinces for post-secondary education [which has amounted] to a loss of income of $800 million per year for Quebec."[41] Federal funds that could be used for investing in higher education have instead been reallocated to support the conservative government's tough-on-crime agenda and either squandered on prison expansion or diverted into a growing Canadian military budget.

Current tuition fee increases would raise about $200 million from students; yet such fees could be completely eliminated and free education provided to all students if the Canadian government cut back on its bloated military budget. Former Quebec premier Jean Charest and his fellow apostles of neoliberalism had no trouble contributing $4.5 billion in 2011 to the $24.7 billion that "the Canadian government is spending . . . on its military budget, a budget that is proportionally higher today than it was during the Cold War" and places Canada fourteenth in global military spending.[42] Offloading more costs to the provinces, the federal government refuses assistance that could offset rising student tuition fees and pushes ahead with a military budget that is still considering an astronomical expenditure on F-35 fighter jets that will cost as much as $45.8 billion.[43] The asymmetry of the situation would be laughable if it weren't so grotesque: students are vilified as irresponsible for protesting against tuition fee increases while the Department of National Defence spends billions at will and remains mostly unopposed. What isn't laughable is the students' demands for free education. At the core of the demand for free education is a rethinking of education as a right, a public good, rather than an entitlement. As a number of studies have pointed out, when education is understood as a public good, you get an educated society; people have the opportunity to develop analytic skills to be actively engaged agents; moreover, people are healthier, there is less crime, and various conditions are put into place that allow an educated society to work.[44]

Commentators in the national newspapers bleat about the putative naïveté or selfishness of Quebec youth but remain conspicuously mute about the increased militarization of the culture, even as Canada attempts to extricate itself from a disastrous and costly war in Afghanistan. In fact, neoliberal governments in the United States, United Kingdom, and Canada express little to no concern about providing students with quality higher education or supporting investment in universities, libraries, health care, or a job creation program for young people. Increasingly, it appears such social investments are viewed as far less important than siphoning off billions to fund a culture of violence and a permanent war machine. Misplaced priorities that shut down economic, educational, and political opportunities suggest that these countries have become societies that are waging a war on their children, even as government policies increasingly reveal the savagery of a system that considers profits more important than the lives of its citizens.

Confronting the Backlash of Smears, Insults, and Police Violence

The student strike in Quebec emerged in February 2012, when it became clear that then-premier Charest and the Quebec government were not interested in opening up a dialogue with the province's major student unions. Various student groups joined hands and organized a massive strike of forty thousand students on February 21, 2012. As the strike became more cohesive under the leadership of the CLASSÉ—the Coalition large de l'Association pour une Solidarité Syndicale Étudiante, Quebec's largest student association and the most vocal in supporting direct action and rejecting the regime of neoliberal capitalism—the tactics employed by the students became both more disruptive and more effective. The strike in turn alarmed a number of business elites, conservative media pundits, and members of the Charest government.

Not surprisingly, the business community in the province supported both the government's effort to raise tuition and its use of state force to crush the strike. Roger Annis notes that "The Conseil du Patronat du Québec (Employers Council of Quebec) issued the results of a survey of its members on June 1 showing 95 percent support for the government's proposed hike in tuition fees that sparked the student strike last February and 68 percent support for Bill 78"—the latter referring to legislation whose purpose was largely viewed as an attempt to break the student unions, suppress democratic expression, bankrupt individuals, and undermine the unity and solidarity that had been forged among the largest student groups.[45]

A massive progovernment smear campaign emerged against the students, labeling them as "self-seeking brats, whining about modest tuition increases and seeking mayhem for its own sake."[46] Margaret Wente, writing for the *Globe and Mail*, echoed the sentiments of many mainstream journalists and derided the student protesters by referring to them as "kids" who "are on another planet."[47] According to Wente, the students were too immature to understand the nature of their own actions, never mind put forth a serious criticism of both market-based higher education and the wider neoliberal order. She judged their complaints about tuition increases as meaningless since, as she put it to her well-heeled readership, not only do the students have "the lowest tuition fees in North America [but] the total increase would amount to the cost of a daily grande cappuccino."[48] Of course, this would make sense if education were literally about nothing more than consuming a product. Wente has a long history of blaming young people for being narcissistic and invoking clichés of "dangerous" youth. For example, in previous articles, she criticized unemployed young men (code for poor minority youth) for creating what she calls a "huge social problem" because "they refuse to work."[49] Yet Wente has appeared strangely untroubled by the billion-dollar crimes committed by corrupt corporations, thus exhibiting what Alain Badiou calls "zero tolerance" for youthful protesters and "infinite tolerance for the crimes of bankers and government embezzlers which affect the lives of millions."[50]

For Wente, the victims of social inequality are now blameworthy. In this view, the real culprits behind an ailing society are the youth—characterized by their alleged moral turpitude and declining values—instead of a global financial meltdown caused by the willingness of finance capitalism to sacrifice the future of young people for short-term political and economic gains. Accordingly, the issue that the protesters should really be addressing is the necessity to rid higher education of those academic disciplines not directly tied to the market because the only purpose of education, in Wente's instrumentalist world view, is to train people to take their place in the neoliberal order she so fervently defends.

Some critics went further than Wente and called for outright violence to be used against the protesters. Roger Annis claimed that not only were many business leaders in favor of using the police to crush the strike but also many "politicians and editorialists were calling for greater use of police violence and court injunctions to break up student picket lines."[51] Michael Den Tandt, writing in the *National Post*, was quite explicit in calling for the government to crack down on the protesters, going so far as to suggest dishing out medieval forms of punishment such as "caning."[52] Bernard Guay, a member of the Quebec Liberal Party and head of the tax office in the Municipal Affairs Department, published a letter on the website of *Le Soleil* in which, according to Andrew Gavin Marshall, he unapologetically recommended

> using the fascist movements of the 1920s and 1930s as an example in how to deal with "leftists" in giving them "their own medicine." He suggested organizing a political "cabal" to handle the "wasteful and anti-social" situation, which would mobilize students to not only cross picket lines, but to confront and assault students who wear the little red square (the symbol of the student strike).[53]

Imitating fascist thuggery, Guay suggested, would "help society 'overcome the tyranny of Leftist agitators.'"[54] In spite of their differences, these attacks all share what *New York Times* columnist Frank Bruni has called, in a different context, an "emphasis on personal advantage over the public good."[55] One might conclude that they all exhibit a hatred for democracy itself.[56]

While Premier Charest eventually agreed to open up talks with the main student groups, he held fast to student tuition increases, though he later made a paltry offer to lower the rate of increase. It is impossible to determine if the bellicose assault against the protesters in the mainstream media, along with the support of a large portion of Quebec's business community, encouraged the Charest government to resort to repressive measures. However, the Charest government did just that by passing Bill 78 into law on May 18, 2012—and proceeding to implement antiprotest legislation that gave sweeping powers to the police and was designed to suppress peaceful protests and shut down student opposition while violating the most basic rights of free speech, association, and assembly.[57]

Representing the dissent expressed by the students "as a criminal rather than political issue," the emergency legislation was a desperate attempt to portray the protest movement as an act of criminality and students as figures of lawlessness, despite the validity of the issues being raised and the general peacefulness of the student demonstrations.[58] In the service of legitimating an alarmist set of regulations and substituting an emotional discourse for a reasoned and thoughtful attempt at dialogue, Law 12 (formerly Bill 78) proved to be a draconian piece of legislation so extreme that Montreal police expressed reluctance about enforcing certain parts of it.[59]

The most prohibitive and irresponsible measures of Law 12 included giving the police eight hours' notice and a precise itinerary for any demonstration involving more than fifty people; fines running as high as $125,000 for unions and student federations and $35,000 for individuals who violate the law; giving police the power to prosecute a person if he or she offers support or encouragement to protesters at a school; making it illegal for any demonstration to be held within fifty meters of any school campus; giving the government the right to order faculty and staff to show up for work on any designated day; and doubling all fines for repeat offenders. But Law 12 was much more than a gross violation of the rights of students to engage in peaceful assembly and protest austerity measures aimed at curtailing access to postsecondary education. It also provided a green light for police violence, making clear that the state was willing to employ aggressive levels of force against students and others in order to sustain its refusal to address major social and economic problems through peaceful public dialogue and debate.

Broadening the Struggle from an Event to a Social Strike

The government's decision to assume a defensive posture on behalf of rich elites and corporate power backfired and the passage of Bill 78 in May 2012 signified a major turning point for the Quebec protest movement. Rather than creating a climate of fear in order to intimidate students, faculty, and other sympathizers, the law outraged both civil libertarians and ordinary citizens and became a catalyst for attracting a much wider following of nonstudent supporters. Not only did public anger explode in a massive demonstration on May 25, in which an estimated five hundred thousand people marched, it also inaugurated nightly demonstrations in Montreal neighborhoods in which people in the streets and on balconies banged their pots and pans at 8:00 p.m. to protest the law as an act of public support and solidarity for the students.

Inspired by the "pots and pans" movement that developed in Chile in the '70s, the "casseroles" demonstrations in Montreal and other cities functioned as a mode of collective performance and a loud but peaceful way to express public outrage and disgust at the Charest government. In addition, crowds of supporters embraced the red square as a symbol of resistance to a future of debt (being "squarely in the red"), pinning it on their clothing and waving red flags from their balconies, donning a powerful symbolic image of defiance as a way to demonstrate their anger over a generation of young people being trapped in a ruinous system of usurious credit and loans.

As public support shifted in favor of the strikers, what initially emerged as a specific set of concerns over tuition hikes evolved into a broader narrative of complaint and resistance toward a global neoliberal order, further providing an opportunity for students to connect their limited set of grievances to a comprehensive set of social problems. What began as a student protest morphed into a social strike in which the assault on the university could be addressed as part of a wider attack on the social state, the environment, unemployed workers, the land rights of indigenous peoples, and young people across the globe. The changing nature of both the debate and the politics that informed it was evident in the CLASSÉ's three-pronged action plan and the "Manifesto for a Maple Spring."[60]

These documents situated the Quebec movement in a broader historical context of social resistance, illuminating a shared opposition to "the laws of an unjust global economy that is mortgaging the future of all of us [and mortgaging] its youth as nothing more than an exploitable resource."[61] In CLASSÉ's "Share Our Future Manifesto," the call for a social strike was presented passionately through a more capacious political narrative as imaginative as it is daring in its call to forge sustainable communal bonds, treat human beings with dignity, build democratic social relations, and construct a new vision of the future. One gets a glimpse of this daring embrace of a revolutionary ideal in the following section from the manifesto, which is worth repeating in full:

> This burden is one that we all shoulder, each and every one of us, whether we are students or not: this is one lesson our strike has taught us. For we, students, are also renters and employees; we are international students, pushed aside by discriminating public services. We come from many backgrounds, and, until the color of our skin goes as unnoticed as our eye color, we will keep on facing everyday racism, contempt and ignorance. We are women, and if we are feminists it is because we face daily sexism and roadblocks set for us by the patriarchal system; we constantly fight deep-rooted prejudice. We are gay,

straight, bisexual, and proud to be. We have never been a separate level of society. Our strike is not directed against the people. We are the people. Our strike goes beyond the $1625 tuition-fee hike. If, by throwing our educational institutions into the marketplace, our most basic rights are being taken from us, we can say the same for hospitals, Hydro-Québec, our forests, and the soil beneath our feet. We share so much more than public services: we share our living spaces, spaces that were here before we were born. We want them to survive us....This is the meaning of our vision, and the essence of our strike: it is a shared, collective action whose scope lies well beyond student interests. We are daring to call for a different world, one far removed from the blind submission our present commodity-based system requires. Individuals, nature, our public services, these are being seen as commodities: the same tiny elite is busy selling everything that belongs to us. And yet we know that public services are not useless expenditures, nor are they consumer goods.[62]

In Badiou's terms, these documents demonstrate a strategy for changing a temporary event into a political organization capable of mobilizing a united idea in the service of a historical awakening.[63]

In both its ideas and actions, the Quebec protest movement was clearly channelling more than the defanged spirit of revolt that Slavoj Žižek warned might dilute the Occupy Wall Street movement. Not only did the Quebec movement symbolize "the awakening of democratic values," but it also signaled the birth of a revolutionary idea grounded in the reality of burgeoning collective organizations and a "minimal positive program of socio-political change."[64] Debates about rising tuition rates were effectively tied to debates about inequality, economic injustice, racial discrimination, the corporatization of education, the destruction of public spheres, and the expanding number of societies willing to wage war on their youth. At the same time, the transformation of the student movement in Montreal into a social movement did not proceed without challenges.

As the Quebec student movement gained in strength and developed into a broad popular uprising intent on transforming government policy and reconfiguring the lines of political and economic power, state-sanctioned law enforcement resorted to more violence. Thousands of students were arrested, one young person lost an eye, and numerous reports surfaced of excessive force used on peaceful demonstrators. Such violence appeared to replay the horrific attacks by the police on students occupying university campuses in the United States. In both instances, the emerging specter of a police state canceled out the fictive portrayal of young people, manufactured by the conservative media, pundits, and government officials, as insignificant whiners and self-indulgent brats. Quite to the contrary, students were making themselves increasingly visible as the harbingers of a social movement willing and capable of challenging the neoliberal nightmare. And because they had become more visible, they were more vulnerable to state violence.

Another distinctive characteristic of the Quebec movement was that it clearly positioned young people as part of the 99 percent. In doing so, it connected with and went far beyond the limited tactic of mass mobilizations. Protesting students opted instead for a permanent presence and media profile through ongoing demonstrations, democratic assemblies, study groups, media outreach, community engagement, policy interventions, and performance art. Thinking otherwise in order to act beyond the boundaries of the given was a characteristic of the Quebec student movement from its inception. These brave young students not only appropriated the language of the dare by displaying their civic courage but also provided a concrete expression of what can be called "educated hope."

The student protesters consequently gave new meaning to what the philosopher Ernst Bloch once referred to as "something that is missing," and, in so doing, resurrected a claim on a future that does not imitate the present. And while the Quebec resistance movement shared the spirit of direct democracy evident in the Occupy movement, it extended its critique of neoliberalism and its embrace of the principles of participatory democracy beyond the boundaries of the nation-state, singular political issues, and temporary political organizations. It connected its democratic project to other student movements in Chile,[65] England, and the United States as well as to a growing worldwide resistance to global capitalism. And it discerningly provided an overarching discourse in which it could begin to address a number of related political and economic issues responsible for mass suffering and human hardships.

In offering the public a new language through which to challenge neoliberal prerogatives, Quebec youth made clear that the financial and corporate interests at work in the drive to raise tuition and push thousands of students into bankruptcy were also responsible for privatizing public services, raising and creating new user fees for health care, eliminating public sector jobs, closing factories, exploiting natural resources for financial gain, extending the retirement age, curbing the power of trade unions while slashing their benefits, promoting tax cuts that benefit the rich, and criminalizing social problems along with anyone who dares to protest such actions. Moreover, the Quebec student movement raised important questions about the role of the university in society and what relationships will exist in the future between corporate power and all aspects of public and political life.

What was also unique about the Quebec movement was its level of organization—a reflection of how the students prepared for the demonstrations before they actually took place by networking and mobilizing small groups to talk to peers, faculty, staff, union representatives, and workers. In addition, the students made use of existing broad-based and powerful associations through which they could advocate for issues directly related to educational reform, rather than outward-facing advocacy movements such as those organized by US students, one example of which is the antisweatshop movement. By activating student unions around demands rooted in knowledge gained from their own lived experiences and the plight of the university, it became easier for the protesters to retain a distinct identity while reaching outside of the university to create a broad-based movement. Moreover, the students organized around an idea—simply that tuition hikes need to be addressed within the suffering and injustices produced by neoliberal austerity measures—which proved revolutionary in its scope, flexible in its ability to connect to other forms of oppression, and decisive in mobilizing other students and the public at large. The Occupy movement began with a slogan about the 99 percent but it lacked the student unions, organizational skills, and sustainable strategies employed by Quebec youth. Of course, the system of higher education in the United States is more complex, given its mix of public and private universities, but this should not prevent the emergence of massive and shared organizational initiatives to develop student organizations at local, state, and national levels.

In addition, the Quebec students developed what Peter Hallward called a "culture of solidarity and confrontation."[66] This strategy was designed to win over students and public opinion while refusing to compromise with official power. For instance, when the leadership of the more moderate student unions suggested the students accept a government offer that would not have lowered tuition fees, the students refused what they thought was a compromising position taken by the unions. They also rejected as insignificant a government offer "to reduce the proposed tuition hike by $35.00 a year over seven years."[67] At the same time, the ongoing strike and widening boycott confronted daily the oppressive power of the state. In doing so, the students made visible on a continuing basis their concerns and the need to extend the ideological and political parameters of their grievances against the state and neoliberalism in general. Clearly, the Quebec students' organizing strategy could provide some useful lessons for the Occupy movement that might enable it to focus on sustained resistance rather than largely disparate and isolated events.

The Quebec resistance movement developed a series of strategies and tactics that awakened society to an ideal of both what a radical democracy might look like and how crucial free, accessible higher education is to such a struggle. What the organizers recognized was that being faithful to this ideal demanded tactics that focused on more than temporary disruptions, occupations, and slogans. It necessitated a new kind of politics in which people become unified around both a collective sense of justice, freedom, and the hope of building a new society. It did not simply criticize the dominant order but pointed to alternatives designed to overthrow it. By engaging in a social strike, the Quebec protesters reopened history, articulated a call for collective and shared struggles, and made visible those groups who are increasingly ignored or viewed as disposable—"people, who are present in the world but absent from its meaning and decisions about its future."[68]

The Quebec student protests against rising university tuition will continue to face a number of crucial challenges, despite the ousting of Charest and his neoliberal government in the 2012 provincial election by the Parti Quebecois (PQ) and leader Pauline Marois. One of Marois's election campaign promises included a planned summit with student unions regarding the province's higher education policies. The day after the election, Marois announced the party's decision to repeal the student tuition fee hike instituted by the Charest government and a plan to cancel Law 12.[69] Yet, at the promised February 2013 education summit, the new provincial leadership was viewed by many as failing to defend the role of higher education as a crucial democratic public sphere when it announced a 3 percent tuition hike (indexed to the rate of inflation) and sparked a protest demonstration by ten thousand students.[70] In spite of this rebuttal, the party announced that the student tuition protests were over. It has also become evident that police repression in Quebec is still being used to restrict public expressions of dissent, and the criminalization of social protests appears no less restrained since the PQ came to power. On the national level, the Harper government has both cut back crucial research on the environment and censored scientists critical of the government's policies on "climate change, fisheries, and aquaculture [that] affect Canadian ocean biodiversity."[71] The Harper government has also withdrawn public funds from scientists, archivists, statisticians, and librarians who use their research and scholarship to address crucial issues that affect the public good. Ideology now trumps evidence, and science gives way to the brutal demands of neoliberalism.

Increasing tuition costs, student debt, and the growing inaccessibility of postsecondary education along with the corporatization of education remain crucial concerns. And additional pressing matters loom on the horizon for higher education in Canada and other democratic states affected by the global economic crisis. As employment opportunities diminish and the baby boomer generation reaches retirement age, there will be significant battles over whether public funding will go to higher education or other valuable public services. One of the most important questions to ask is whether the students will continue to organize and take a progressive stand on a range of social and economic issues extending from the demand for free education to the rebuilding of the social state. In other words, what role will the students take in developing organizations that will push the PQ to reverse the neoliberal politics and policies that have dominated the province and Canada for far too long while expanding the demands of a radical democratic society? Regardless of how the Quebec movement turns out, the protesters have demonstrated a degree of courage, skill, organization, and solidarity that will not easily fade away. A revolutionary idea has been born and now waits for the conditions through which it can become a more powerful, inspiring political and moral force.

Learning from the Quebec Student Resistance: Student Unionism in the United States

Clearly, more was at stake in Quebec than tuition increases, however important the issue in galvanizing students who would be most impacted by them. As Eric Pineault has pointed out, "Neoliberalism has nothing original to offer outside of austerity" and the redeployment of progressive alternatives by students must include a broader sense of struggle that connects "environment and labour struggles to the student struggle."[72] Student organizations in the United States have been working toward forging such connections, taking their cues from the recent student movements in Quebec and Chile. Rather than wait for the leadership of business unions or rely solely on "spectacular politics" of protest demonstrations, as student Marianne Garneau argues, groups of students have been organizing themselves around a range of issues extending from labor rights to education to social justice.[73]

Graduate students at New York University are working with labor leaders from the United Auto Workers to unionize graduate student teaching assistants, which would set a precedent for private universities in the United States.[74] A group called All in the Red emerged as an activist collective in New York City in the wake of solidarity marches inspired by the Quebec student strike. The group challenges "policies that limit access to higher education and financial entities that profit from the burgeoning student debt crisis."[75] As documented in biweekly updates in the *Nation*, recent student activism has addressed not only tuition hikes, university budget cuts, the imposition of new student fees, and rising student debt, but also cutbacks of ethnic studies programs, labor union and outsourcing struggles within the university, and the funding of universities by corporations and right-wing organizations (for example, New York Students Rising). Students along with faculty supporters are also mobilizing more broadly in favor of election campaign-finance reform (for example, 99Rise), harsh anti-immigrant legislation (for example, Freedom University), and divestiture of shares in fossil fuel companies (a nationwide movement led by Bill McKibben and 350.org).[76]

What becomes clear is that the new student activism encompasses student-focused issues as well as wider social, educational, and workforce issues. In this way, the goals and organizing strategies of the US movement have been inspired by the Quebec students, whom they watched exercise legitimate power in public and political arenas, express solidarity without imposing uniformity, mobilize broader public support, and sit down with politicians and major policy decision-makers. Although organizing is still in its initial stages and must be adapted to US contexts, a number of student voices have drawn lessons from the Quebec movement's use of information campaigns, town hall meetings, mobilization training camps, and joint actions with other universities.[77] Of particular interest has been Quebec student unionism and the federation model of organization deployed to organize the student resistance movement. In the federated model, smaller student groups voted autonomously on issues to address their local contexts but also worked to forge connections with other groups as part of a larger movement.[78]

According to Zachary Bell, this structure allowed for greater student participation across the political spectrum, accountability, and collective action—three critical hallmarks of any genuine democratic process.[79] Across the United States, student groups have been challenging the representation of traditional student governments and business unions. At the University of California, Berkeley, a grassroots activist group called Academic Workers for a Democratic Union ousted its "previously bureaucratic" union leadership and now controls the UC Student-Workers Union UAW Local 2865. It is forming coalitions with other student activist groups to protest the privatization of public education in advance of negotiating a new contract in summer 2013.[80] A common principle vocalized by several of the new student activists (like the more radical Quebec student union, ASSÉ) is the ultimate goal of achieving an egalitarian and free university—as well as the need for students to establish mechanisms for achieving real power within their institutions and the broader society.

One of the major recent examples of US student organizing was the National Student Power Convergence held in Columbus, Ohio, in August 2012. As Kathryn Seidewitz suggests, students attending the massive summit-style meeting expressed a desire to build "power for themselves, within their institutions" in order to demand a greater role in their education and the decision-making structures of the campus.[81] Notably, the students recognize the need for a combination of local campaigns (and the broad-based training and support these require) and horizontal networking at the state level. They are also working to form state-wide and nationwide associations capable of addressing state legislatures thatcontrol education budgets.[82] For instance, a number of student groups have organized to challenge new discriminatory laws against undocumented students, enacted when several state legislatures responded to President Obama's June 2012 Executive Order on "Deferred Action for Childhood Arrivals" by preventing undocumented students from applying for financial aid and requiring them to pay higher out-of-state tuition, or, in the case of Georgia, excluding undocumented youth from attending state universities altogether.[83] As Seidewitz observes, as a result of organizing, undocumented students feel empowered to view themselves as "intellectual workers with rights and agency."[84] Whether emerging student movements in the United States will be able to organize in a sustainable way and continue to engage in ideological and political struggle remains to be seen, but the promise of change now appears on the horizon.

Both the Occupy movement and the Quebec student resistance have ignited a new generation of young people who now face the ongoing challenge of developing a language and a politics that both integrate a meaningful consideration of public life and public values and imagine the possibilities of an insurrectionist democracy not wedded to the dictates of global capitalism.[85] The key challenge for these movements will be to continue to circulate and advance their views in the public sphere through forms of political organization that are as coordinated as they are flexible and open to new ideas. In addition, there is the crucial need to develop sustainable educational institutions and enlarge public spaces in which matters of knowledge, desire, identity, and social responsibility become central to creating a democratic formative culture—understood as the very precondition for the modes of agency and engaged citizenship necessary for any just and inclusive society. This formative culture must make pedagogy central to its understanding of politics and work diligently to provide alternative narratives, stories, subjects, power relations, and values that point to a future when young people and all those others excluded from the savage politics of casino capitalism will create a society in which justice and dignity mutually inform each other.

CHAPTER SEVEN

Democracy Unsettled:
From Critical Pedagogy to the War on Youth

**AN INTERVIEW WITH HENRY A. GIROUX
BY MICHAEL A. PETERS**

*I want to conclude with an interview that provides a histor-
ical context for much of the work on critical pedagogy, youth
studies, social justice, cultural politics, and higher education
that I have addressed in this book. For me, this work has not
been easy. As a working-class intellectual, I found myself at
an institution that was largely hostile to my experiences, cultural capital, and the critical scholarship that informed my
work at the university. I believe that such narratives and
struggles need to be made visible in order to articulate the
broader pressures that many academics marginalized by their
backgrounds experience when they push against the grain or
find themselves under assault as part of a hidden curriculum
that has a powerful and invisible order of politics. At the same
time, my own struggle is not meant to reaffirm the often
dystopian nature of the university but to make clear that such*

181

spaces are not without their contradictions and that power is never absolute—social and political change is always possible. Moreover, the interview provides a glimpse into how the interaction between the private and the public have informed my role as a public intellectual in higher education and my attempts to develop an understanding of critical pedagogy as central to the very nature of agency, politics, and democracy itself. Amid the pressures of an institution rife with the legacy of cultural elitism, class structures, racism, and repression, the interview provides an archive and a narrative of critique and possibility, despair and hope, and a glimpse into a particular kind of memory work that illuminates past struggles and the problems of a new historical conjuncture as well as what it means to address them.

Michael Peters: Henry, it is a great pleasure to do this interview with you, as a colleague and friend I have much admired over the years and someone who helped me enormously to develop my work and professional self when I was a young academic. As a young New Zealand academic, I remember reading your work in the 1980s. I was a graduate fresh from a philosophy department, hungry for material that took a critical look at the world. I discovered your early work on postmodern criticism and used the book you wrote with Stanley Aronowitz, *Education Under Siege*, as a text in one of the classes I was teaching. You expressed eloquently many ideas that I was then grappling with and led the way, I suspect, for a generation when you developed as a public intellectual and cultural critic concerned for the fate of young people. In particular, you generously mentored and supported me in publishing my first book, *Education and the Postmodern Condition* (foreword by Lyotard) in your Bergin and Garvey series coedited with Paulo Freire. The experience really kick-started my academic career and, under your auspices, I went on to publish some six books in your series. This was a generous and collegial act for which I am very grateful. I know there must be many other scholars whom you mentored and helped along the way. And this speaks to your role as a public intellectual located increasingly in a networked environment that transforms the concept of intellectual collaboration and enhances the notions of collegiality and the public space of knowledge development.

Let me start this interview by asking you to reflect on your childhood, upbringing, and undergraduate experience. What was it in your background that predisposed you to issues of social justice? Tell us when and under what circumstances you felt outraged at social injustice and became determined to do something about it.

Henry Giroux: I grew up in a working-class neighborhood in the 1950s and '60s that was marked by an ongoing juxtaposition of violence, loyalty, and solidarity. On the one hand, it was a neighborhood where people defined themselves in terms of specific communities, places, and spaces. The notion of the detached individual going it alone and defining his or her existence in mostly individualistic and competitive terms was an anomaly in such a neighborhood. People helped each other in times of need, socialized together, and looked out for each other. At the same time, there was a lot of violence in the neighborhood, often inflicted by the police and other repressive institutions such as the schools. One could not survive in that neighborhood without friends, without recognizing that the protections that offered one a sense of agency and freedom came from the group, not the isolated uncommitted individual so celebrated today. Social justice for me was forged in the bonds of solidarity and the need to recognize both some notion of the common good and the importance of the social.

As a working-class male in a neighborhood where masculinity was a shifting marker of courage, brutality, and identity, the body became the most resourceful tool I had. It was the ultimate source of agency, required in order to survive, ensure respect, and provide a framing mechanism to mediate between oneself and the larger world. Violence in that neighborhood was both personal and institutional. People were poor, many unemployed, and their lives were often lost before they had any chance of maturing. Young people existed in a kind of dead time, waiting to graduate from high school and hoping to get a job, perhaps as a priest, firefighter, or police officer and eventually go on disability. Gender was a dividing line and the violence that permeated our relations with women was rarely ever physical as much as it was ideological and political. Women just didn't matter much outside of very traditional roles. I saw a lot of hardship and love in that neighborhood, and it affected me deeply. On a personal level, my family was very poor, and my father struggled tirelessly to feed us and make sure we had the basic necessities, though he was not always successful. We usually ran out of food by Thursday, one day before my dad got paid. But at least we were not homeless, and we managed to survive less as victims than as a family fighting against larger systemic forces that we were not in a position to control. Such hardships created enormous problems, but they also strengthened our resolve to struggle, embrace the warmth of others, and develop a sense of both humility and outrage in the face of such unnecessary and systemically determined deprivations. But poverty does not just build character, it also produces tensions, injustices, and violence. Surviving was not made for reality TV, it was an effort that put one on guard constantly; it turned time into a deprivation rather than a luxury, and it redefined the parameters of agency, learning, and survival. Justice came quickly in that neighborhood, and it was not always on the side of the angels. Much of my youth until I went to high school was based on getting by, surviving in a world in which my biggest strength was talking fast rather than proving myself as a neighborhood fighter. At six feet and 145 pounds, that wasn't a viable option.

What I lacked at that time was a language to mediate the inequalities, suffering, and modes of solidarity I saw all around me. I got a glimpse of the need for such a discourse when I went to high school, which ironically was named Hope High School. At the time, Hope High School was segregated along class and racial lines. Poor white and Black kids were in what were labeled as the "junk" courses, played sports, and were seen for the most part as both deficit-ridden and delinquent. Most of us entered the school through the back entrance; wealthy white kids came through the front door. It was hard for me to miss the class and racial dimensions of all of this, especially as I was a basketball player and hung out with many of the Black kids on my team. Visiting their neighborhood and playing in gyms on their turf was relatively easy, but they could not come into my neighborhood without suffering the indignities of racial slurs or much worse.

My sense of social justice began at that moment when the lived experience of solidarity and loyalty rubbed up against my own unquestioned racism and sexism, which had a long history in the daily encounters of my youth. Sometimes the contradictions that characterize the "common sense" of racism and sexism were challenged and became unraveled. Treating people as objects or understanding them through established stereotypes was being constantly tested as I moved through high school and met Black men and women who refuted those stereotypes and had the kindness and intelligence to open my eyes through both their own lived experiences and their access to a critical language that I lacked.

Everything changed when I went to college, at least on my second attempt. The first time I left for college, I attended a junior college on a basketball scholarship, but I was not ready for the cultural shift. I felt terribly insecure in that space, did not know how to navigate the cultural capital of middle-class kids, and within a short time dropped out. After working for two years in odd jobs, I got another basketball scholarship to a small school in Maine. This all took place in the sixties—a time in which language, social relations, and culture itself were changing at an accelerated rate. It was hard to miss the changes, ignore the civil rights struggles, and not feel the collective hope that was driving student protests against the Vietnam War and middle-class mores. I got caught up in it very quickly. Knowledge took on a new register for me, just as the changing cultural mores deeply affected my sense of both the present and the future. As a result, knowledge was not just powerful but sexy; language became my weapon of choice. Social justice as a means to live in a better world was the preeminent issue touching the lives of most of the people around me at the time. In college, I read avidly, moving between Marx and James Baldwin, immersing myself in Beat literature and trying to figure out how all of this made sense in terms of my own critical agency and what role I might play in shaping a better world.

Enrolling in a teacher education program was enormously important for me because I quickly realized the ethical and political dimensions of teaching and how important the issue of developing a critical consciousness and formative culture was to any viable democratic society. After graduating, I went to Appalachian State University for an MA in history and became a research assistant for a young and passionate assistant professor named Bob Sandels. Bob was an incredibly sharp leftist intellectual, and he did more than anyone at the time to connect the dots for me around a number of domestic and foreign policy issues in which social and economic justice were central. Once I graduated, I ended up teaching at the high school level for several years and started reading Paulo Freire and Howard Zinn, both of whom eventually became close friends. From that point, I was on fire, and fortunately the fire never went out.

MP: So your working-class credentials have stayed with you. I'm interested in the tensions and contradictions of those born into the working class who become professors. May I hear your reflections on your own experience of education as self-transformation? I suspect the reason that Paulo Freire and Howard Zinn resonated with you was in part because of your background. Perhaps you could also detail the nature of your relationships with these two thinkers.

HG: Being an academic from the working class is, of course, impacted by many registers, extending from ideology and cultural capital to politics. When I first started teaching at Boston University I did not have the knowledge, theoretical tools, or the experience to move into a world largely dominated by middle- and ruling-class cultural capital. I was constantly confronted with faculty and students who assumed a god-given right of privilege and power, especially with regards to their academic credentials, middle-class language skills, and lifelong experience in which people like me were defined through our deficits and largely as outsiders—as imaginary others incapable of narrating ourselves. Or, even worse, our very presence in the academy meant that we had to assimilate mentally to the middle class, or at least act as if we were. This often meant dressing a particular way, speaking in elaborate code, and immersing oneself into the cultural circuits that middle-class people enjoyed.

All of these requisite changes were brought home to me during my second semester. My father had just died of a heart attack, and I had returned to the campus after attending his funeral. My dean at the time was a guy named Bob Dentler, an Ivy League–educated scholar. I ran into him on the street shortly after my father's death and he said to me, "I am sorry to hear about your father. It must have been difficult settling his estate." Estate? My father left a hundred dollars in an envelope taped behind a mirror. That was his estate. I was immediately struck by how out of touch so many academics are with respect to those others who are not replicas of themselves. But as I began to understand how class was mapped onto academia, I was determined not to play the role of the subservient, aspiring-to-be-middle-class professional. I had no intention of letting myself morph into a golf-playing suburbanite living a politically irrelevant academic life. I viewed myself as being on the left, and my politics provided me with the tools to be not only self-reflective but also critical of the cultural capital that dominated the academy and passed itself off as entirely normalized. I had no interest in narrowly defined, almost-choking specializations, stifling forms of professionalism, appeals to positivism, or a politics that largely removed the university from the society.

I was also lucky in that before I became an academic, I lived in Providence, Rhode Island, and took advantage of the many free lectures Brown University offered. Watching the radical lawyer William Kunstler and scholar-activist Stanley Aronowitz in many ways saved my life. Here were two working-class intellectuals whose cultural capital was unmistakable. And they knew much more than most of the Ivy League types who invited them. They were passionate, brilliant, and spoke directly to public issues. Of course, I had a certain familiarity with the discourses of radical education, history, and the civil rights movement, having read Paulo Freire, Howard Zinn, and James Baldwin, but it was the existential grounding of such work that quickened in me a willingness to fight for social justice that changed my life. I had been told all my life that the body should not connect with one's head, that passion was a liability in making an argument or taking a position. These figures uprooted that myth very quickly, and I never let go of my working-class sensibility, even though I had to learn middle-class skills and knowledge in order to be a border-crosser—to cross over into a middle-class institution such as academia without burning the bridges that enabled me to get there.

I also remember having a conversation with Joe Kincheloe, who had a similar background. Joe was always such a pleasure to be around because we shared a cultural capital that defined us both within and outside of the academy as outsiders: we were working class and allegedly deficient, unsanctified by Ivy League degrees and harboring a pedigree that connected the body and mind in a way that was often defined by the overly scrubbed and passionless as lacking civility. Of course, it was this shared space that allowed us not only to reject an easy and unproductive sense of resentment but also to interrogate the strengths of the resources hard-wired into our working-class backgrounds, along with what it meant to develop a more expansive and democratic politics. We got along with many different kinds of people, but we were especially sensitive to poor white and minority kids who shared our background and sometimes found a model in what we represented that changed their lives and prepared them for the long struggle ahead.

The starting point for my politics began with questioning what the middle- and ruling-class types alleged were working-class "deficiencies." It was necessary to flip the script on this type of stereotyping aimed at working-class kids. I began to see that my cultural capital could not be reduced to deficits or lack. In fact, I had learned some time back that while my background was problematic in terms of a range of issues extending from violence to sexism, it also provided me with a deep commitment to solidarity and a humility that recognized that people had different capacities and intellectual strengths. My sense of what constitutes a crisis is generally different from my peers. I never bought the arrogance and I never bought the notion that if one were educated in an Ivy League school that guaranteed superior knowledge and a strong set of skills. In due time, the university seemed, with some exceptions of course, to produce academics who were uptight, conservative politically, and personally arrogant. When accompanied by rigorous modes of reflection and discrimination, these alleged lacks became for me a formidable resource and source of strength for a more viable sense of critical agency and democratic political commitment. Neither Joe nor I ever faltered on this issue, and I think it served us and our working-class students well.

I have often laughed over the seeming incongruity of being a working-class intellectual, and how such a term often rubbed against the grain of many colleagues whose cultural capital seemed to mark them less by what they knew than by how much they had to unlearn. It was often difficult to listen to, experience, and tolerate the pompous self-flattery, the impenetrable discourses, the rigid specializations, the flat affect, and the decidedly antipolitical posturing that characterized so many in the academy. These were academics who were both clever and frivolous, antipolitical, and often indifferent to the growing plight of human suffering. Their academic work was often utterly privatized and unconnected to important social issues and always haughty—and they were quite unaware of the caricatures they had become. For others, intellectual courage had given way to the comfortable space of accommodation, and the notion of the public intellectual had been replaced by the "public relations intellectual," the overheated talking head spewing out sound bites and providing "scholarshit" to various media outlets. I increasingly came to believe that I was in an educational setting where most academics had withdrawn into a world in which the measure of theoretical prowess was determined by the degree to which it escaped from any sense of responsibility, or for that matter any notion of consequential thinking.

Being in the academy for me was a form of soft exile. I have always felt as if I did not belong there, though I was far from alienated over the issue. I simply did my work, published, taught, and used the academy as a site from which to do what I was thought was important educational and democratically inspired political work. I realized early that coming from a working-class background gave me at least a couple of advantages in academia. Because I did not have to unlearn all of the cultural junk that came with middle- and ruling-class ideologies, I had more time to be reflective about my own work, politics, and the role I would play in furthering the discourses of critical agency, education, pedagogy, politics, and hope.

I have felt isolated, but not alone, in the academy. Fortunately, a number of friends, including Joe Kincheloe, Richard Quantz, Paulo Freire, Stanley Aronowitz, Roger Simon, Peter McLaren, and Donaldo Macedo helped me to find solidarity in often dark places. These spaces are no longer as dark for me as they were when I was first teaching at Boston University, and I believe being an outsider in the academy offers both the possibility for developing an opening to consider critical insights forged within a working-class sensibility and the never ending challenge presented by class lines.

MP: Thanks.This is exactly the kind of reflection and autobiographical detail I was hoping would emerge. There is a need for those traditionally excluded from the academy to be able to identify with those who have negotiated the class experience so successfully as you have. I am also interested in your remarks about privilege and the way in which many professors simply take class position for granted. To what extent is the university a class-based institution? One other aspect that you allude to in your experience is the way university administrations are often out of sync with the professoriate. I know that you have been targeted because of your beliefs. I know also that you have theorized the institution and its development under the conditions of neoliberalism. Please share with us your thoughts on the neoliberal and neoconservative attacks on the Left and the rise of the neoliberal university.

HG: Higher education in the United States has the appearance of a meritocracy, but that belies the ways in which wealth and power shape the hierarchical nature of the system. Working-class kids in the United States, if they have aspirations of getting a college diploma, generally do not have the funds to support such an endeavor, particularly given the spiralling tuition rates of the last few decades. And when they do go on to some form of higher education, many of them wind up in community colleges or technical schools. Of course, in the past we had programs like the GI Bill that made access easier, but those days are over. Economic inequality is now hardwired into the central core and structure of the university thanks to neoliberalization, though mass access to higher education has always been a kind of holy grail. So access is largely a class issue, but also a racial issue. The culture of much of higher education has little to do with the histories, experiences, languages, and cultural backgrounds of many working-class and minority kids. Middle- and upper-class cultural capital tends to crush these kids, and the damage is inflicted more heavily when there are no remedial programs available to compensate for the poor education they often receive in underfunded and neglected schools that largely serve to contain and criminalize the behaviors of the disenfranchised. For many working-class youth, time is a burden, not a luxury, and they have to often work while trying to take classes and make the requisite grades. College for these kids is an uphill battle. They often compete with middle-class kids who can spend most of their time studying or attending classes.

In terms of the university itself, the attack on higher education by right-wing ideologues and corporate power has been going on for a long time, but at the current historical conjuncture it has gotten much worse. As a democratic public sphere, it offers students the skills, knowledge, and values to develop the capacity for critique, dialogue, and informed judgment. Increasingly in a market-driven and militarized society, such capacities are viewed as irrelevant, if not dangerous. As public funds are drained from university budgets, the liberal arts downsized, and tuition increases, higher education aligns itself more closely with the culture, values, and incentives of the business world. One consequence is that economic Darwinism is now undermining the civic and intellectual promises that make higher education a public good. Managerial modes of governance, the rise of part-time faculty, and the prevalence of an empirically based audit culture now drives the mission of higher education, which increasingly is about training the elite and low-paid workers for the global workforce. Moreover, the most important value of higher education is now tied to the need for credentials. In the search for adopting market values and cutting costs, classes have ballooned in size, and there is an increased emphasis on rote learning and standardized testing. Disciplines and subjects that do not fall within the purview of mathematical utility and economic rationality are now seen as dispensable. Like most neoliberal models of education, higher education only matters to the extent that it promotes national prosperity and drives economic growth, technical innovation, and market transformation.

In the United States, this neoliberal model can be understood through a number of corporatizing tendencies. Under the rubric of austerity, higher education has for all intents and purposes adopted the organizational structure, values, and culture of medium-sized or big corporations. University presidents now speak in the name of big ideas or inspiring social visions, they now align themselves with business values, and they openly associate themselves with corporate interests. As business culture permeates higher education, all manner of school practices from food services to specific modes of instruction and the hiring of temporary faculty are now outsourced to private contractors. In some universities, new college deans are shifting their focus outside of the campus in order to take on fundraising and establish industry partnerships that were once the job of the university president. Academic leadership now draws less from the reservoir of democratic ideals, struggles, and modes of witnessing than from the corporate playbook of strategic planning and fundraising. This is not meant to wholeheartedly condemn the necessity for fundraising, which can also be productive, as much as it is to insist that it cannot take priority over modes of leadership rooted in more democratic, emancipatory, and noncommodified values.

Neoliberal austerity and disciplinary measures now dominate most major universities. Moreover, as higher education becomes more corporatized it becomes more conservative, more willing to bend to right-wing ideological interests that would have been anathema to higher education just a few decades ago. For instance, the prestigious Washington University in St. Louis gave a doctorate in 2008 to Phyllis Schlafly. This is the same person who opposes "the Equal Rights Amendment, the United Nations, Darwinism . . . blamed the Virginia Tech massacre on the English department [and] advocated banning women from traditionally male occupations like construction, firefighting, and the military."[1] At the same time, one of the most serious threats to higher education is the increasing reliance on part-time faculty—who generally have no power, are paid starvation wages, lack benefits, and have no prestige. Currently more than 70 percent of undergraduate college instruction is in the hands of part-time faculty who are overworked and underpaid. Not only is the quality of instruction, the welfare of students, and the democratic function of the university undermined under such circumstances, but the governance structure of the university is largely in the hands of a corporate-oriented managerial class that has little respect for the liberal arts and has harnessed the future of higher education to a business culture that mimics the culture of the corporate boardroom. This new class of precarious academic labor and growing pool of students who define themselves largely as consumers cancels out the democratic mission of the university and has potentially disastrous consequences for the future of higher education, wherever this model is emulated.

As higher education is increasingly restructured by the interests of corporations and the security state, academic freedom is compromised and faculty live in fear of losing their jobs for being too critical of established authority. The loss of faculty autonomy breeds academic unfreedom and makes the faculty vulnerable to outside right-wing interests who are increasingly monitoring what faculty teach, what they say, and what they publish. For example, Republican Party legislators in Wisconsin have used the courts to gain access to faculty e-mails—a new form of digital terrorism designed to keep academics in their place or in a state of constant fear about what they say or publish. As state spending is slashed to the bone, the university is transformed into a training ground for corporate and military interests, as I have pointed out in *The University in Chains: Confronting the Military-Industrial-Academic Complex.* In addition, the university is transformed into a credentializing factory, one that eschews teaching students the skills necessary for them to be engaged critical citizens and to keep democracies alive. As management principles drive the organization and culture of higher education, research becomes more entrepreneurial, student access is driven by purchasing power, public values are replaced by market values, departmental resources are determined by how close the latter align with corporate interests, and teaching is geared toward producing human capital for the global economy.

If it is viewed as simply a training ground for the corporate order and the national security state, then higher education will default on its promise of a democratic future for young people and its investment in a social state. The antipublic social formation that has emerged with neoliberalism has no interest in fostering the formative cultures and social relationships necessary for young people to imagine themselves as critically engaged and socially responsible citizens. While the difficulty of overcoming these conditions cannot be exaggerated, it is time for educators and concerned citizens to develop a new political language that connects the dots between the wars abroad and the war happening at home—a language that understands the assault on higher education as part of a broader assault on the welfare state, critical thought, and democracy itself. The consequences of such an egregious assault on the university will be the destruction of any vestige of higher education as a public good and democratic public sphere. Clearly, there is more at stake here than the abrogation of workers' bargaining rights and skyrocketing university tuition rates. There are also questions regarding what kind of society we want to become and what is going to have to be done to stop the arrogant and formidable assault on all aspects of democratic life now being waged by the financial elite, corporations, conservatives, reactionary think tanks, authoritarian politicians, and a right-wing media that ignores every principle of honor, decency, and truth. Of course, the point is for intellectuals and others to make it clear that neoliberal and neoconservative forces are transforming the university into an antidemocratic public sphere and to provide a discourse of possibility that challenges this terrible reconfiguration of higher education. Let me mention a few possibilities informed by my own work on the neoliberalization of the university.

First, educators and others need to figure out how to defend more vigorously higher education as a public good. If we can't do that, we're in trouble. Secondly, we need to address what the optimum conditions are for educators, artists, activists, and so on, to perform their work in an autonomous and critical fashion. In other words, we need to think through the conditions that make academic labor fruitful, engaging, and relevant. Third, we need to turn the growing army of temporary workers now swelling the ranks of the academy into full-time, permanent staff. The presence of so many part-time employees is scandalous and both weakens the power of the faculty and exploits them. Fourth, we need to educate students to be critical agents, to learn how to take risks, engage in thoughtful dialogue, and address what it means to be socially responsible. Pedagogy is not about training; it is about educating people to be self-reflective, critical, and self-conscious about their relationship with others and to know something about their relationship with the larger world. Pedagogy in this sense not only provides important thoughtful and intellectual competencies; it also enables people to act effectively upon the societies in which they live.

Pedagogy also takes on a new dimension and impact with the rise of digital technologies and the endlessly multiplying forms of screen culture, each attempting to win over new and larger audiences and more often than not mark them as potential consumers. These new technologies and the proliferating sites in which they are appearing constitute powerful configurations of what C. Wright Mills termed "cultural apparatuses" engaged in modes of popular education. They represent more specifically pervasive forms of public pedagogy that increasingly function to divorce learning from any vestige of critical thought. These powerful forms of public pedagogy need to be addressed, both for how they distort and how they can create important new spaces for emancipatory forms of pedagogy. Not only do we need to understand who controls these cultural apparatuses and how they mobilize new desires, needs, modes of identity, and social relations, we also need to challenge the new media in terms of their power, what they represent and how they present it. Public pedagogy is a site of struggle in which critically engaged intellectuals can address broader audiences and raise in the public domain a number of important social and political issues. The articulation of knowledge to experience, the construction of new modes of agency, the production of critical knowledge, the recovery of critical histories, and the possibility of linking knowledge to social change cannot be limited to influencing students in the classroom. Everyone, but especially those of us working in education, have to extend our roles as public intellectuals to other pedagogical sites, audiences, and institutions. It is politically imperative to organize a whole range of people outside of the academy. For this, as I mentioned above, we need a new political language with broader narratives. I am not against identity politics or single-based issues, but we need to find ways to connect these issues to more encompassing, global narratives about democracy so we can recognize their strengths and limitations in building broad-based social movements. In short, it is imperative that as educators and socially responsible intellectuals, artists, parents, and concerned citizens, we must act for justice and against injustice. And such a call to pursue the truth with a small "t" must be shaped by informed judgments, self-reflection, searing forms of critique, civic courage, and a deep commitment to education as central to the struggle for democracy and social change. Needless to say, we need to find new ways to connect education to the struggle for a democratic future, which is now being undermined in ways that were unimaginable thirty years ago.

MP: Thanks, Henry. I appreciate the way in which your analysis proceeds from a combination of personal experience and critical theory. Your works have sustained us for many decades now and the thrust of your work in terms of critical pedagogy, cultural studies, youth culture, and global studies in communication provides both a powerful theoretical lens and a practical critique of contemporary neoliberal society. I know these interests did not develop chronologically and there are many overlapping characteristics. It would be interesting to hear of the evolution of your thought in terms of these perspectives and what you think is required to be a critical thinker today, in an age of global media.

HG: My interest in critical pedagogy grew out of my experience as a secondary school teacher. I came of age in the 1960s as a teacher and there was a great deal of latitude in what we were allowed to teach then. I taught a couple of seminars in social studies and focused on feminist studies, theories of alienation, and a range of other important social issues. While I had no trouble finding critical content, including progressive films I used to rent from the Quakers (Society of Friends), I did not know how to theorize the various approaches to teaching I tried in the classroom. This all came to a head when an assistant principal confronted me after class once and demanded that I not put the students in a circle while teaching the class. I really could not defend my position theoretically. Fortunately, I was introduced to Paulo Freire's *Pedagogy of the Oppressed*, and from then on my interest in radical pedagogy began to develop. My interest in young people also developed during that time, though I don't believe I had any idea that it would later become a serious object of scholarship and political intervention for me. After graduating from Carnegie-Mellon University in 1977, I became deeply involved with the work being produced around the sociology of education in England, the work of Bowles and Gintis on the political economy of schooling as well as the Marxist ethnographic work developed by Paul Willis at the Birmingham Center for Cultural Studies. All of this scholarship was heavily influenced by various shades of Marxism, and while I learned a great deal from it, I felt that it erred on the side of political economy and did not say enough about either resistance, pedagogy, or the importance of cultural politics. The structural nature of this work was gloomy, overdetermined, and left little room for seizing upon contradictions, developing a theory of power that did not collapse into domination or imagining a language of struggle and hope.

I began to look elsewhere for theoretical models to develop a more comprehensive understanding of schooling and its relationship to larger social, economic, and cultural forces and found it in the work of contemporary critical theorists, especially those of the Frankfurt School. I drew upon critical theory to challenge the then dominant culture of positivism as well as the overemphasis on the political economy of schooling. *Theory and Resistance in Education* was the most well-known outcome of that investigation. And while it is considered a classic in some quarters, I must say that I had a hard time publishing my work in the late 1970s and early 1980s. Work in educational theory and practice in the United States was dominated by Routledge Press, which was inclined to publish mostly scholarship that moved safely within the parameters of Marxism and political economy. I was fortunate at that time to meet Roger Simon, who not only published my work in the prestigious journal *Curriculum Inquiry* but also taught me a great deal about how to theorize matters of pedagogy and schooling. Roger was brilliant, and his work in my estimation far exceeded anything being published on critical education at the time, especially his book *Teaching Against the Grain*. I believe that *Theory and Resistance in Education* would never have been written if it had not been for my ongoing conversations with Roger.

In the 1970s and '80s, I developed a friendship with Donaldo Macedo and Paulo Freire, and we soon started an education series with Bergin and Garvey that later became the Greenwood series. It opened up a new space for publishing a variety of work from theorists dealing with critical pedagogy and educational theory more broadly. Crucial to my own conception of pedagogy is that I saw it as a moral and political practice that was about more than analyzing classrooms and schools. Pedagogy for me was central to proclaiming the power and necessity of ideas, knowledge, and culture as central to any viable definition of politics, and the goal of living in a just world with others. Pedagogy remains a crucial political resource in theorizing the importance of establishing a formative culture conducive to creating subjects and values that can sustain a substantive democracy.

I was also deeply influenced in the 1980s by the cultural studies movement in the United States and England, particularly the work of Larry Grossberg, Meaghan Morris, Paul Gilroy, Paul Willis, Angela McRobbie, Richard Johnson, and Stuart Hall. The early work in cultural studies on education and youth was very important to my own theoretical development. Not only did it emphasize the importance of pedagogy inside of the academy, but Raymond Williams opened up the concept with an exploration of what he called "permanent education" and offered the beginning of a theoretical framework for taking seriously the educational force of the wider culture. At that point, I attempted to revive the centrality of pedagogy for cultural studies, particularly given that many of the theorists who followed Williams seem either to display little interest in it or to assume that it meant teaching cultural studies in schools. Pedagogy in this case had become the present absence in cultural studies, just as youth had become the present absence among left theorizing in general. While there was considerable talk about class, race, and gender, there were very few people writing in the United States about the plight of young people and the transformation from a society of production to a society of consumption, or, as Zygmunt Bauman points out, the move from solid modernity to liquid modernity. Young people, especially minorities of class and color, were under siege in a particularly harsh way at the beginning of the 1980s, and there were very few people addressing what I called the "war on youth." I argued then and continue to insist that since the 1980s we have seen a series of political, economic, and cultural shifts that mark the beginning of a form of economic Darwinism, on the one hand, and the rise of the punishing state, on the other. And one consequence of the merging of these two movements is this war on youth. I have attempted to chart and engage the shifting parameters of the war on youth in a number of books, with the recent and perhaps most definitive being *Youth in a Suspect Society: Democracy or Disposability?*

In the aftermath of Reagan and Thatcher, neoliberalism was becoming normalized all over the globe. This was particularly evident to me by the early 1990s, as neoliberal capitalism became more ruthless, consolidated, and poisonous in its ever-expanding support for a culture of cruelty and a survival-of-the-fittest ethic in which market-driven values and relations acted as the template for judging all aspects of social life. By transforming society into the image of the market, the space and conditions for thinking outside of market values and relations became more difficult, and one particularly grim consequence was the demolition of nonmarket values, public spheres, and forms of community. As democratic social forms diminished, so did social values, the public good, social responsibility, and the very nature of politics. This was a very destructive moment for both the United States and the rest of the world. Just as corporate sovereignty replaced or weakened political sovereignty, the attack on the social state intensified, the power of capital became detached from the traditional politics of the nation state, the punishing state was on the rise, and there emerged a new set of economic and social formations in which social protections were weakened, social problems were increasingly criminalized, and all public spheres were subjected to the forces of privatization and commodification, especially public and higher education.

Under neoliberalism, we have witnessed the rise of an unfettered free-market ideology and economic Darwinism in which market values supplant civic values. Everything is for sale. A hyper-individualism is celebrated. Profit-making is seen as the essence of democracy, and the obligations of citizenship are reduced to the practice of consuming. This is a system in which a dehumanizing mode of consumerism and the unencumbered concentration of capital are matched by the endless disposing not only of goods, but also human beings, many of whom as flawed consumers, immigrants, or low-income whites and poor minorities are considered redundant and disposable. This is also a system in which everything is privatized, with one grave consequence being that the public collapses into the private. It becomes increasingly difficult to translate private concerns into public issues. My work in the last decade has aimed at connecting neoliberal forms of public pedagogy and authoritarian disciplinary practices with the rise of new modes of individualism and what it means to make such forces visible in order to collectively resist them. This project has been deeply influenced by the work of diverse figures such as Pierre Bourdieu, Angela Davis, Edward Said, Zygmunt Bauman, Hannah Arendt, Nancy Fraser, C. Wright Mills, Stanley Aronowitz, and more recently David L. Clark.

Bourdieu's work on neoliberalism and Bauman's work on liquid modernity and the transformation of the public sphere are treasure troves of insight regarding the changing conditions of modernity, the politics of consumerism, and the call for new modes of ethical responsibility. Arendt's work on authoritarianism and its potentially recurring conditions, albeit in new forms, along with Nancy Fraser's brilliant work on feminist public spheres provided me with a new language to think about the institutions and spaces necessary for a formative culture that makes democratic modes of agency and subjectivity possible. Said's and Bourdieu's work on the responsibility of academics as public intellectuals had a profound effect on my scholarship. Similarly, C. Wright Mills deeply influenced me on the importance of connecting private issues to public considerations, the centrality of cultural apparatuses in the transformation of political culture, and the role public intellectuals might play as agents of change.

Stanley Aronowitz may be one of the most brilliant public intellectuals in North America. His broad understanding of various domains of knowledge and his ability to bring vastly different issues together and to engage them in relation to a larger totality is a model for how to do scholarship that is public, rigorous, and dialectical. Finally, I would be remiss to not underscore the more recent influence of my colleague David L. Clark. His erudition—which never fails to astound me—has been instrumental in fine-tuning my knowledge of critical theory, Derrida, and a range of other theoretical traditions that he engages and writes about in ways that are as insightful as they are poetic. David's sense of solidarity and commitment is remarkable in an academy that increasingly seems addicted to the insularities of careerism, cronyism, and the need to comfort students—now viewed as customers with rights rather than obligations—rather than prepare them intellectually for a world that needs to be engaged, not merely enjoyed.

To be an intellectual in the current historical juncture is not only to rethink the profound changes wrought by the rise and power of the new media and the ways in which it has transformed the very concept of the social, communal, and political but to redefine what it means to be a public intellectual capable of working across a number of disciplines and speaking to a variety of audiences. The old model of the intellectual writing and speaking in a narrow and obtuse theoretical language seems unproductive at this particular point in history. Theory needs to be rigorous *and* accessible, and it needs to address not merely the outer limits of disciplinary scholarship but also important social problems. Equally important, it needs to include and engage people who are not versed in the specialized disciplinary vocabularies of the academy. Theory is neither a metaphor for scholasticism and formalism nor is it politically irrelevant. Nor can it be dismissed as something distinctly American or French, or a thing exotic or foreign. Theory is essential and inescapable and cannot be so neatly abstracted from the responsibilities of political criticism, but how we do it and for what reason is a more problematic and troubling issue. What does it mean to *use* theory rather than simply apply it as many graduate students and professors tend to do?

Theory is the enemy of "common sense," and hence hated by many of our newly minted anti-intellectual authoritarian populists who ran against Obama in the 2012 elections. Of course, there is another important question regarding when theory becomes toxic, an immunity against immunity, turning in on itself, functioning, to use Derrida's term, as kind of autoimmunity. Given the bankruptcy of the current anti-intellectual politics of the "self-evident," theory is all we have left and functions as a kind of toolbox to be used to break the consensus of common sense, develop better forms of knowledge, and promote more just social relations. Theory is an indispensable resource in the task of thinking through and developing new modes of agency, power, and action in the service of connecting knowledge and power, meaning and social relevance, and private troubles and public issues. Clearly, self-reflection, mastering broad bodies of knowledge, and engaging with new technologies as a way to reach broader audiences all matter—just as it is only through theory that we can recover what survives of the defeated, the repressed, the marginalized, and those ideas relegated as obsolete, un-American, and indigestible. But there is also something more fundamental at work in this project. The global Left doesn't need to abandon theory; it needs to find a new language in order to move away from the kinds of fractured politics that have dominated Western societies since the 1980s.

In a similar manner, the politics of identity has to guard against becoming exclusionary and needs to be rethought of as part of a much broader set of connections and projects. In the 1980s, I believe that a group of highly influential feminist theorists in education did a great deal of damage politically and ethically to the understanding of both critical pedagogy and radical education as a practice of transformation and freedom. Rather than build upon and critically engage the complex traditions out of which this work developed, interrogating both its strengths and weaknesses, treating it as a developing and ongoing theoretical discourse and practice, they falsely labeled critical pedagogy as the enemy of empowerment. Operating out of comforting absolutes on the model of us versus them, this rhetoric of simplistic oppositions furthered a manipulative discourse and a climate for political opportunism. A crude type of essentialism and reductionism structured this work. Rather than engage a complex tradition of work, it simply demonized it, reducing it to one side of a binarism in which all doubt, mediation, complexity, and nuance disappeared.

What made this intervention even worse was that it was followed by an endless stream of endorsements by supine white male academics who cited this work to prove their own faux feminist credentials. This was truly as ideologically disingenuous as it was politically reactionary, or even worse, dangerous. Unaware of its own refusal to engage in nuanced and thoughtful analytic and deconstructive work, this type of feminist educational theory put forth its own mechanical and positivist calculations as if such work offered political guarantees, buttressed by the absolutism and vitriol in which it was sometimes delivered. This was symptomatic of what a particular version of identity politics can become when it is driven by moralism, a politics of purity, a logic of certainty, and a disregard for critical and scholarly exchange. There is more at work here than simply hubris and a denial of the complexity of the work under review; there is also a claim to moral and political clarity that actually produces its opposite. Fortunately, some of this work was offset by a smaller number of feminist scholars working in critical pedagogy who rejected this type of friend/enemy distinction. This was particularly evident at the time in the brilliant work by Linda Brodkey, bell hooks, Deborah Britzman, Sharon Todd, Chandra Mohanty, Sharon Crowley, Lynn Worsham, and later by Robin Truth Goodman and Susan Searls Giroux.

Rather than fire missiles at each other, public intellectuals need to address how we can effectively understand our differences as part of a broader and more powerful movement for engaging in critical exchanges, pushing the frontiers of transformative knowledge, extending democratic struggles, and addressing the massive suffering and hardships, particularly for young people, now being caused by various fundamentalist and authoritarian institutions, policies, and practices. As my partner, Susan Searls Giroux, has stated with characteristic precision, "As a consequence of our devastatingly misguided priorities and our negligence we have, in short, produced smart bombs and explosive children."

We need to make connections, build broad social movements, make pedagogy central to politics, and dismantle the reactionary forms of neoliberalism, racism, and media culture that have become normalized. We need to take up and develop more relational theories concerned with broader totalities and the ways in which the forces of difference, identity, local politics, cultural pedagogy, and other social formations interact in ways that speak to new and more threatening forms of global politics. Power is now free floating; it has no allegiances except to the accumulation of capital and is not only much more destructive but also more difficult to contain. Any viable notion of politics has to be relational and connected; it has to think within and beyond the boundaries of nation-states, invent new vocabularies, invest in more broad-based groups beyond simply workers, address the plight of young people, and resurrect the power of the social state and democracy as a radical mode of governance and politics. This suggests taking matters of specificity and context seriously, while at the same time changing the level of magnification to a more global view.

One of the most important considerations necessary for a new vision of politics is incorporating economic rights and social protections into the political sphere. Political and personal rights become dysfunctional without social rights. As Zygmunt Bauman reminds us, freedom of choice and the exercise of political and personal rights become a cruel joke in a society that does not provide social rights—that is, some form of collectively endorsed protections that provide the time and space for the poor and disenfranchised to participate in the political sphere and help shape modes of governance. In order to exercise any real sense of civic agency, people need protections from those misfortunes and hardships that are not of their own doing. At the same time, a movement for democracy must challenge the erosion of social bonds, the crumbling of communal cohesion, and the withering of social responsibility that have taken place under a neoliberal apparatus that promotes deregulation, privatization, and individualization. We also need to think in terms of what it means to create the formative cultures necessary to fight racism, celebrity culture, the culture and institutions of casino capitalism, the assault on the environment, and the growing inequality in wealth and income that is destroying every vestige of democratic politics in the world. We need a language that takes both history and the current dangerous authoritarian period seriously, one that recognizes, as Bauman points out, that shared humanity is the lifeboat. Too many people on the left are acting as if they are living in the nineteenth century and are completely out of touch with the new technologies, modes of domination, and emerging social formations that are taking shape all over the world.

A viable politics in the present has to take seriously the premise that knowledge must be meaningful in order to be critical, in order to be transformative. This is about more than reclaiming the virtues of dialogue, exchange, and translation. It is about recovering a politics and inventing a language that can create democratic public spheres in which new subjects and identities can be produced that are capable of recognizing and addressing the plight of the other and struggling collectively to expand and deepen the ongoing struggle for justice, freedom, and democratization. The global Left needs to be thorough, accessible, and rigorous in our critiques, especially amid the political and cultural illiteracy produced by neoliberalism's cultural apparatuses. But we also need a language of hope, one that is realistic rather than romantic about the challenges the planet is facing and yet electrified by a realization that things can be different, that possibilities can not only be imagined but engaged, fought for, and realized in collective struggles.

Opposing the forces of domination is important, but it does not go far enough. We must move beyond a language of pointless denunciations and offer instead a language that moves forward with the knowledge, skills, and social relations necessary for the creation of new modes of agency, social movements, and democratic economic and social policies. We need to open up the realm of human possibility, recognize that history is open, that justice is never complete, and that democracy can never be fully settled. I fervently believe in the need for both critique and hope, and have faith that the Left can develop the public spheres that make such possibilities possible, whether they be schools, classrooms, workshops, newspapers, online journals, community colleges, or other spaces where knowledge, power, ethics, and justice merge to create new subjectivities, new modes of civic courage, and new hope for the future.

Introduction: Neoliberalism's War on Democracy

1. These themes are taken up extensively in David Harvey, *A Brief History of Neoliberalism* (New York: Oxford University Press, 2005), David Harvey, *The Enigma of Capitalism* (New York: Oxford University Press, 2010), and Colin Crouch, *The Strange Non-Death of Neoliberalism* (Cambridge: Polity, 2011).

2. This quote is from Andrew Reszitnyk, "Beyond Difference and Becoming: Towards a Non-Differential Practice of Critique," a paper presented as part of his 2013 doctoral comprehensive exam. For other sources on neoliberalism, see Manfred B. Steger and Ravi K. Roy, *Neoliberalism: A Very Short Introduction* (New York: Oxford University Press, 2010); Juliet B. Schor, *Plenitude: The New Economics of True Wealth* (New York: Penguin Press, 2010); Henry A. Giroux, *Against the Terror of Neoliberalism* (Boulder, CO: Paradigm, 2008); Harvey, *Brief History of Neoliberalism*; and John Comaroff and Jean Comaroff, eds., *Millennial Capitalism and the Culture of Neoliberalism* (Durham, NC: Duke University Press, 2001). On the moral limits and failings of neoliberalism, see Michael J. Sandel, *What Money Can't Buy* (New York: Farrar, Straus and Giroux, 2012). And for positing a case for neoliberalism as a criminal enterprise, see Jeff Madrick, *Age of Greed: The Triumph of Finance and the Decline of America, 1970 to the Present* (New York: Vintage, 2011); Charles Ferguson, *Predator Nation: Corporate Criminals, Political Corruption, and the Hijacking of America* (New York: Crown Business, 2012); Henry A. Giroux, *Zombie Politics in the Age of*

Casino Capitalism (New York: Peter Lang, 2010).

3. João Biehl, *Vita: Life in a Zone of Social Abandonment* (Berkeley and Los Angeles: University of California Press, 2005). These zones are also brilliantly analyzed in Chris Hedges and Joe Sacco, *Days of Destruction, Days of Revolt* (New York: Knopf, 2012).

4. For instance, see Henry A. Giroux, *Youth in a Suspect Society* (New York: Routledge, 2010) and Annette Fuentes, *Lockdown High* (New York: Verso, 2013).

5. Zygmunt Bauman, "Does 'Democracy' Still Mean Anything? (And in Case It Does, What Is It?)" *Truthout*, January 21, 2011, http://truth-out.org/index.php?option=com_k2&view=item&id=73:does-democracy-still-mean-anything-and-in-case-it-does-what-is-it.

6. Lauren Berlant cited in Michael Dawson, *Blacks In and Out of the Left* (Cambridge, MA: Harvard University Press, 2013), 181–182.

7. George Lakoff and Glenn W. G. Smith, "Romney, Ryan and the Devil's Budget," *Reader Supported News*, August 22, 2012, http://blogs.berkeley.edu/2012/08/23/romney-ryan-and-the-devils-budget-will-america-keep-its-soul/.

8. Robert Reich, "Mitt Romney and the New Gilded Age," *Reader Supported News*, June 30, 2012, http://robertreich.org/post/26229451132.

9. David Theo Goldberg, "The Taxing Terms of the GOP Plan Invite Class Carnage," *Truthout*, September 20, 2012, http://truth-out.org/news/item/11630-the-taxing-terms-of-the-gop-plan-invite-class-carnage.

10. Paul Krugman, "Galt, Gold, and God," *New York Times*, August 23, 2012.

11. Ibid.

12. Marian Wright Edelman,"Ending Child Poverty: Child Poverty in America: 2011," Children's Defense Fund, http://www.childrensdefense.org/child-research-data-publications/data/2011-child-poverty-in-america.pdf.

13. Marian Wright Edelman, "Ryanomics Assault on Poor and Hungry Children," *Huffington Post*, September 14, 2012, http://www.huffingtonpost.com/marian-wright-edelman/ryanomics-assault-on-poor_b_1885851.html.

14. Richard D. Wolff, "The Truth about Profits and Austerity," *MR Zine*, March 31, 2013, http://mrzine.monthlyreview.org/2013/wolff310313.html. Wolff develops this position in Richard D. Wolff, *Democracy at Work: A Cure for Capitalism* (Chicago: Haymarket Books, 2012).

15. Igor Volsky, "Pick Your Poison," *Progress Report*, March 4, 2013, http://thinkprogress.org/progress-report/pick-your-poison/?mobile=nc.

16. ThinkProgress War Room, "Sequester: 'A Fancy Word for a Dumb Idea," *Think Progress*, March 1, 2013, http://thinkprogress.org/progress-report/?mobile=nc.

17. Reich, "Mitt Romney and the New Gilded Age"; Ferguson, *Predator Nation*; Daisy Grewal, "How Wealth Reduces Compassion: As Riches Grow, Empathy for Others Seems to Decline," *Scientific American*, April 10, 2012, http://www.scientificamerican.com/article.cfmid=how-wealth-reduces-compassion.

18. Bauman, "Does 'Democracy' Still Mean Anything?"

19. Lewis H. Lapham, "Feast of Fools: How American Democracy Became the Property of a Commercial Oligarchy," *Truthout*, September 20, 2012, http://truth-out.org/opinion/item/11656-feast-of-fools-how-american-democracy

-became-the-property-of-a-commercial-oligarchy.

20. Ibid.

21. Zygmunt Bauman, *This Is Not a Diary* (Cambridge: Polity Press, 2012), 102.

22. Lapham, "Feast of Fools."

23. Eric Lichtblau, "Economic Downturn Took a Detour at Capitol Hill," *New York Times*, December 26, 2011, http://www.nytimes.com/2011/12/27/us/ politics/economic-slide-took-a-detour-at-capitol-hill.html?pagewanted=all.

24. Peter Grier, "So Much Money, So Few Lobbyists in D.C.: How Does the Math Work?" *DC Decoder*, February 24, 2012, http://www.csmonitor.com/USA/ DC-Decoder/Decoder-Wire/2012/0224/So-much-money-so-few-lobbyists-in -D.C.-How-does-that-math-work.

25. Bill Moyers and Bernard Weisberger, "Money in Politics: Where Is the Outrage?" *Huffington Post*, August 30, 2012, http://www.huffingtonpost.com/ bill-moyers/money-in-politics_b_1840173.html.

26. Erika Eichelberger, "See How Citigroup Wrote a Bill So It Could Get a Bailout," *Mother Jones*, May 24, 2013, http://www.motherjones.com/politics/2013/ 05/citigroup-hr-992-wall-street-swaps-regulatory-improvement-act.

27. The inhumanity of such modes of punishment are captured brilliantly in Lorna A. Rhodes, *Total Confinement: Madness and Reason in the Maximum Security Prison* (Berkeley and Los Angeles: University of California Press, 2004).

28. It is difficult to access this study because Citigroup does its best to make it disappear from the Internet. See the discussion of it by Noam Chomsky in "Plutonomy and the Precariat: On the History of the U.S. Economy in Decline," *Truthdig*, May 8, 2012, http://www.truthdig.com/report/item/plutonomy_ and_the_precariat_the_history_of_the_us_economy_in_decline_201205/.

29. Chrystia Freeland, *Plutocrats: The Rise of the New Global Super-Rich and the Fall of Everyone Else* (New York: Penguin, 2012).

30. See Olivia Ward's interview with Chrystia Freeland. Olivia Ward, "The Rise of the Super-rich: Is the Economy Just Going Through a Bad Patch?" *Truthout*, April 1, 2013, http://truth-out.org/news/item/15452-the-rise-of-the-super-rich -is-the-economy-just-going-through-a-bad-patch.

31. Salvatore Babones, "To End the Jobs Recession, Invest an Extra $20 Billion in Public Education," *Truthout*, August 21, 2012, http://truth-out.org/opinion/item/ 11031-to-end-the-jobs-recession-invest-an-extra-$20-billion-in-public-education.

32. John Atcheson, "The Real Welfare Problem: Government Giveaways to the Corporate 1%," *Common Dreams*, September 3, 2012, http://www.commondreams .org/view/2012/09/03-7.

33. John Cavanagh, "Seven Ways to End the Deficit (Without Throwing Grandma Under the Bus)," *Yes! Magazine*, September 7, 2012, http://www.yesmagazine.org/ new-economy/seven-ways-to-end-the-deficit-without-throwing-grandma-under -the-bus.

34. Ibid.

35. Joseph Stiglitz, "Politics Is at the Root of the Problem," *European Magazine*, April 23, 2012, http://theeuropean-magazine.com/633-stiglitz-joseph/634 -austerity-and-a-new-recession.

36. Lynn Parramore, "Exclusive Interview: Joseph Stiglitz Sees Terrifying Future for America If We Don't Reverse Inequality," *AlterNet,* June 24, 2012, http://www .alternet.org/economy/155918/exclusive_interview%3A_joseph_stiglitz_sees _terrifying_future_for_america_if_we_don%27t_reverse_inequality.

37. Editorial, "America's Detainee Problem," *Los Angeles Times,* September 23, 2012, http://articles.latimes.com/2012/sep/23/opinion/la-ed-detention-20120923.

38. Glenn Greenwald, "Unlike Afghan Leaders, Obama Fights for Power of Indefinite Military Detention," *Guardian,* September 18, 2012, www.guardian .co.uk/commentisfree/2012/sep/18/obama-appeals-ndaa-detention-law. See also Glenn Greenwald, "Federal Court Enjoins NDAA," *Salon,* May 16, 2012, www.salon.com/2012/05/16/federal_court_enjoins_ndaa/. See also Henry A. Giroux, *Hearts of Darkness: Torturing Children in the War on Terror* (Boulder, CO: Paradigm, 2010).

39. Charlie Savage, "Judge Rules against Law on Indefinite Detention," *New York Times,* September 12, 2012, www.nytimes.com/2012/09/13/us/judge-blocks -controversial-indefinite-detention-law.html?_r=0.

40. Karen J. Greenberg, "Ever More and Ever Less," *TomDispatch,* March 18, 2012, www.tomdispatch.com/archive/175517/.

41. Catherine Poe, "Federal Judge Emails Racist Joke about President Obama," *Washington Times,* March 1, 2012, http://communities.washingtontimes.com/ neighborhood/ad-lib/2012/mar/1/federal-judge-emails-racist-joke-about -president-o/.

42. Amanda Turkel and Sam Stein, "Mitt Romney, on *60 Minutes,* Cities Emergency Room as Health Care Option for Uninsured," *Huffington Post,* September 23, 2012, www.huffingtonpost.com/2012/09/23/mitt-romney-60-minutes- health-care_n_1908129.html?.

43. Editorial, "Why Romney Is Slipping," *New York Times,* September 25, 2012.

44. Brennan Keller, "Medical Expenses: Top Cause of Bankruptcy.in the United States," *GiveForward,* October 13, 2011, www.giveforward.com/blog/medical -expenses-top-cause-of-bankruptcy-in-the-united-states.

45. Stanley Aronowitz, *Against Schooling: For an Education That Matters* (Boulder, CO: Paradigm Publishers, 2008), xviii.

46. Reuters, "Goldman Sachs CEO Lloyd Blankfein Says Banks Do 'God's Work,'" *Daily News,* November 9, 2009, http://articles.nydailynews.com/2009-11-09/ news/17938614_1_year-end-bonuses-goldman-sachs-lloyd-blankfein.

47. Paul Krugman, "Defining Prosperity Down," *New York Times,* August 1, 2010.

48. Zygmunt Bauman is the most important theorist writing about the politics of disposability. Among his many books, see *Wasted Lives* (London: Polity Press, 2004).

49. Bauman, *Wasted Lives,* 5.

50. Robert Reich, "The Rebirth of Social Darwinism," *Robert Reich's Blog,* November 30, 2011, http://robertreich.org/post/13567144944.

51. Tony Judt, *Ill Fares the Land* (New York: Penguin, 2010).

52. This argument has been made against academics for quite some time, though it has either been forgotten or conveniently ignored by many faculty. See, for example, various essays in C. Wright Mills, "The Powerless People: The Role of

the Intellectual in Society" in C. Wright Mills, *The Politics of Truth: Selected Writings of C. Wright Mills* (Oxford: Oxford University Press, 2008), 13–24; Edward Said, *Humanism and Democratic Criticism* (New York: Columbia University Press, 2004); and Henry A. Giroux and Susan Searls Giroux, *Take Back Higher Education* (New York: Palgrave, 2004).

53. On the university's relationship with the national security state, see David Price, "How the CIA Is Welcoming Itself Back Onto American University Campuses: Silent Coup," *CounterPunch*, April 9–11, 2010, www.counterpunch.org/price04092010.html. See also Nick Turse, *How the Military Invades Our Everyday Lives* (New York: Metropolitan Books, 2008); and Henry A. Giroux, *The University in Chains: Confronting the Military-Industrial-Academic Complex* (Boulder, CO: Paradigm Publishers, 2007).

54. Robert McChesney, *The Problem of the Media* (New York: Monthly Review Press, 2004). See the interesting table by Ashley Lutz, "These Six Corporations Control 90% of the Media in America," *Business Insider*, June 14, 2012, www.businessinsider.com/these-6-corporations-control-90-of-the-media-in-america-2012-6.

55. See, for instance, Chris Mooney, *The Republican War on Science* (New York: Basic Books, 2005).

56. Frank Rich, "Could She Reach the Top in 2012? You Betcha," *New York Times*, November 20, 2010.

57. Cornelius Castoriadis, "Democracy as Procedure and Democracy as Regime," *Constellations* 4, no. 1 (1997): 5.

58. Toni Morrison, "How Can Values Be Taught in This University," *Michigan Quarterly Review* (Spring 2001): 278.

59. Stephen Holden, "Perils of the Corporate Ladder: It Hurts When You Fall," *New York Times*, December 10, 2010.

60. Hart Research Associates, *American Academics: Survey of Part Time and Adjunct Higher Education Faculty* (Washington, DC: AFT, 2011);Steve Street, Maria Maisto, Esther Merves, and Gary Rhoades, *Who Is Professor "Staff" and How Can This Person Teach So Many Classes?* (Los Angeles: Center for the Future of Higher Education, 2012).

61. Andrew Martin and Andrew W. Lehren, "A Generation Hobbled by the Soaring Cost of College," *New York Times*, May 12, 2012.

62. Paul Buchheit, "Five Ugly Extremes of Inequality in America—the Contrasts Will Drop Your Chin to the Floor," *AlterNet*, March 24, 2013, www.alternet.org/economy/five-ugly-extremes-inequality-america-contrasts-will-drop-your-chin-floor.

63. For an excellent defense of critical thinking not merely as a skill, but as a crucial foundation for any democratic society, see Robert Jensen, *Arguing for Our Lives* (San Francisco: City Lights Books, 2013).

64. Cited in Richard J. Bernstein, *The Abuse of Evil: The Corruption of Politics and Religion since 9/11* (London: Polity Press, 2005), 7–8.

65. Paul Buchheit, "Now We Know Our ABCs and Charter Schools Get an F," *CommonDreams*, September 24, 2012, https://www.commondreams.org/view/2012/09/24-0.

66. See Giroux, *The University in Chains*.

67. See, for instance, Robert B. Reich, "Slashed Funding for Public Universities Is Pushing the Middle Class Toward Extinction," *AlterNet*, March 5, 2012, www.alternet.org/education/154410/slashed_funding_for_public_universities_is_pushing_the_middle_class_toward_extinction. For a brilliant argument regarding the political and economic reasons behind the defunding and attack on higher education, see Christopher Newfield, *Unmaking the Public University: The Forty-Year Assault on the Middle Class* (Cambridge, MA: Harvard University Press, 2008).

68. Les Leopold, "Crazy Country: 6 Reasons America Spends More on Prisons Than on Higher Education," *AlterNet*, August 27, 2012, www.alternet.org/education/crazy-country-6-reasons-america-spends-more-prisons-higher-education?paging=off. On this issue, see also the classic work by Angela Y. Davis, *Are Prisons Obsolete?* (New York: Open Media, 2003) and Michelle Alexander, *The New Jim Crow: Mass Incarceration in the Age of Colorblindness* (New York: New Press, 2012).

69. Leopold, "Crazy Country."

70. Zygmunt Bauman, *The Individualized Society* (London: Polity, 2001), 4.

71. See, for instance, Rebecca Solnit, "Rain on Our Parade: A Letter to the Dismal Left," *TomDispatch*, September 27, 2012, www.tomdispatch.com/blog/175598/tomgram%3A_rebecca_solnit,_we_could_be_heroes/. *TomDispatch* refers to this article as a call for hope over despair. It should be labeled as a call for accommodation over the need for a radical democratic politics. For an alternative to this politics of accommodation, see the work of Stanley Aronowitz, Chris Hedges, Henry Giroux, Noam Chomsky, and others.

72. This term comes from Daniel Bensaïd. See Sebastian Budgen, "The Red Hussar: Daniel Bensaïd, 1946–2010," *International Socialism* 127 (June 25, 2010), http://www.isj.org.uk/?id=661.

73. Castoriadis, "Democracy as Procedure," 5.

74. Archon Fung, "The Constructive Responsibility of Intellectuals," *Boston Review*, September 9, 2011, www.bostonreview.net/BR36.5/archon_fung_noam_chomsky_responsibility_of_intellectuals.php.

75. Heather Gautney, "Why Do Political Elites All Hate Democracy?" *LA Progressive*, September 19, 2012, www.laprogressive.com/hate-democracy.

76. Stuart Hall and Les Back, "In Conversation: At Home and Not at Home," *Cultural Studies* 23, no. 4 (July 2009), 681.

77. Guy Standing, *The Precariat: The New Dangerous Class* (New York: Bloomsbury, 2011), 20.

Chapter One: Dystopian Education in a Neoliberal Society

1. Some important sources include: Henry A. Giroux, *Education and the Crisis of Public Values* (Boulder, CO: Paradigm Publishers, 2012); Kenneth J. Saltman, *The Failure of Corporate School Reform* (Boulder, CO: Paradigm Publishers,

2012); Diane Ravitch, *The Death and Life of the Great American School System: How Testing and Choice Are Undermining Education* (New York: Basic Books, 2011); Gaston Alonso, Noel S. Anderson, Celina Su, and Jeanne Theoharis, *Our Schools Suck: Students Talk Back to a Segregated Nation on the Failures of Urban Education* (New York: NYU Press, 2009).

2.   Graeme Turner, *What's Become of Cultural Studies* (New York: Sage, 2011), 183.

3.   See, for example, Madrick, *Age of Greed: The Triumph of Finance and the Decline of America*; Ferguson, *Predator Nation*; Giroux, *Zombie Politics in the Age of Casino Capitalism*.

4.   David Theo Goldberg, "The Taxing Terms of the GOP Plan Invite Class Carnage," *Truthout*, September 20, 2012, http://truth-out.org/news/item/11630 -the-taxing-terms-of-the-gop-plan-invite-class-carnage.

5.   Jolle Fanghanel, *Being an Academic* (New York: Routledge, 2012), 15.

6.   See, for example, Gaye Tuchman, *Wannabe U: Inside the Corporate University* (Chicago: University of Chicago Press, 2009); Martha C. Nussbaum, *Not for Profit: Why Democracy Needs the Humanities*, (Princeton, NJ: Princeton University Press, 2010); Michael Bailey and Des Freedman, eds., *The Assault on Universities: A Manifesto for Resistance* (London: Pluto Press, 2011); Henry A. Giroux, *Twilight of the Social: Resurgent Politics in the Age of Disposability* (Boulder, CO: Paradigm Publishing, 2012).

7.   On the religious Right, see Chris Hedges, *American Fascists: The Christian Right and the War on America* (New York: Free Press, 2008) and Clyde Wilcox and Carin Robinson, *Onward Christian Soldiers? The Religious Right in American Politics* (Boulder, CO: Westview Press, 2010).

8.   I have taken up the attack on higher education in a number of books. See, for example, Giroux and Searls Giroux, *Take Back Higher Education* and *The University in Chains* (Boulder, CO: Paradigm, 2009).

9.   David Theo Goldberg, "The University We Are For," *Huffington Post*, November 28, 2011, http://www.huffingtonpost.com/david-theo-goldberg/university -california-protests_b_1106234.html.

10.   Marc Bousquet, *How the University Works: Higher Education and the Low-Wage Nation* (New York: NYU Press, 2008).

11.   For a sustained analysis of how inequality undermines democracy and public services, see Richard Wilkinson and Kate Pickett, *The Spirit Level: Why Equality Is Better for Everyone* (New York: Penguin, 2010).

12.   John Atcheson, "The Real Welfare Problem: Government Giveaways to the Corporate 1%," *Common Dreams*, September 3, 2012, www.commondreams.org/ view/2012/09/03-7.

13.   See Joseph E. Stiglitz, *The Price of Inequality* (New York: W. W. Norton, 2012) and Michael Sandel, *What Money Can't Buy* (New York: FSG Publishing, 2012).

14.   Goldberg, "The Taxing Terms of the GOP Plan."

15.   Sandel, *What Money Can't Buy*.

16.   Les Leopold, "Hey Dad, Why Does This Country Protect Billionaires, and Not Teachers?" *AlterNet*, May 5, 2010, www.alternet.org/module/printversion/146738.

17.   David Glenn, "Public Higher Education Is 'Eroding from All Sides,' Warns Po-

litical Scientists," *Chronicle of Higher Education*, September 2, 2010, http://chronicle.com/article/Public-Higher-Education-Is/124292/.

18. Noam Chomsky, "Public Education Under Massive Corporate Assault—What's Next? *AlterNet*, August 5, 2011, www.alternet.org/story/151921/chomsky%3A _public_education_under_massive_corporate_assault_%E2%80%94_what's_next.

19. Peter Seybold, "The Struggle Against the Corporate Takeover of the University," *Socialism and Democracy* 22, no. 1 (March 2008): 1–2.

20. Nancy Hass, "Scholarly Investments," *New York Times*, December 6, 2009.

21. Diane Ravitch, "Two Visions for Chicago's Schools," *Common Dreams*, September 14, 2012, www.commondreams.org/view/2012/09/14-3?print.

22. See Christopher Robbins, *Expelling Hope: The Assault on Youth and the Militarization of Schooling* (Albany: SUNY Press, 2008); Giroux, *Youth in a Suspect Society*; Fuentes, *Lockdown High*; Sadhbh Walshe, "US Education Orientation for Minorities: The School-to-Prison Pipeline," *Guardian*, August 31, 2012, www.guardian.co.uk/commentisfree/2012/aug/31/us-education-orientation -minorities. See also the ACLU report *Locating the School-to-Prison Pipeline*, www.aclu.org/racial-justice/school-prison-pipeline.

23. I have taken this issue up in Henry A. Giroux (co-authored with Susan Searls Giroux), "Scandalous Politics: Penn State and the Return of the Repressed in Higher Education," *JAC* 32, no. 1–2.

24. Charles M. Blow, "Plantations, Prisons and Profits," *New York Times*, May 25, 2012, www.nytimes.com/2012/05/26/opinion/blow-plantations-prisons-and -profits.html. For a detailed analysis of the racist prison-industrial complex, see Angela Y. Davis, *Abolition Democracy: Beyond Empire, Prisons, and Torture* (Seven Stories Press, 2005); Michelle Brown, *The Culture of Punishment: Prison, Society and Spectacle* (New York: NYU Press, 2009); Alexander, *The New Jim Crow*.

25. Amanda Terkel, "Arizona Expands Its Discrimination: Teachers with Heavy Accents Can't Teach English, Ethnic Studies Are Banned," *ThinkProgress*, April 30, 2010, http://thinkprogress.org/politics/2010/04/30/94567/arizona-teachers/.

26. Miriam Jordan, "Arizona Grades Teachers on Fluency," *Wall Street Journal*, April 30, 2010, http://online.wsj.com/article/SB10001424052748703572 5 04575213883276427528.html.

27. Zygmunt Bauman, *Society under Siege* (Malden, MA: Blackwell, 2002), 170.

28. Salvatore Babones, "To End the Jobs Recession, Invest an Extra $20 Billion in Public Education," *Truthout*, August 21, 2012, http://truth-out.org/ opinion/item/11031-to-end-the-jobs-recession-invest-an-extra-$20-billion-in -public-education.

29. FT's Lex blog, "U.S. Defense Spending: What's the Real Figure?," *Globe and Mail*, May 28, 2012, www.theglobeandmail.com/report-on-business/international -business/us-defence-spending-whats-the-real-figure/article4217831/.

30. Daniel Trotta, "Cost of War $3.7 Trillion and Counting, 258,000 Dead," Reuters, June 28, 2011, http://uk.reuters.com/article/2011/06/29/uk-usa-war -idUKTRE75S76R20110629.

31. Dominic Tierney, "The F-35: A Weapon That Costs More Than Australia," *Atlantic*, November 11, 2011, www.theatlantic.com/national/archive/

2011/03/the-f-35-a-weapon-that-costs-more-than-australia/72454/.

32. Babones, "To End the Jobs Recession."

33. Cited in Zygmunt Bauman, *Liquid Life* (Cambridge: Polity Press, 2005), 138.

34. Bill Readings *The University in Ruins* (Cambridge, MA: Harvard University Press,) 11, 18.

35. Zygmunt Bauman, *In Search of Politics* (Stanford, CA: Stanford University Press, 1999), 170.

36. Bauman, *Society under Siege*, 70.

37. Lynn Worsham and Gary A. Olson, "Rethinking Political Community: Chantal Mouffe's Liberal Socialism," *Journal of Composition Theory* 19, no. 2 (1999): 178.

38. Cavanagh, "Seven Ways to End the Deficit."

39. Ibid.

40. Noam Chomsky, "Paths Taken, Tasks Ahead," *Profession* (2000): 34.

41. Pierre Bourdieu, "For a Scholarship of Commitment," *Profession* (2000): 44.

42. Jacques Derrida, "Intellectual Courage: An Interview," trans. Peter Krapp, *Culture Machine* 2 (2000): 9.

43. A Conversation between Lani Guinier and Anna Deavere Smith, "Rethinking Power, Rethinking Theater," *Theater* 31, no. 3 (Winter 2002): 34–35.

Chapter Two: At the Limits of Neoliberal Higher Education

1. This theme is taken up powerfully by a number of theorists. See C. Wright Mills, *The Sociological Imagination* (New York: Oxford University Press, 2000); Richard Sennett, *The Fall of Public Man* (New York: Norton, 1974); Zygmunt Bauman, *In Search of Politics* (Stanford, CA: Stanford University Press, 1999); and Henry A. Giroux, *Public Spaces, Private Lives* (Lanham, MD: Rowman and Littlefield, 2001).

2. Stuart Hall interviewed by James Hay, "Interview with Stuart Hall," *Communication and Critical/Cultural Studies* 10, no. 1 (2013): 11.

3. Vivian Yee, "Grouping Students by Ability Regains Favor in Classroom," *New York Times*, June 10, 2013, www.nytimes.com/2013/06/10/education/grouping-students-by-ability-regains-favor-with-educators.html?pagewanted=all&_r=0.

4. Craig Calhoun, "Information Technology and the International Public Sphere," in *Shaping the Network Society: The New Role of Society in Cyberspace*, ed. Douglas Schuler and Peter Day (Cambridge, MA: MIT Press, 2004), 241.

5. Michael D. Yates, "Occupy Wall Street and the Significance of Political Slogans," *Counterpunch*, February 27, 2013, www.counterpunch.org/2013/02/27/occupy-wall-street-and-the-significance-of-political-slogans/.

6. Zaid Jilani, Faiz Shakir, Benjamin Armbruster, George Zornick, Alex Seitz-Wald, and Tanya Somanader, "Rewarding Corporations While Punishing Workers," *Progress Report*, March 18, 2011, http://pr.thinkprogress.org/2011/03/pr20110318/index.html.

7. Jeffrey Sachs, "America's Deepening Moral Crisis," *Guardian*, October 4, 2010, www.guardian.co.uk/commentisfree/belief/2010/oct/04/americas-deepening -moral-crisis.

8. Classic examples of this can be found in the work of Milton Friedman and the fictional accounts of Ayn Rand. It is a position endlessly reproduced in conservative foundations and institutes such as the American Enterprise Institute, Heritage Foundation, Hudson Institute, Manhattan Institute for Policy Research, and the Hoover Institute. One particularly influential book that shaped social policy along these lines is Charles Murray, *Losing Ground* (New York: Basic, 1994).

9. Jacques Rancière, *Hatred of Democracy* (London: Verso 2006).

10. Ellen Schrecker, *The Lost Soul of Higher Education* (New York: The New Press, 2010), 3.

11. A number of important critiques of the Browne Report and the conservative-liberal attack on higher education include: Simon Head, "The Grim Threat to British Universities," *New York Review of Books*, January 13, 2011, www.nybooks .com/articles/archives/2011/jan/13/grim-threat-british-universities/; Anthony T. Grafton, "Britain: The Disgrace of the Universities," *New York Review of Books*, March 10, 2010, 32; Nick Couldry, "Fighting for the Life of the English University in 2010," unpublished manuscript; Stefan Collini, "Browne's Gamble," *London Review of Books* 32, no. 21 (November 4, 2010) 23–25; Stanley Fish, "The Value of Higher Education Made Literal," *New York Times*, December 13, 2010, http://opinionator.blogs.nytimes.com/2010/12/13/the-value-of-higher-education -made-literal/; Aisha Labi, "British Universities and Businesses Are Forming Stronger Research Ties," *Chronicle of Higher Education*, October 4, 2010, http://chronicle.com/article/British-Universities-and/124814; and Terry Eagleton, "The Death of Universities," *Guardian*, December 17, 2010, www.guardian .co.uk/commentisfree/2010/dec/17/death-universities-malaise-tuition-fee.

12. Michael Collins, "Universities Need Reform—but the Market Is Not the Answer," *OpenDemocracy.net*, November 23, 2010, www.opendemocracy.net/ ourkingdom/michael-collins/universities-need-reform-but-market-is-not-answer.

13. Luke Johnson, "Marco Rubio on Climate Change: 'The Government Can't Change the Weather,'" *Huffington Post*, February 13, 2013, www.huffingtonpost .com/2013/02/13/marco-rubio-climate-change_n_2679810.html.

14. Ibid.

15. Collini, "Browne's Gamble."

16. Head, "The Grim Threat to British Universities."

17. Stanley Aronowitz, "Introduction," *Against Schooling: For an Education That Matters* (Boulder, CO: Paradigm, 2008), xv.

18. Kathryn Masterson, "Off Campus Is Now the Place to Be for Deans," *Chronicle of Higher Education*, March 6, 2011, http://chronicle.com/article/For-Deans -Off-Campus-Is-Now/126607/.

19. Jason Del Gandio, "Neoliberalism and the Academic-Industrial Complex," *Truthout*, August 12, 2010, www.truth-out.org/neoliberalism-and-academic -industrial-complex62189.

20. Scott Jaschik, "New Tactic to Kill Faculty Unions," *Inside Higher Ed*, March 3,

2011, www.insidehighered.com/news/2011/03/03/ohio_bill_would_kill_faculty
_unions_in_unexpected_way.

21. The Coalition on the Academic Workforce, *A Portrait of Part-Time Faculty Members: A Summary of Findings on Part-Time Faculty Respondents to the Coalition on the Academic Workforce Survey of Contingent Faculty Members* (Washington, DC: CAW, June 2012), www.academicworkforce.org/CAW_portrait_2012.pdf.

22. Schrecker, *The Lost Soul of Higher Education*, 206–215.

23. Evan McMorris-Santoro, "Conservative Think Tank Seeks Michigan Profs' Emails About Wisconsin Union Battle . . . and Maddow," *Talking Points Memo*, March 29, 2010; Paul Krugman, "American Thought Police," *New York Times*, March 27, 2011, A27.

24. I take up these attacks in great detail in *The University in Chains*.

25. Stanley Aronowitz, "The Knowledge Factory," *Independent*, March 16, 2011, www.indypendent.org/2011/03/17/the-knowledge-factory/.

26. John Pilger, "The Revolt in Egypt Is Coming Home," *Truthout*, February 10, 2011, www.truth-out.org/the-revolt-egypt-is-coming-home67624.

27. Courtney E. Martin, *Do It Anyway: A New Generation of Activists* (Boston: Beacon Press, 2010).

28. Courtney E. Martin, "Why Class Matters in Campus Activism," *American Prospect*, December 6, 2010, www.prospect.org/cs/articles?article=why_class
_matters_in_campus_activism.

29. Cited in ibid.

30. Mark Edelman Boren, *Student Resistance: A History of the Unruly Subject* (New York: Routledge, 2001), 227.

31. Simeon Talley, "Why Aren't Students in the U.S. Protesting Tuition, Too?" *Campus Progress*, December 23, 2010, http://www.campusprogress.org/articles/why
_arent_students_in_the_u.s._protesting_tuition_too.

32. Susan Searls Giroux, *Between Race and Reason: Violence, Intellectual Responsibility, and the University to Come* (Stanford: Stanford University Press, 2010), 79.

33. Edelman Boren, *Student Resistance*, 228.

34. Robert Reich, "The Attack on American Education," *Reader Supported News*, December 23, 2010, www.readersupportednews.org/opinion2/299-190/4366
-the-attack-on-american-education.

35. Ibid.

36. There are many books and articles that take up this issue. One of the most incisive commentators is Jeffrey Williams, "Student Debt and the Spirit of Indenture," *Dissent* (Fall 2008), www.dissentmagazine.org/article/?article=1303.

37. David Mascriotra, "The Rich Get Richer and the Young Go into Deep Debt," *BuzzFlash*, December 6, 2010, http://blog.buzzflash.com/node/12045.

38. Head, "The Grim Threat to British Universities."

39. Jean-Luc Nancy, *The Truth of Democracy*, trans. Pascale-Anne Brault and Michael Naas (New York: Fordham University Press, 2010), 9.

40. Tom Engelhardt, "An American World War: What to Watch for in 2010," *Truthout*, January 3, 2010, www.truth-out.org/topstories/10410vh4. See also Andrew Bacevich, *The New American Militarism* (New York: Oxford University

Press, 2005); and Chalmers Johnson, *Nemesis: The Last Days of the American Empire* (New York: Metropolitan Books, 2006).

41. Eric Gorski, "45% of Students Don't Learn Much in College," *Huffington Post*, January 21, 2011, www.huffingtonpost.com/2011/01/18/45-of-students-don't -learn_n_810224.html. The study is taken from Richard Arum and Josipa Roksa, *Academically Adrift: Limited Learning on College Campuses* (Chicago: University of Chicago Press, 2011).

42. Surely there is a certain irony in the fact that the work of Gene Sharp, a little-known American theorist in nonviolent action, is inspiring young people all over the world to resist authoritarian governments. Yet his work is almost completely ignored by young people in the United States. See, for instance, Sheryl Gay Stolberg, "Shy U.S. Intellectual Created Playbook Used in Revolution," *New York Times*, February 16, 2011, A1. See, in particular, Gene Sharp, *From Dictatorship to Democracy* (London: Serpent's Tail, 2012).

43. Sheldon S. Wolin, *Democracy Incorporated: Managed Democracy and the Specter of Inverted Totalitarianism* (Princeton, NJ: Princeton University Press, 2008), 259–260.

44. Zygmunt Bauman, *Does Ethics Have a Chance in a World of Consumers?* (Cambridge MA: Harvard University Press, 2008), 159.

45. Ibid., 235. I have also taken up this theme in great detail in *Youth in a Suspect Society*.

46. Zygmunt Bauman, *The Individualized Society* (London: Polity, 2001), 55.

47. Alex Honneth, *Pathologies of Reason* (New York: Columbia University Press, 2009), 188.

48. John Comaroff and Jean Comaroff, "Reflections on Youth from the Past to the Postcolony," in *Frontiers of Capital: Ethnographic Reflections on the New Economy*, ed. Melissa S. Fisher and Greg Downey (Durham, NC: Duke University Press, 2006), 268.

49. Ibid.

50. Cited in Pascale-Anne Brault and Michael Naas, "Translator's Note," in Nancy, *The Truth of Democracy*, xii.

Chapter Three: Intellectual Violence in the Age of Gated Intellectuals

1. This issue has been taken up in detail in Schrecker, *The Lost Soul of Higher Education*, and Edward J. Carvalho and David Downing, eds., *Academic Freedom in the Post-9/11 Era* (New York: Palgrave, 2011).

2. Theodor Adorno, *Authoritarian Personality* (New York: Harper & Row, 1950).

3. Lutz Koepnick, "Aesthetic Politics Today—Walter Benjamin and Post-Fordist Culture," *Critical Theory—Current State and Future Prospects*, ed. Peter Uwe Hohendahl and Jaimey Fisher (New York: Berghahn Books: 2002), 96.

4. Mumia Abu-Jamal, "The U.S. Is Fast Becoming One of the Biggest Open-Air

Prisons on Earth," *Democracy Now!*, February 1, 2013, www.democracynow.org/2013/2/1/mumia_abu_jamal_the_united_states.

5. Michel Foucault, *Society Must Be Defended: Lectures at the College de France 1975–1976*, (New York: Picador, 2003), 47.

6. Ibid., 256.

7. Ibid., 56.

8. On this see, in particular, Bauman, *Society under Siege*.

9. Brad Evans and Mark Duffield, "Biospheric Security: How the Merger Between Development, Security & the Environment [Desenex] Is Retrenching Fortress Europe," in *A Threat Against Europe? Security, Migration and Integration,* eds. Peter Burgess and Serge Gutwirth (VUB Press: Brussels, 2011).

10. This critique of instrumental reason was a central feature of the Frankfurt School and is most notable in the work of Herbert Marcuse. See also Zygmunt Bauman's brilliant critique in *Modernity and the Holocaust* (Ithaca, NY: Cornell University Press, 2010), reprint edition.

11. See, for example, World Bank and Carter Centre, *From Civil War to Civil Society*, (Washington, DC: World Bank and Carter Centre, 1997).

12. Cited in Matt Phillips, "Goldman Sachs' Blankfein on Banking: 'Doing God's Work,'" *Marketbeat* (blog), *Wall Street Journal*, November 9, 2009, http://blogs.wsj.com/marketbeat/2009/11/09/goldman-sachs-blankfein-on-banking-doing-gods-work/.

13. C. Wright Mills, *The Politics of Truth: Selected Writings of C. Wright Mills* (New York: Oxford University Press, 2008), 200.

14. Aronowitz, *Against Schooling*, xii. See also http://archive.truthout.org/the-disappearing-intellectual-age-economic-darwinism61287 - 13.

15. Kate Zernike, "Making College 'Relevant,'" *New York Times*, January 3, 2010.

16. While this critique has been made by many critics, it has also been made recently by the president of Harvard University. See Drew Gilpin Faust, "The University's Crisis of Purpose," *New York Times*, September 6, 2009.

17. Harvey cited in Stephen Pender, "An Interview with David Harvey," *Studies in Social Justice* 1, no. 1 (Winter 2007): 14.

18. See, in particular, Giorgio Agamben, *Homo Sacer: Sovereign Power and Bare Life* (Stanford, CA: Stanford University Press, 1995); and Giorgio Agamben, *State of Exception* (Chicago: University of Chicago Press, 2005).

19. This term is first developed in Henry A. Giroux, *Twilight of the Social* (Boulder, CO: Paradigm, 2012).

20. David Theo Goldberg, *The Threat of Race: Reflections on Racial Neoliberalism* (Malden, MA: Wiley-Blackwell, 2009), 338-339.

21. Zygmunt Bauman, "Has the Future a Left?" *The Review of Education/Pedagogy/Cultural Studies* (2007): 2. Henry Giroux takes up the issue of gated intellectuals in greater detail in Henry A. Giroux, *The Education Deficit and the War on Youth* (New York: Monthly Review Press, 2013).

22. Judith Butler, *Frames of War: When Is Life Grievable?* (London: Verso, 2009), 3,4.

23. Ibid., 4.

24. Henry Giroux, "Counter-Memory & the Politics of Loss," *Truthout*, September 13, 2011, www.truth-out.org/counter-memory-and-politics-loss-after-911/1315595429.

25. Marjorie Cohn, ed., *The United States and Torture: Interrogation, Incarceration, and Abuse* (New York: NYU Press, 2011); Medea Benjamin, *Drone Warfare* (London: Verso Press, 2013); Nick Turse and Tom Englehardt, *Terminator Planet: The First History of Drone Warfare, 2001–2050* (New York: Dispatch Press, 2012).

26. Roger Simon, "A Shock of Thought," *Memory Studies* (February 21, 2011).

27. See Michael Hardt and Antonio Negri, *Declaration* (New York: Argo Navis Author Services, 2012).

28. Simon Critchley, "September 11 and the Cycle of Revenge," *The Stone* (blog), *New York Times*, September 8, 2011, http://opinionator.blogs.nytimes.com/2011/09/08/the-cycle-of-revenge/.

29. Jacques Derrida, *On Cosmopolitanism and Forgiveness* (New York: Routledge, 2005), 32.

30. Ibid., 37.

31. Brad Evans, *Liberal Terror* (Cambridge: Polity Press, 2013).

32. Leo Lowenthal, "Atomization of Man," *False Prophets: Studies in Authoritarianism* (New Brunswick, NJ: Transaction Books, 1987), 181–82.

33. Walter Benjamin, "Critique of Violence," in *Reflections: Essays, Aphorisms, Autobiographical Writings*, ed. Peter Demetz (Schocken Books: New York, 1986), 277–300.

34. Stanley Aronowitz, "Introduction," in Paulo Freire, *Pedagogy of Freedom* (Boulder, CO: Rowman and Littlefield, 1998), 7.

35. Michel Foucault, "Preface," in Gilles Deleuze and Felix Guattari, *Anti-Oedipus: Capitalism and Schizophrenia* (London: Continuum, 2003), xv.

36. Gilles Deleuze, *Desert Islands and Other Texts, 1953–1974*, ed. David Lapoujade, trans. Michael Taormina (New York: Semiotext[e], 2004), 139–40.

37. Stuart Hall, "Epilogue: Through the Prism of an Intellectual Life," in *Culture, Politics, Race, and Diaspora: The Thought of Stuart Hall*, ed. Brian Meeks (Miami: Ian Rundle Publishers, 2007), 289–90.

38. See also Giroux and Searls Giroux, *Take Back Higher Education*.

39. Jacques Rancière, *On the Shores of Politics* (London: Verso Press, 1995), 3.

40. Edward Said, *Humanism and Democratic Criticism* (New York: Columbia University Press, 2004), 50.

41. C. Wright Mills, "Culture and Politics: The Fourth Epoch," in *The Politics of Truth: Selected Writings of C. Wright Mills* (New York: Oxford University Press, 2008), 199.

42. Editors, "A Conversation with David Harvey," *Logos: A Journal of Modern Society & Culture* 5, no. 1 (2006).

Chapter Four: Universities Gone Wild

1. Elizabeth Stone, "Student Private Loan Debt Tops 1 Trillion?" *Examiner*, April 16, 2012, www.examiner.com/article/student-private-loan-debt-tops-1-trillion-dollars.

2. Stanley Aronowitz, *The Knowledge Factory: Dismantling Corporate Education and Creating True Higher Learning* (Boston: Beacon Press, 2001). See also Giroux, *The University in Chains.*

3. Anya Kamenetz, *Generation Debt* (New York: Riverhead, 2006); Alan Collinge, *The Student Loan Scam: The Most Oppressive Debt in U.S. History and How We Can Fight Back* (Boston: Beacon Press, 2009).

4. Larry Wilmore, "Newt Gingrich's Poverty Code," *The Daily Show with Jon Stewart* (video), December 13, 2011.

5. Russell Goldman, "Looking to 2012, Gingrich Strikes an Old Chord and Assails the Unemployed," *ABC News.com*, December 22, 2010, http://abcnews .go.com/Politics/2012-gingrich-strikes-chord-assails-unemployed/ story?id=12453191.

6. See, for instance, Ferguson, *Predator Nation*; John Bellamy Foster and Robert W. McChesney, *The Endless Crisis: How Monopoly-Finance Capital Produces Stagnation and Upheaval from the USA to China* (New York: Monthly Review Press, 2012).

7. Clark Kerr, "Shock Wave II: An Introduction to the Twenty-First Century," in *The Future of the City of Intellect: The Changing American University*, ed. Steven Brint (Stanford, CA: Stanford University Press, 2002), 1–19.

8. Paul Krugman, "Depression and Democracy," *New York Times*, December 12, 2011.

9. See the Centre County Grand Jury Indictment against Gerald A. Sandusky, www.freep.com/assets/freep/pdf/C4181508116.PDF, 3.

10. Tim Rohan, "Sandusky Gets 30 to 60 Years for Sexual Abuse," *New York Times*, October 9, 2012, www.nytimes.com/2012/10/10/sports/ncaafootball/penn -state-sandusky-is-sentenced-in-sex-abuse-case.html.

11. Krugman, "Depression and Democracy."

12. Associated Press, "Casey Says He Received Death Threats," *ABC Sports*, December 13, 2002, http://espn.go.com/abcsports/bcs/s/2001/0516/1200265.html.

13. Brentin Mock, "The Other Penn State Cover-Up: Death Threats Against Black Students," *Huffington Post*, November 16, 2011, www.huffingtonpost.com/2011/ 11/16/penn-state-racism_n_1098237.html.

14. "Jerry Sandusky Arrested on New Charges of Child Sex Abuse: The Former Penn State Assistant Football Coach Faces More than 50 Child Sex Abuse Charges," *Los Angeles Times*, December 7, 2011, www.latimes.com/sports/la -sp-newswire-20111208,0,265641,print.story. See also "Penn State Charges: News on the Cases against Sandusky, Curley and Schultz," *StateCollege.com*, December 20, 2011, www.statecollege.com/news/penn-state-charges-sandusky -curley-schultz/.

15. Michael Bérubé. "At Penn State, a Bitter Reckoning," *New York Times*, November 17, 2011.

16. Ibid.

17. Cary Nelson and Donna Potts, "The Dangers of a Sports Empire," *AAUP Newsroom*, November 2011, www.aaup.org/AAUP/newsroom/2011PRs/psu.htm.

18. J. Bryan Lowder, "The Danger of Joe Paterno's 'Father-Figure' Mystique," *Slate*, November 10, 2011, www.slate.com/blogs/xx_factor/2011/11/10/the_danger

_of_joe_paterno_s_father_figure_mystique.html.

19. Katherine Greenier, "From Fear to Safety: Confronting Sexual Assault and Harassment on Campuses," *RH Reality Check*, November 21, 2011, www.rhrealitycheck .org/article/2011/11/18/schools-must-protect-students-from-sexual-violence.

20. Penn State Division of Student Affairs, "Know the Facts—Rape and Sexual Assault," Penn State Center for Women Students, December 20, 2011, http://studentaffairs.psu.edu/womenscenter/awareness/rapeandassault.shtml.

21. Brent Kallest, "Fired College Band Head Warned of Hazing," *Time*, November 28, 2011, www.time.com/time/nation/article/0,8599,2100507,00.html.

22. Joe Nocera, "It's Not Just Penn State," *New York Times*, December 2, 2011.

23. Steve Kettmann, "Are We Not Man Enough?" *New York Times*, December 17, 2011.

24. Ibid.

25. Claire Potter, "The Penn State Scandal: Connect the Dots Between Child Abuse and the Sexual Assault of Women on Campus," *Chronicle of Higher Education*, November 10, 2011, http://chronicle.com/blognetwork/tenuredradical/2011/ 11/1401/.

26. Katha Pollitt, "Penn State's Patriarchal Pastimes," *The Nation*, November 16, 2011, www.thenation.com/article/164655/penn-states-patriarchal-pastimes.

27. Sophia A. McClennen,"Is There a Way to Be Good Again? How to Be a Man after the Penn State Pedophilia Scandal," *Truthout*, November 28, 2011, www.truth-out.org/there-way-be-good-again-how-be-man-after-penn-state -pedophilia-scandal/1322491679.

28. J. Bryan Lowder, "The Danger of Joe Paterno's 'Father-Figure' Mystique," *Slate*, November 10, 2011, www.slate.com/blogs/xx_factor/2011/11/10/the_danger _of_joe_paterno_s_father_figure_mystique.html.

29. Stefan Collini, "Browne's Gamble," *London Review of Books* 32, no. 21 (November 4, 2010).

30. Kathy N. Davidson, "A Plea to College Presidents: Exercise Your Moral Leadership," *Chronicle of Higher Education*, November 21, 2011, http://chronicle .com/article/A-Plea-to-College-Presidents-/129863/.

31. Goldie Blumenstyk and Jack Stripling, "Leaders' Choices Put Colleges in Uneasy Spot,"*Chronicle of Higher Education*, November 27, 2011, http://chronicle .com/article/Questionable-Decisions-Cast/129901/.

32. Jack Stripling, "Farewell Payout to Spanier Made Him Priciest President," *Chronicle of Higher Education*, May 17, 2013.

33. Juan Cole, "The Koch Brothers and the End of State Universities," *Informed Comment*, May 13, 2011, www.juancole.com/2011/05/the-koch-brothers-and -the-end-of-state-universities.html.

34. Jean Comaroff and John Comaroff, "Reflections of Youth: From the Past to the Postcolony," in *Frontiers of Capital: Ethnographic Reflections on the New Economy*, ed. Melissa S. Fisher and Greg Downey (Durham, NC: Duke University Press, 2006), 268.

35. Alex Honneth, *Pathologies of Reason*,(New York: Columbia University Press, 2009), 188.

36. Giroux, *The University in Chains.*

37. Peter Seybold, "The Struggle against Corporate Takeover of the University," *Socialism and Democracy* 22, no. 1 (March 2008): 1–11.

38. Steven Higgs, "The Corporatization of the American University," *CounterPunch*, November 21, 2011, www.counterpunch.org/2011/11/21/the-corporatization -of-the-american-university/. See also Seybold, "The Struggle against Corporate Takeover of the University."

39. Sydney University Academics, "Sydney University Academics Speak Out," *New Matilda*, December 5, 2011, http://newmatilda.com/2011/12/05/sydney -university-academics-speak-out.

40. Nick Turse, *The Complex: How the Military Invades Our Everyday Lives* (New York: Metropolitan Books, 2008). See also David H. Price, *Weaponizing Anthropology*, (Oakland, CA: AK Press, 2011).

41. Henry Giroux, *Against the Terror of Neoliberalism* (Boulder, CO: Paradigm, 2008).

42. Remarks of Louis Freeh in Conjunction with Announcement of Publication of Report Regarding the Pennsylvania State University. Community Voices, July 12, 2012, http://communityvoices.sites.post-gazette.com/index.php/news/154 -ipso-facto-pr/33663-remarks-of-louis-freeh-in-conjunction-with-announcement -of-publication-.

43. Editorial, "The Rotten Heart of Finance," Economist, July 7, 2012, www.economist.com/node/21558281.

44. Quoted in Amy Goodman, "Penn State Students Bear Brunt of NCAA Sanctions for Sandusky Cover-Up as Trustees Emerge Unscathed," *Democracy Now!*, July 24, 2012, www.democracynow.org/2012/7/24/penn_state_students_bear _brunt_of.

45. Quoted in ibid.

46. Ibid.

47. Robin Wilson, "As Students Return, Penn State Begins the Year Under a Cloud," *Chronicle of Higher Education*, September 3, 2012, http://chronicle.com/ article/Penn-State-Begins-Academic/134062/.

48. Joe Drape, "Penn State to Pay Nearly $60 Million to 26 Abuse Victims," *New York Times*, October 28, 2013, www.nytimes.com/2013/10/29/sports/ncaafootball/ penn-state-to-pay-59-7-million-to-26-sandusky-victims.html?hp.

49. Alexandra Sifferlin, "Breaking Down GlaxoSmithKline's Billion-Dollar Wrongdoing," *Time*, July 5, 2012, http://healthland.time.com/2012/07/05/breaking -down-glaxosmithklines-billion-dollar-wrongdoing/.

50. Aronowitz, *Against Schooling*, xviii.

Chapter Five: On the Urgency
for Public Intellectuals in the Academy

1. Audre Lorde, "Poetry is not a Luxury," *Sister Outsider: Essays and Speeches* (Freedom, CA: The Crossing Press, 1984), 38.

2. I have taken this idea of linking Lorde's notion of poetry to education from Martha Nell Smith, "The Humanities Are a Manifesto for the Twenty-First Century," *Liberal Education* (Winter 2011): 48–55.

3. Debra Leigh Scott, "How the American University Was Killed, in Five Easy Steps," The Homeless Adjunct Blog, August 12, 2012, http://junctrebellion .wordpress.com/2012/08/12/how-the-american-university-was-killed-in-five -easy-steps/.

4. Ferguson, *Predator Nation*, 21.

5. Nicholas Lemann, "Evening the Odds: Is There a Politics of Inequality?" *New Yorker*, April 23, 2012, www.newyorker.com/arts/critics/atlarge/2012/04/23/ 120423crat_atlarge_lemann.

6. Reihaneh Hajibeigi, "Resisting Corporate Education: Is 'Business Productivity' Coming to the University of Texas?" *Nation of Change*, June 13, 2013, www .nationofchange.org/resisting-corporate-education-business-productivity-coming -university-texas-1371133921.

7. Joseph E. Stiglitz, "The Price of Inequality," *Project Syndicate*, June 5, 2012, www.project-syndicate.org/commentary/the-price-of-inequality.

8. Ibid.

9. Ferguson, *Predator Nation*, 8

10. Ibid.

11. Andrew Gavin Marshall, "The Shocking Amount of Wealth and Power Held by 0.001% of the World Population," *AlterNet*, June 12, 2013, www.alternet.org/ economy/global-power-elite-exposed?akid=10567.40823.Q_uvw_&rd=1&src =newsletter854356&t=3.

12. Alex Honneth, *Pathologies of Reason* (New York: Columbia University Press, 2009), 188.

13. Buchheit, "Five Ugly Extremes."

14. Zygmunt Bauman, *Collatoral Damage: Social Inequalities in a Global Age* (Cambridge, UK: Polity Press, 2011), 39.

15. I have taken these figures from Paul Buchheit, "Five Facts That Put America to Shame," *Common Dreams*, May 14, 2012, www.commondreams.org/view/ 2012/05/14-0.

16. Cornelius Castoriadis, *A Society Adrift: Interviews & Debates 1974–1997*, trans. Helen Arnold (New York: Fordham University Press, 2010), 7.

17. The genealogy from anti-intellectualism in American life to the embrace of illiteracy as a virtue is analyzed in the following books: Richard Hofstadter, *Anti-Intellectualism in American Life* (New York: Vintage, 1966); Susan Jacoby, *The Age of American Unreason* (New York: Pantheon, 2008); Charles P. Piece, *Idiot America: How Stupidity Became a Virtue in the Land of the Free* (New York: Anchor Books, 2009).

18. Castoriadis, *A Society Adrift*, 8.

19. Mills, *The Politics of Truth*, 200.

20. Frank B. Wilderson III, "Introduction: Unspeakable Ethics," in *Red, White, & Black* (London, UK: Duke University Press, 2012), 2.

21. Stanley Aronowitz, "Against Schooling: Education and Social Class," in *Against*

Schooling (Boulder, CO: Paradigm, 2008), xii.

22. See most recently Kelly V. Vlahos, "Boots on Campus," *AntiWar.com*, February 26, 2013, http://original.antiwar.com/vlahos/2013/02/25/boots-on-campus/; and David H. Price, *Weaponizing Anthropology* (Oakland, CA: AK Press, 2011).

23. Kelley B. Vlahos, "Boots on Campus: Yale Flap Highlights Militarization of Academia," *Truthout*, February 27, 2013, http://truth-out.org/news/item/ 14837-boots-on-campus-yale-flap-highlights-militarization-of-academia.

24. Ibid.

25. Greg Bishop, "A Company that Runs Prisons Will Have Its Name on a Stadium," *New York Times*, February 19, 2013, www.nytimes.com/2013/02/ 20/sports/ncaafootball/a-company-that-runs-prisons-will-have-its-name-on-a -stadium.html?_r=0.

26. Dave Zirin, "Victory! The Stopping of Owlcatraz," *Common Dreams,* April 3, 2013, www.commondreams.org/view/2013/04/03.

27. Ibid.

28. Scott Travis, "GEO Withdraws Gift, Naming Rights for FAU Stadium," *South Florida Sun-Sesntinel*, April 1, 2013, www.sun-sentinel.com/news/palm-beach/ fl-fau-geo-stadium-20130401,0,6857150.story.

29. Zirin, "Victory! The Stopping of Owlcatraz."

30. Zernike, "Making College 'Relevant.'"

31. Scott Jaschik, "Making Adjuncts Temps—Literally," *Inside Higher Education*, August 9, 2010, www.insidehighered.com/news/2010/08/09/adjuncts.

32. Martha C. Nussbaum, *Not for Profit: Why Democracy Needs the Humanities* (Princeton, NJ: Princeton University Press, 2010), 142.

33. Greig de Peuter, "Universities, Intellectuals, and Multitudes: An Interview with Stuart Hall," in *Utopian Pedagogy: Radical Experiments against Neoliberal Globalization,* eds. Mark Cote, Richard J. F. Day, and Greig de Peuter (Toronto: University of Toronto Press, 2007), 111.

34. Nussbaum, *Not for Profit*.

35. On the militarization of higher education, see Giroux, *The University in Chains*. See also Philip Zwerling, ed., *The CIA on Campus: Essays on Academic Freedom and the National Security State* (Jefferson, NC: McFarland and Company, 2011); David H. Price, *Weaponizing Anthropology* (Petrolia, CA: CounterPunch, 2011).

36. Castoriadis, "Democracy as Procedure and Democracy as Regime," 5.

37. George Scialabba, *What Are Intellectuals Good For?* (Boston: Pressed Wafer, 2009) 4.

38. Toni Morrison, "How Can Values Be Taught in This University," *Michigan Quarterly Review* (Spring 2001): 278.

39. Scialabba, *What Are Intellectuals Good For?*

40. James Baldwin interview by Mel Watkins, *New York Times Book Review*, September 23, 1979, 3.

41. Zoe Williams, "The Saturday Interview: Stuart Hall," *Guardian*, February 11, 2012, www.guardian.co.uk/theguardian/2012/feb/11/saturday-interview -stuart-hall.

42. Sheldon S. Wolin, *Democracy, Inc.: Managed Democracy and the Specter of In-

verted Totalitarianism (Princeton, NJ: Princeton University Press, 2008), 43.

43. Morrison, "How Can Values Be Taught in This University," 276.

44. On this issue, see the brilliant essay by Susan Searls Giroux, "On the Civic Function of Intellectuals Today," in *Education as Civic Engagement: Toward a More Democratic Society,* eds. Gary Olson and Lynn Worsham (Boulder, CO: Paradigm Publishers, 2012), ix–xvii.

45. Martin Luther King, Jr., "The Trumpet of Conscience," in *The Essential Writings and Speeches of Martin Luther King, Jr.*, ed. James M. Washington (New York: Harper Collins, 1991), 644.

46. Arundhati Roy, *Power Politics* (Cambridge, MA: South End Press, 2001), 6.

47. de Peuter, "Universities, Intellectuals, and Multitudes," 113–14.

48. Ibid., 117.

49. Cited in Madeline Bunting, "Passion and Pessimism," *Guardian*, April 5, 2003, http:/books.guardian.co.uk/print/0,3858,4640858,00.html.

50. Irving Howe, "This Age of Conformity," *Selected Writings 1950–1990* (New York: Harcourt Brace Jovanovich, 1990), 27.

51. Giovanna Borriadori, ed., "Autoimmunity: Real and Symbolic Suicides—a Dialogue with Jacques Derrida," in *Philosophy in a Time of Terror: Dialogues with Jurgen Habermas and Jacques Derrida* (Chicago: University of Chicago Press, 2004), 121.

52. Cornelius Castoriadis, "Democracy as Procedure and Democracy as Regime," *Constellations* 4, no. 1 (1997): 10.

53. Edward Said, *Out of Place: A Memoir* (New York: Vintage, 2000), 294–99.

54. Said, *Out of Place,* 7.

55. Stephen Howe, "Edward Said: The Traveller and the Exile," *Open Democracy*, October 2, 2003, www.opendemocracy.net/articles/ViewPopUpArticle.jsp?id=10&articleId=1561.

56. Hannah Arendt, *Between Past and Future: Eight Exercises in Political Thought* (New York: Penguin, 1977), 149.

57. Edward Said, "On Defiance and Taking Positions," *Reflections on Exile and Other Essays* (Cambridge, MA: Harvard University Press, 2001), 504.

58. Edward Said, *Humanism and Democratic Criticism* (New York: Columbia University Press, 2004), 70.

59. Howe, "This Age of Conformity," 36.

60. See, especially, Christopher Newfield, *Unmaking the Public University: The Forty-Year Assault on the Middle Class* (Cambridge, MA: Harvard University Press, 2008).

61. See Henry A. Giroux, "Academic Unfreedom in America: Rethinking the University as a Democratic Public Sphere," in Edward J. Carvalho, ed., "Academic Freedom and Intellectual Activism in the Post-9/11 University," special issue of *Works and Days* 51–54 (2008–2009): 45–72. This may be the best collection yet published on intellectual activism and academic freedom.

62. Gayatri Chakravorty Spivak, "Changing Reflexes: Interview with Gayatri Chakravorty Spivak," *Works and Days* 28, no. 55/56 (2010): 8.

63. Bill Moyers, "Interview with William K. Black," *Bill Moyers Journal*, April 23,

2010, www.pbs.org/moyers/journal/04232010/transcript4.html.

64. Ibid.

65. See, especially, Hannah Arendt, *The Origins of Totalitarianism*, third edition, revised (New York: Harcourt Brace Jovanovich, 1968); and John Dewey, *Liberalism and Social Action* (New York: Prometheus Press, 1999/1935).

66. See Frederick Douglass, "West India Emancipation," speech delivered at Canandaigua, New York, August 4, 1857, in *The Life and Writings of Frederick Douglass*, vol. 2, ed. Philip S. Foner (New York: International, 1950), 437.

67. Aronowitz, "The Winter of Our Discontent," 68.

68. Jacques Derrida, "No One Is Innocent: A Discussion with Jacques About Philosophy in the Face of Terror," The Information Technology, War and Peace Project, www.watsoninstitute.org/infopeace/911/derrida_innocence.html.

69. Howe, "The Age of Conformity," 49.

Chapter Six: Days of Rage

1. I want to thank Grace Pollock, Maya Sabados, Danielle Martak, and David L. Clark for their excellent editing suggestions for this chapter.

2. For some excellent sources on the emergence of new social movements in 2011 and afterward, see Paul Mason, *Why It's Kicking Off Everywhere: The New Global Revolutions* (London: Verso, 2012); Manuel Castells, *Networks of Outrage and Hope: Social Movements in the Internet Age* (London: Polity Press, 2012); and Henry A. Giroux, *Youth in Revolt* (Boulder, CO: Paradigm, 2013).

3. David Harvey, "Is This Really the End of Neoliberalism?" *CounterPunch*, March 13–15, 2009, www.counterpunch.org/2009/03/13/is-this-really-the-end-of-neoliberalism/print.

4. Eric Cazdyn, "Bioeconomics, Culture, and Politics after Globalization," in *Cultural Autonomy: Frictions and Connections*, ed. Petra Rethmann, Imre Szeman, and William D. Coleman (Vancouver: UBC Press, 2010), 64.

5. Alain Badiou, *The Rebirth of History*, trans. Gregory Elliott (London: Verso, 2012), 12.

6. Stuart J. Murray, "The Voice of the We Yet to Come," *Canadian Journal of Communication* 37, no. 3 (2012): 495–97.

7. Bruce Campbell, "Rising Inequality, Declining Democracy," *Canadian Centre for Policy Alternatives*, December 12, 2011, www.policyalternatives.ca/publications/commentary/rising-inequality-declining-democracy.

8. Zygmunt Bauman, *This Is Not a Diary* (Cambridge: Polity Press, 2012), 103.

9. Joseph Stiglitz, *The Price of Inequality: How Today's Divided Society Endangers Our Future* (New York: W. W. Norton, 2012).

10. Some recent and important literature on this issue includes Ferguson, *Predator Nation*; Jacob Hacker and Paul Pierson, *Winner-Take-All Politics: How Washington Made the Rich Richer—and Turned Its Back on the Middle Class* (New York: Simon & Schuster, 2011); David Harvey, *The Enigma of Capital and the Crises of Capitalism* (New York: Oxford University Press, 2011); Paul Krugman,

8. Zygmunt Bauman, *This Is Not a Diary* (Cambridge: Polity Press, 2012), 103.

9. Joseph Stiglitz, *The Price of Inequality: How Today's Divided Society Endangers Our Future* (New York: W. W. Norton, 2012).

10. Some recent and important literature on this issue includes Ferguson, *Predator Nation*; Jacob Hacker and Paul Pierson, *Winner-Take-All Politics: How Washington Made the Rich Richer—and Turned Its Back on the Middle Class* (New York: Simon & Schuster, 2011); David Harvey, *The Enigma of Capital and the Crises of Capitalism* (New York: Oxford University Press, 2011); Paul Krugman, *End This Depression Now!* (New York: W. W. Norton, 2012); Madrick, *Age of Greed*; Stiglitz, *The Price of Inequality*; and Richard D. Wolff and David Barsamian, *Occupy the Economy: Challenging Capitalism* (San Francisco: City Lights Open Media, 2012).

11. Ferguson, *Predator Nation*, 2.

12. Ibid.

13. Zygmunt Bauman, *Living on Borrowed Time: Conversations with Citlali Rovirosa-Madrazo* (Cambridge: Polity, 2010), 68.

14. Bauman, *Wasted Lives*, 76.

15. Ibid.

16. I have borrowed the term "zones of social abandonment" from João Biehl, *Vita: Life in a Zone of Social Abandonment* (Los Angeles and Berkeley: University of California Press, 2005); see also Giroux, *Disposable Youth* and Alexander, *The New Jim Crow*.

17. Biehl, *Vita*, 14.

18. Etienne Balibar, *We, the People of Europe? Reflections on Transnational Citizenship* (Princeton, NJ: Princeton University Press, 2004), 128.

19. Editorial, "Global Youth Jobless Rates Still High," *Hamilton Spectator*, May 23, 2012, A17.

20. Jordan Weissmann, "53% of Recent College Grads Are Jobless or Underemployed–How?" *Atlantic*, April 23, 2012, www.theatlantic.com/business/archive/2012/04/53-of-recent-college-grads-are-jobless-or-underemployed-how/256237/.

21. Bauman, *Liquid Modernity*.

22. See Zygmunt Bauman, *Collateral Damage: Social Inequalities in a Global Age* (Cambridge: Polity, 2011); Stiglitz, *The Price of Inequality*; Lynn Parramore, "Exclusive Interview: Joseph Stiglitz Sees Terrifying Future for America If We Don't Reverse Inequality," *AlterNet*, June 24, 2012, www.alternet.org/economy/155918/exclusive_interview%3A_joseph_stiglitz_sees_terrifying_future_for_america_if_we_don%27t_reverse_inequality; Buchheit, "Five Facts That Put America to Shame"; and Peter Elderman, *So Rich, So Poor: Why It's So Hard to End Poverty in America* (New York: New Press, 2012).

23. Bauman, *Living on Borrowed Time*, 39–40.

24. See the brilliant work of Angela Davis on the prison-industrial complex and the emerging punishing state in the United States, especially *Are Prisons Obsolete?*

25. Report by National Association of Consumer Bankruptcy Attorneys (NACBA), *The Student Loan "Debt Bomb": America's Next Mortgage-Style Economic Crisis*,

February 7, 2012, http://nacba.org/Portals/0/Documents/Student%20Loan%20Debt/020712%20NACBA%20student%20loan%20debt%20report.pdf; Andy Kroll, "Shut Out: How the Cost of Higher Education Is Dividing Our Country," *Truthout*, April 2, 2012, http://archive.truthout.org/040209T; and Collin Harris, "The Student Debt Bubble: Interview with Alan Nasser," *ZSpace*, December 18, 2011, www.zcommunications.org/the-student-debt-bubble-interview-with-alan-nasser-by-collin-harris.

26. Jonathan Simon, *Governing Through Crime: How the War on Crime Transformed American Democracy and Created a Culture of Fear* (New York: Oxford University Press, 2007). See also Giroux, *Youth in a Suspect Society.*

27. Martin Lukacs, "Quebec Student Protests Mark 'Maple Spring' in Canada," *Guardian*, May 2, 2012, www.guardian.co.uk/commentisfree/cifamerica/2012/may/02/quebec-student-protest-canada.

28. David Camfield, "Quebec's "Red Square" Movement: The Story So Far," *Socialist Project*, no. 680, August 13, 2012, www.socialistproject.ca/bullet/680.php. Since the "Quiet Revolution" of the 1960s, Quebec has been developing its own distinct political culture. A full understanding of the conditions of possibility that have produced this distinct contemporary student movement would require its contextualization within this history. This is beyond the scope of this chapter.

29. Mark Cardwell, "Quebec Students Begin Strike Action," *University Affairs*, February 21, 2012, www.universityaffairs.ca/quebec-students-begin-strike-action.aspx.

30. Lukacs, "Quebec Student Protests Mark 'Maple Spring.'"

31. Peter Hallward, "The Threat of Quebec's Good Example," *Socialist Project*, no. 647, June 6, 2012, www.socialistproject.ca/bullet/647.php.

32. Andrew Gavin Marshall, "10 Things You Should Know About the Quebec Student Movement," *CounterPunch*, May 23, 2012, www.counterpunch.org/2012/05/23/10-things-you-should-know-about-the-quebec-student-movement/. For a brilliant commentary on the history of debt and its effect on the economy, see David Graeber, *Debt: The First 5,000 Years* (Brooklyn, NY: Melville House Publishing, 2011).

33. Randy Boyagoda, "For Student Protesters in Quebec, It's About More Than Tuition," *Chronicle of Higher Education*, June 3, 2012, http://chronicle.com/article/For-Student-Protesters-Its/132089/.

34. Malav Kanuga, "The Quebec Student Strike Celebrates 100th Day," *In These Times*, May 23, 2012, http://inthesetimes.com/uprising/entry/13252/the_quebec_student_strike_celebrates_its_100th_day/.

35. Alain Badiou cited in John Van Houdt, "The Crisis of Negation: An Interview with Alain Badiou," *Continent* 1, no. 4 (2011): 234.

36. Lukacs, "Quebec Student Protests Mark 'Maple Spring.'"

37. Ibid.

38. Ibid.

39. Erika Shaker, "Don't Kid Yourself: We All Pay for the Defunding of Higher Education," *Common Dreams*, May 12, 2012, www.commondreams.org/view/2012/05/12-3.

40. Ibid.

41. Pierre Graveline, "The Strange Disappearance of the Canadian State from the Debate on the Student Strike," *Canadian Dimension*, June 17, 2012, http://canadiandimension.com/articles/4770/.

42. Ibid.

43. CBC News, "Fighter Jet Plan 'Reset' as F-35 Costs Soar," *CBC News*, December 12, 2012, www.cbc.ca/news/canada/story/2012/12/12/pol-f-35-kpmg-report-release.html.

44. For an interesting commentary on this issue, see Shaker, "Don't Kid Yourself." See also W. Craig Riddell, "The Social Benefits of Education: New Evidence on an Old Question," paper prepared for the conference "Taking Public Universities Seriously," University of Toronto, December 3-4, 2004, www.utoronto.ca/president/04conference/downloads/Riddell.pdf.

45. Roger Annis, "Update on Quebec Student Strike: Summer of Protest Ahead," *rabble.ca*, June 4, 2012, http://rabble.ca/blogs/bloggers/campus-notes/2012/06/update-quebec-student-strike-summer-protest-ahead.

46. J. F. Conway, "Quebec: Making War on Our Children," *Socialist Project*, e-Bulletin no. 651, June 10, 2012, www.socialistproject.ca/bullet/651.php.

47. Margaret Wente, "Quebec's University Students Are in for a Shock," *Globe and Mail*, May 1, 2012, http://www.theglobeandmail.com/commentary/quebecs-university-students-are-in-for-a-shock/article4104304/.

48. Ibid.

49. Margaret Wente, "Young Men Without Work," *Globe and Mail*, November 11, 2011, www.theglobeandmail.com/commentary/young-men-without-work/article4183419/.

50. Badiou, *The Rebirth of History*, 18–19.

51. Roger Annis, "Quebec Students Mobilize Against Draconian Law Aimed at Breaking Four-Month Strike," *Socialist Project*, e-Bulletin no. 637, May 19, 2012, www.socialistproject.ca/bullet/637.php. Also see Annis, "Update on Quebec Student Strike."

52. Michael Den Tandt, "It's Time for Tough Treatment of Quebec Student Strikers," *National Post*, May 12, 2012, http://fullcomment.nationalpost.com/2012/05/11/michael-den-tandt-its-time-for-tough-treatment-of-quebec-student-strikers/.

53. For an account of the Bernard Guay letter, see Marshall, "10 Things You Should Know About the Quebec Student Movement." The original letter is no longer posted on Le Soleil's website, but can be downloaded here: http://jhroy.ca/Article-Bernard-Guay.pdf.

54. Ibid.

55. Frank Bruni, "Individualism in Overdrive," *New York Times*, July 17, 2012.

56. Jacques Rancière, *Hatred of Democracy* (London: Verso, 2006).

57. For a critique and summary of the bill, see Annis, "Quebec Students Mobilize"; Common Dreams Staff, "'Biggest Act of Civil Disobedience in Canadian History,'" *Common Dreams*, May 23, 2012, www.commondreams.org/headline/2012/05/23-5; Linda Gyulai, "Bill 78 Contravenes Charter, Lawyer Says," *Montreal Gazette*, May 23, 2012, www.montrealgazette.com/business/Bill+contravenes+charter+lawyer+says/6662877/story.html; Laurence Bherer and Pascale Dufour,

"Our Not-So-Friendly Northern Neighbor," *New York Times*, May 23, 2012, A31; and Ian Austen, "Emergency Law Broadens Canada's Sympathy for Quebec Protests," *New York Times*, June 5, 2012, A4.

58. Hallward, "The Threat of Quebec's Good Example."

59. CBC News, "Montreal Police Cagey about Enforcing Bill 78," *CBC News*, August 11, 2012, www.cbc.ca/news/canada/montreal/story/2012/08/11/montreal -police-bill-78-12-enforcement.html.

60. See "Manifesto for a Maple Spring," *rabble.ca*, April 26, 2012, http:// rabble.ca/news/2012/04/quebecs-spring-manifesto-printemps-%C3%A9rable. See also "The CLASSE Manifesto: Share Our Future," *rabble.ca*, July 12, 2012, http://rabble.ca/taxonomy/term/20878.

61. "Manifesto for a Maple Spring."

62. "The CLASSE Manifesto: Share Our Future."

63. Badiou, *The Rebirth of History*.

64. Slavoj Žižek, "Occupy Wall Street: What Is to Be Done Next?" *Guardian*, April 24, 2012, www.guardian.co.uk/commentisfree/cifamerica/2012/apr/24/occupy -wall-street-what-is-to-be-done-next.

65. Students in Chile followed a similar path politically and also have taken to the streets over the neoliberalization of higher education. Students have occupied schools and taken to the streets en masse to protest Chile's president, Sebastián Piñera, who has "defined education as a consumer good." In opposition to Piñera's business-oriented model of education as a consumer product, the students have fiercely argued "that education is a basic right." The government has held firm and the student protests "have been marked by severe brutality, including shooting the students in the face with paintballs and indiscriminately beating them with truncheons [and] during the removal of students from the prestigious Carmela Carvajal school police dragged girls out by their hair." All of these student- and youth-led movements view education as a basic right and central to any viable notion of educational reform and as crucial to the struggle for democracy itself. Jonathan Franklin, "The 18-Year-Old Voice of Chile's Nationwide Student Uprising Moisés Paredes Speaks for a Movement Which Has Defied Police Brutality to Put Education Reform High on the Election Agenda," *Guardian*, June 28, 2013, www.theguardian.com/world/2013/jun/28/chile -student-uprising-election.

66. Hallward, "The Threat of Quebec's Good Example."

67. Sarah Jaffe, "Red Squares Everywhere: Will Quebec's Maple Spring Come South?" *In These Times*, July 9, 2012, www.inthesetimes.com/article/13470/ red_squares_everywhere.

68. Badiou, *The Rebirth of History*, 56.

69. Canadian Press, "It's Official: Quebec's Tuition Hikes Are History," *Macleans.ca*, September 20, 2012, http://oncampus.macleans.ca/education/2012/09/20/ its-official-quebec-tuition-hikes-are-history/.

70. CBC News, "Quebec Education Summit Ends without Consensus," *CBC News*, February, 2013, www.cbc.ca/news/canada/montreal/story/2013/02/26/montreal -quebec-education-summit-student-fee-protest.html.

71. Jeffrey Hutchings, "Harper Government's Muzzling of Scientists a Mark of Shame for Canada," *Toronto Star*, March 15, 2013, www.thestar.com/opinion/commentary/2013/03/15/harper_governments_muzzling_of_scientists_a_mark_of_shame_for_canada.html.

72. Eric Pineault, "Message from Quebec's Student Movement: Austerity Can Be Fought," *rabble.ca*, May 4, 2012, http://rabble.ca/blogs/bloggers/progressive-economics-forum/2012/05/message-qu%C3%A9becs-student-movement-austerity-can-be.

73. *Class War University*, "Could Students in the US Pull Off a Strike Like in Montreal? An Interview with Marianne Garneau," August 21, 2012, http://classwaru.org/2012/08/31/could-students-in-the-us-pull-off-a-strike-like-in-montreal/. Garneau contrasts the potential of an emerging democratic movement with the traditional representation of student interests by student associations that rely on university administrations to collect and hand them their dues. On business unionism in the context of public education in the United States, see Lois Weiner, *The Future of Our Schools: Teacher Unions and Social Justice* (Chicago: Haymarket, 2012). Weiner argues that teacher unions should not only challenge neoliberal reforms and the corporate assault on public education but also work with other organizations as part of a larger social movement rooted in matters of equity and social justice.

74. Scott Jaschik, "Students or Employees?" *Inside Higher Ed*, July 24, 2012, www.insidehighered.com/news/2012/07/24/organized-labor-and-higher-education-line-opposite-sides-grad-union-issue. NYU, other private universities, and the American Council on Education insist that graduate students are students who are assessed based on academic standards, rather than employees assessed on labor standards, and therefore are not entitled to collective bargaining. Similarly, Brown University argued against reversing a landmark decision in 2004 that prohibited the unionization of graduate students. A brief in favor of student unionization submitted by the largest federation of labor organizations in the United States, the AFL-CIO, was backed by the American Association of University Professors, the American Federation of Teachers, and the National Education Association. On the same issue, see also Peter Schmidt, "College Leaders and Labor Organizers Spar over Possible Graduate Student Unionization," *Chronicle of Higher Education*, July 24, 2012, http://chronicle.com/article/College-LeadersLabor/133119/.

75. Ibid.

76. See, for example, "Dispatches from the US Student Movement: March 1," *Nation*, March 1, 2013, www.thenation.com/blog/173144/dispatches-us-student-movement-march-1.

77. Zachary A. Bell, "Why Don't American Students Strike?" *Nation*, August 12, 2012, http://www.thenation.com/blog/169378/why-dont-american-students-strike.

78. See, for example, Jasper Conner, *Towards a New Student Unionism*, www.lizardelement.com/unionism/unionisminsidewebread.pdf. See also Biola Jeje and Isabelle Nastasia, "Student Activism, Reborn," *Salon*, May 21, 2012, www.salon.com/2012/05/21/student_activism_reborn/.

79. Bell, "Why Don't American Students Strike?" See also Isabelle Nastasia and Biola Jeje, "New York Students Speak on International Protests and Student Power in the U.S.," *Student Voice*, August 18, 2012, www.stuvoice.org/2012/08/18/two-student-organizers-speak-on-internationac-protests-and-student-power-in-the-u-s/.

80. "Dispatches from the US Student Movement," *Nation*, January 18, 2013, www.thenation.com/blog/172303/dispatches-us-student-movement.

81. Kathryn Seidewitz, "What Comes First—Student Issues or Student Power?" *Waging Nonviolence*, February 13, 2013, http://wagingnonviolence.org/feature/what-comes-first-student-issues-or-student-power-2-2/.

82. Kathryn Seidewitz, "Where Is the U.S. Student Movement? Ohio Wants to Know," *Waging Nonviolence*, December 17, 2012, http://wagingnonviolence.org/feature/where-is-the-student-movement-ohio-wants-to-know/.

83. "Dispatches from the US Student Movement," *Nation*, January 18, 2013.

84. Seidewitz, "Where Is the U.S. Student Movement?"

85. Chris Hedges, "Northern Light," *TruthDig*, June 3, 2012, www.truthdig.com/report/item/northern_light_20120603.

Chapter Seven: Democracy Unsettled

1. Katha Pollitt, "Backlash Spectacular," *Nation*, May 26, 2008, www.thenation.com/article/backlash-spectacular.

INDEX

"Passim" (literally "scattered") indicates intermittent discussion of a topic over a cluster of pages.

About the Author

SUSAN SEARLS GIROUX

Henry A. Giroux currently holds the Global TV Network Chair Professorship at McMaster University in the English and Cultural Studies Department and a Distinguished Visiting Professorship at Ryerson University. His most recent books include *Youth in Revolt: Reclaiming a Democratic Future* (Paradigm, 2013) and *America's Educational Deficit and the War on Youth* (Monthly Review Press, 2013).

OLD AGE IS NOT FOR SISSIES

OLD AGE IS NOT FOR SISSIES

Jocelyn Reichel

Illustrated by
Martha Reichel Hekman

MOODY PRESS

CHICAGO

© 1976, 1981 by
THE MOODY BIBLE INSTITUTE
OF CHICAGO
Revised Edition

Reichel, Jocelyn.
    Old age is not for sissies.

    Previously published as: We're traveling light.
c1976.
    1. Aged—United States—Anecdotes, facetiae,
satire, etc. I. Title.
HQ1064.U6R4   1981   305.2'6'0973   81–11003
ISBN 0-8024-9311-4   AACR2

Printed in the United States of America

Contents

1

Old Age Is Not for Sissies

I'M SO GLAD I can't take it with me when I shuffle off this
mortal coil. I'm so relieved that there will be no luggage to
pack, no effects to crate, no shopping bags to stuff. Because if it
were so, I might never get to heaven; and if I did, I might never
make it through the turnstyle—for I happen to be an
"eventuality" packer. I toss in boots and parkas for a trip to
Phoenix and snakebite remedy and suntan oil for a weekend in
New York City. My put-upon husband is so intimidated by the
mountain of baggage that accompanies us on every trip that he
feels it necessary to explain to the train conductors, the
cabbies, and the airline clerks, "My wife doesn't want to get
caught away from home without the kitchen sink!"

I have tried to reform, believe me. Especially since my
husband's third herniorraphy. On the eve of a trip, I cull, I
weed, I determine to do without; but my insecurity invariably
triumphs, and in go the longies and the seersucker suit, the
vaporizer and the insect spray, the books and the Scrabble
board.

"You call that a suitcase?" Everett asked me on one
occasion, abandoning his own Spartan packing to discourage
my enthusiasm. He poked around the weekender that I had
just dragged down from a closet shelf, sniffed in exasperation
at the first aid kit, and shook his head disgustedly at the family

"This time we are traveling light," Everett warned.

photograph album. He cued me again. "You call that a suitcase?"

"Well, what do *YOU* call it?" I countered, bristling and ready to defend my *semper paratus* philosophy right down to the three boxes of animal crackers for the grandchildren.

"Ha!" he snorted derisively. "It's not a *suit*case. It's an *in*case!"

Overload was never a problem for concern when the children were growing up. Granted, even on a short jaunt between Chicago and Milwaukee we managed to look like a royal entourage embarking on the first leg of an African safari; but since our four children did most of the toting, my idiosyncrasy was indulged. However, now that our offspring are long gone and far away, and my husband's patience, along with his strength, has diminished with the years, I try, more resolutely than ever before, to think small. I imagined I was succeeding until we made a trip to Quebec last year to spend Christmas with our oldest daughter's family.

The night before our departure Everett wagged a finger under my nose. "This time we are traveling light!"

I nodded, mentally shifting clothing priorities—an extra dress for me, one less shirt for him.

"Look," he continued, taking hold of my wrists, "we have only four hands between the two of us. So that means no more than four bags—and that includes that miniature Gladstone you call a purse."

I agreed with alacrity.

He was not convinced. "None of this tuck-it-under-your-arm, last-minute, can't-do-without-it merchandise," he warned.

I was with him 100 percent, I assured him. After all, we had three train connections to make in the twenty-five-hour journey, and no baggage accommodations along the way.

9

"We will take only what we can carry," I promised.

That was not enough for Everett. "In our hands," he amended.

It is amazing how much one can carry in one's hands. There we were, at 5:00 the next morning, sitting on a bench in Union Station, flushed, breathless, and a little dismayed; we two old-enough-to-know-better grandparents were barricaded behind enough baggage to warm the hearts of a half-dozen redcaps. But redcaps were no more, I reminded myself. It was the two of us against a self-service system.

I cast a covert glance at Everett. *How could I have done this to him?* I worried.

His expression was bleak and full of self-reproach. *How could I have let you do this to me?* he telegraphed back.

A sweat-shirted, paunchy janitor shuffled past us, wearing bedroom slippers and pushing a longhandled broom. He looked at our luggage, at us, back at our luggage, shook his head, and moved on, in obvious bewilderment. I couldn't blame him. At our feet were two pullman cases, a bulging garment bag, a train case, a rope-tied carton containing Christmas presents for the grandchildren, two pairs of skis, and a cane. The cane was an unpremeditated addition; in the hectic hours of shopping and packing and tidying our apartment I had reactivated a dormant spur on my left foot. The self-reproach was almost as painful as the injury. I felt an apology was in order.

"I'm sorry about my heel acting up," I tendered.

Everett didn't bother to answer; he was too busy eating his heart out watching a carefree couple walk by with only two pieces of luggage between them.

"You know," I continued, "you could go home and get the car. We can drive to Quebec in the same time the train trip takes."

10

"And what about your knees?" he reminded me, referring to the limited confines of our compact car and what we call my "migrating" arthritis, one of the pesty concomitants of middle age that I am learning to live with "in spite of." Two or three hours on the road and I am beating a mad tattoo on the dashboard.

My burdened conscience drove me to make one more sacrificial suggestion. "We can call the whole trip off. It's not too late."

"Don't be foolish," he replied. "We reached the point of no return when I tipped the cab driver."

I was relieved, now that I had shifted the responsibility from my shoulders to Everett's. I sat back and decided to think positively, to tally my blessings. I couldn't get past (a) by this time tomorrow we'd be six hours from our destination and (b) how good it would be to see the grandchildren. Canned Christmas carols began to blare at us from speakers hidden behind the marbled columns. My thoughts slowed to a halt, and I attempted to restore communications.

"What are you thinking about?" I asked. Thirty years of married life have taught me that that is the most unproductive dead-end question a woman can put to her spouse; but in moments of desperation I forget.

"Nothing," Everett responded.

The sleepy janitor made a second pass in our vicinity, giving us another heavy-lidded once-over.

"Well, then, what do you suppose *he's* thinking?"

"He's probably of the opinion that whatever it is you broke, it serves you right, a woman your age out skiing when you should be home taking care of the housework."

"He's right," I said, feeling my age and pains and thinking of the obstacle course we had to run in the next twenty-five

11

hours. "I should be home in bed instead of gallivanting across the continent."

"You're suffering from 'packer's fatigue,'" Everett diagnosed. "Happens every trip. I'll take a walk over to the cafeteria and get us a snack. You'll feel better after you eat."

"Yes," I said, "comfort me with Coke and a doughnut."

"I'll do more than that," he replied. "I'll give you some food for thought. 'Old age is not for sissies!' Remember?"

I propped my aching foot on the train case and reflected on our motto. It wasn't a spiritual one, not even the least bit inspirational. It was a statement of fact that we had picked up somewhere in our travels—a truism that often makes me wonder whatever became of "Grow old along with me; the best is yet to be."

"Old age is not for sissies" is an adage that Everett saves for moments of crisis and accomplishment; for example, when I took and passed my driving test at the age of forty-eight; when I learned to ride a ten-speed bike at forty-nine; when I took up cross-country skiing at fifty; and when I swam for the first time at fifty-one. Getting to Quebec by common carrier could not compare with any of the foregoing; it was not all that much of a challenge. I told him so when he returned with our snacks.

He thought it over, took a quick inventory, and pronounced: "Getting there, no. Intact, yes."

Well, we got there all right. There were helping hands along the way, including the Detroit native who warned us, "The cabbies will rob you!" and persuaded us that it would be wiser to take a bus to the train depot in Windsor. Actually, there were three buses—"even change only" on two of them—and it was the height of the rush hour. Being "ripped off" by a cab driver would have been a kinder fate.

In Toronto we had time between trains to revive our spirits

with cheeseburgers, and by Montreal we had developed a sort of aplomb—we knew who would carry what. When we detrained at Ste. Foy and hugged our suddenly shy grandchildren, we were not only intact, but we had also added a box of cookies picked up somewhere along the way.

"Which proves," I said to Everett that night as we relaxed in our room in a two-hundred-year-old pension in Quebec's Old Town, "that where the spirit is willing, it doesn't make any difference what condition the flesh is in."

"Precisely what I have been telling you," he agreed. "Old age is not for sissies."

I sat in the deep window seat and looked out across the snow-covered park at the imposing Chateau Frontenac, looming like an enchanted castle with its hundreds of illuminated dormers. I expected momentarily to see a cabriolet roll through the medieval archway and to hear the clop of hoofs on the cobblestone courtyard

I was tired but impatient for tomorrow. Our daughter and son-in-law, on vacation from their studies at Laval University, would be taking us sightseeing. They were missionaries with Wycliffe Bible Translators; their ultimate goal was to work with the Montagnais Indians in the northern part of the province of Quebec, transcribing the Scriptures into the native tongue. As "landed immigrants," Martha and Don were required to enroll in an intensive study of the French language. Four-year-old Phyllis and the two-year-old twins, Nathaniel and Benjamin, cared for during the day by a gracious French woman who spoke no English, were rapidly becoming bilingual.

I began to feel the cold probing my bones as I leaned against the windowpane. A few feet from our hotel was the promenade that overlooked the St. Lawrence, and I could hear the faint

13

sound of the whistles as the car ferries passed in mid-channel.

"Tomorrow we must take a ride on that ferry," I said turning to Everett.

He didn't answer; he was sound asleep. Poor guy! It had been a strenuous journey. Come to think of it, I was exhausted too. Now, where did I—? In which suitcase? Or was it in the bottom of the garment bag that I had packed my pajamas? I sighed and began my search.

2

Ein, Zwei, Drei, Spiel!

ONCE UPON A TIME I chuckled at the cartoons that depict the bored husband accompanying his wife to the opera. In those humorous drawings it is always evident that the husband does not share his wife's enthusiasm for music. The "little man" is usually engaged in some devilish trick that will upset the equilibrium of a hefty Valkyrie or disconcert a helmeted Tristan in the middle of a rapturous duet with Isolde.

Now that I have "passed through the waters," I find the theme of those cartoons not at all funny. My sympathy no longer lies with the mischievous husband but with the soon-to-be-embarrassed wife. Let me explain.

Somewhere in my pre-engaged state I must have read a book, or perused an article, or dallied in a daydream that left me with the conviction that in order to achieve a happy marriage both partners must share the same interests, think the same thoughts, enjoy the same foods, and vote the same party. Later, therefore, when I became engaged, it was a matter of real concern to me when I discovered that my fiancé did not share my taste in music. Everett had been brought up on "Casey Jones," "Big Rock Candy Mountain," and "Jatta," whereas I had been nurtured on symphonic concerts, piano and violin lessons, and daily exposure to an aunt who was a

15

concert pianist. It was clear that the only musical selection on which Everett and I could reach any agreement was a certain tune from Lohengrin.

My job was cut out for me; the challenge was plain. Some women would marry a drunkard hoping to reform him. I would marry a musical illiterate and transform him into a Milton Cross. What I neglected to take into consideration was my fiance's origin—the mountains of Pennsylvania. Perhaps it's subsisting on a steady diet of pork shanks and sauerkraut, or growing up in the shadow of hex-marked barns, but whatever—a Dutchman of the Pennsylvania class is set in a stubborn mold.

I began—and ended—my first campaign on a Saturday night. Taking my brand-new husband to a Grant Park concert, I relied heavily on the cool lake breeze and the glow of the setting sun to provide a seductive atmosphere. When he held my hand snugly in his, my confidence soared. For thirty minutes he endured Sibelius and swatted mosquitoes with his free hand. Then, in the second movement of a Mendelssohn concerto, he bolted. And dragged me with him.

"That's it," he declared on the way home. "My first—and last—concert."

I was too unhappy to answer. For a brief moment I entertained visions of poetic justice. I would leave him and run away with a bald-headed bassoonist. On second thought, I would not leave him. I would stay and raise a string quartet! We declared a truce that August evening, but I resolved never to stop trying, and he promised to continue resisting.

My trying began with saving enough to buy a dilapidated old upright, and as the years went by, seeking out teachers who would give me a special rate, three children for the price of two, for example. Everett's resisting consisted mainly of never

16

going to piano recitals and switching to the afternoon shift so that he wasn't home for practice sessions. There were times when I envied his independent spirit.

We maintained this stand-off position for years, and finally I gained a minor victory. Our children were to appear in a piano recital, and I was too ill to attend. Everett would have to go in my place. I commiserated with him, knowing he would be miserable. I could see him squirming through "Poupee Valsante;" sighing heavily during "The Happy Peasant;" walking out, perhaps, in the middle of "Marche Militaire." I assured him he would never have to go through such an ordeal again.

When he returned three hours later, looking none the worse for wear, he brushed aside my condolences with "It wasn't bad at all. In fact, I kind of enjoyed it."

That episode was not the beginning of the "Golden Age of Music" in our household, however; Everett had had what is known in medical circles as a "temporary remission." He returned to normal the next day. That is, he came home from work, turned off the stereo, and then kissed me.

Oh, there is some music that Everett will sit still for. But, as much as I love them, I can't spend the rest of my life listening only to George Beverly Shea and Helen Barth. I need a bit of Chopin and Mozart and Strauss interspersed.

"You are deprived," I sympathized. "You are missing so much that is lovely."

"Can I help it if I was born tone-deaf?" he defended himself.

And he was. It is most evident at church services in the congregational singing. Everett does not let his congenital handicap get in the way of his enthusiasm. In self-defense I hold my own hymnal and keep a safe distance. There was a time when, if he strayed too far off-key, I closed ranks and

17

elbowed him in the ribs. He used to pay attention to my nudge and soft-pedal the fortissimo somewhat. And then one night a few years ago, a visitor in our church, a woman in the pew immediately in front of ours, turned to him at the close of the service and said, "My, I enjoyed listening to you sing! You must be a professional."

We both swung around to see if she was speaking to someone behind us, but no, this positive thinker was addressing Everett.

Do-gooder, I thought. *There'll be no living with him from now on.*

And there hasn't been. He sings with even less inhibition and littler accuracy. The volume has increased and so has the cocksureness. He lives in hope that the miracle will recur, that one of these days another tone-deaf talent scout will turn to him and say, "What a voice! You must have had professional training!" He is even wondering aloud if all these years it hasn't been his wife who has the faulty perception, instead of he.

Ah, well, a happy married life is one of compromise. I continue to accompany Everett to church, and he has made it possible for me to have music whenever I want. He bought me a set of headphones to plug into my stereo! "There is one drawback, though," I told him. "I have to stay put once I'm plugged in."

He gave the problem considerable thought and came up with a solution. He wears the earphones—the plug in his pocket— and is insulated from the sound of music. Also from the sound of my voice. He is twice-blest, he says, ducking as I pretend to throw a Van Cliburn concerto in his direction.

"You must be a professional!"

3

This One You Can Keep

I DIDN'T CRY at my daughter's wedding. It wasn't for lack of hanky that I held back the tears. My family had seen to it that I was provided with everything from absorbent tissues to something that resembled a miniature monogrammed tablecloth. They know well my propensity for tears. Anyone who watches the Waltons each week with a box of Kleenex in her lap could be expected to shed buckets at the nuptials of her firstborn.

But I didn't. I was too busy repressing a grin. Too jubilant to shed a tear. Doesn't the Bible say that there is a time for everything? A time to weep and a time to laugh? To mourn and to dance? Well, Martha's wedding day was no time for weeping or wailing. It was a time to kick up one's heels!

Why was I so indecently exuberant? Had I been in despair that no one would pop the question? Hardly. Martha takes after the women in my husband's family. She's a Janet Lynn, a Dresden figurine of a girl, who never has to open a door or stand on a crowded bus or wait her turn in line.

No, we never worried about Martha's being overlooked. What did concern us was the possibility that Martha might overlook Mr. Right. You see, our young daughter suffered from both a total lack of discrimination and an inordinate compassion for the weak and helpless—excellent qualifications for the mission field or a life of social service but not for the selecting of one's life companion.

We had been aware of her handicap for a long time. Before Martha was five years old, she was in the habit, as it were, of being followed home by stray dogs and undernourished kittens. When she was only seven, her bedroom, which I vainly attempted to keep beruffled and feminine, had become an aviary filled with orphaned sparrows and crippled robins.

We sent her to camp when she was eight years old, and she returned home with sun-bleached tresses, a peeling nose, and a surprise—a collection of Mason jars with perforated lids, containing specimens from an exciting new world—amphibia.

She hammered open her piggy bank at the age of nine to buy a fullgrown garter snake from a classmate with a prejudiced parent—more prejudiced than I, apparently.

By the time she was ten, Martha's reputation had spread to such proportions that her Dad considered building a night depository on our rear porch. All the family was in favor and voted "aye," with one exception. I was still trembling from an encounter with our daughter's latest boarder, a female opossum with a pouch full of young and a vicious snarl.

"She won't hurt you, Mom," Martha insisted, coaxing the protesting creature back into her cage, a temporary shelter until we could take her back to the woods from which she had strayed. Martha and her brother had rescued the animal from some juvenile tormentors.

"We have no one to blame but ourselves," Everett admitted, the day our daughter returned from a school picnic with a moribund bat in her lunchbox. "If we don't start discouraging her, we'll wake up some morning to find ourselves dead of rabies or tularemia."

It was our fault, all right. I suppose it began with my determination that none of our children would grow up with the same irrational fears about animals that I had acquired. Since the children weren't liable to meet anything but the usual cats, dogs, and city birds in our northwest side neighborhood, I encouraged importation and for the most part was able to hide my revulsion as the steady stream of exotic and under-the-rock creatures came to share our bed and board.

There was Jerry the white rat, for example. He may have been a beauty, as the whole family insisted, but I could not forgive him his tail. Martha soon learned that Mommy did not appreciate having him dumped into her lap as a surprise nor smuggled under the bed clothes as a foot warmer and that there wasn't anything their Uncle Pete would like more for a birthday present than Jerry the rat.

The hamsters were a consolation present to make up for the loss of the rat. They were irresistible; they kept us awake all night; and after they had lived out their normal in-captivity life span (which means they eventually disappeared into the woodwork), they were not replaced. Unless the white mouse that Everett brought home from work could be called a replacement.

Everett had rescued the mouse, an escapee from a Railway Express shipment, on the eve of our vacation trip east. We would be traveling by train, and the mouse presented a problem. Martha pleaded, promised, and prevailed. Her dad sat up half the night fashioning a traveling cage out of a wooden cheese box. Doing what came naturally, the mouse began gnawing at his cell just outside of Gary, Indiana, and poked his whiskered head through the tiny aperture as we pulled into Detroit. Martha caught him before he could trigger a stampede in the passenger coach.

It was in Philadelphia that our five-year-old got her first glimpse of genuine hysteria. She walked into our hostess's living room, mouse in hand, eager to introduce her pet to the gathering. A visiting relative, a plump matron about fifty, took one look at the mouse and lost all control. Martha stood there, running her pet from one hand to the other, wondering what had got into the funny lady, who kept screaming from her unsteady perch on the sofa, "Take it away! Oh, please take it away!"

I shared Martha's amazement. Antipathy towards some animals I can readily understand, but how a grown woman could give way to such frenetic behavior, merely at the sight of a mouse—and a white mouse, at that—was beyond my comprehension.

That is, until four years later when I was "tabled" by a garter snake. Martha, whose snake it was, Tom, and Debby were in school. Two-year-old Joanna, clad only in diapers that warm morning, was playing contentedly on the floor when the creaking of the dining room table attracted her attention. She looked up from the block tower she was constructing. There sat her mother, atop the table, waving her arms and trying to speak. Joanna was not so much alarmed as she was curious at the strange perspective.

"Whatamatta?" she lisped.

I pointed to the corner of the room where Martha's twenty-inch serpent was awkwardly propelling itself across the waxed linoleum.

"Uh-huh," she acknowledged. "'nake." And she resumed her construction work.

I took a measure of courage from her unconcern and assessed the situation. I could sit on the table until noon when the children came home for lunch, but that was three hours

24

"Take it away! Oh, please take it away!"

away. In the meantime the telephone might ring, a neighbor might knock, and Joanna would certainly need some attention. Besides, I had no assurance that the snake, now trying unsuccessfully to climb the wall, would not turn next to the ornately carved table leg and find it easier to scale. I did the most heroic thing I could, under the circumstances.

"Joanna," I croaked. "Pick up the snake and put him back into his cage." I tried for a cool, calm delivery—an I'd-do-it-myself-sweetheart-if-I-weren't-so-busy-holding-down-the-table tone of voice. It worked.

"Pick up da 'nake? OK," she said. She knocked down her tower, padded barefoot across the room, and after a brief struggle held the writhing creature tenderly and affectionately against her bare chest, looking for all the world like the infant Hercules. Standing as tall as she could, she strained and grunted and finally was able to drop him into his windowsill terrarium.

"Mommy, you can come down now," she said sympathetically.

That was in June. In July Martha and the snake left for Camp Awana with instructions that only one of them was to return. She agreed with alacrity. I should have been suspicious; the alacrity in this kind of situation was abnormal. Three weeks later when she returned home, we discovered that, yes, she had left the snake in a Wisconsin bog, but she had eased the wrench of the separation by bringing home several additions to her frog and toad collection. I groaned, thinking of the neighbors. Already they were talking about our family's foraging around garbage cans. How does one communicate across the backyard fence that one's husband and children are prowling the alleys in order to provide dinner for a dozen amphibians?

Everett, of whom it can never be said that he wouldn't even

hurt a fly, taught the children the fine art of fly-catching: the cupped palm, the slow approach from the front, and then the surprise rush, followed by the deft removal of a wing and the popping into the milk bottle.

Every time I protested—and I protested every time—he would reply, "Well, it's that or remove the window screens and let the flies come to us." The other alternative never occurred to us: get rid of the fly-eaters.

Yes, on the animal issue we leaned over backward; we wanted the children to experience life to the fullest. We couldn't get out into the countryside, so we encouraged the children to bring the country into our city apartment. I had another motive. I wanted to encourage the faculty of wonder in our youngsters, to get across the message that a mouse or guinea pig or parakeet or snake is "miracle enough to stagger sextillions of infidels."

While all four of the children loved animals, it was Martha whose single-minded dedication worried me. I feared her growing up into a legend of eccentricity—a musty recluse, known to the neighborhood as "The Cat Lady of Irving Park."

"Don't worry," Everett advised. "One of these days she'll discover that boys are a whole lot more interesting than animals, and your troubles will be over."

"Do you really think so?" I grasped eagerly at the prospect.

The day did come, even as he had prophesied. When Martha trembled on the brink of sixteen, sure enough, she discovered the other sex. With what relief we watched as she dispassionately disposed of cages, aquaria, flea powder, and mange medicine! But our relief was premature. True, she may have switched her allegiance from zoology to anthropology, but she had not lost her propensity for rescue and salvage operations.

No potentially rabid bat or tularemic rabbit had ever frightened us as much as her bizarre succession of swains—all

27

of them in desperate need of someone to love them, to understand them, to shelter them from life's wintry blasts. Each time Martha introduced us to another teenage derelict, it was as though she were saying, as in days of yore, "Look what I found! May I keep it?"

This time around we were not permissive; we were tactlessly antagonistic. We could not pretend we were pleased with Tom, the masochist; or Dick, the reformatory alumnus; or Harry, a sullen Heathcliff. How we longed for the good old days when our arguments had centered around such impersonal issues as mouse odors and escaping opossums!

We prayed, of course. We had long, emotional confabs. When words failed, we sent intrafamily notes to each other. Somehow, we survived the ordeal; and when Martha left for college at the age of nineteen, she was unattached, and we were still friends. And I had aged ten years in three.

I was a little uneasy about Martha's being four hundred miles away from our protective custody. As it turned out, I needn't have been. Working twenty to thirty hours a week in addition to carrying a full academic load, she had little time for socializing.

"Besides," she wrote, out of a surprising new fastidiousness, "I don't like what I see." That was in her sophomore year, and I figured she had plenty of time left for looking around.

But when she was in her junior year, I began to fret. "What kind of college is that, anyway? She's not engaged yet."

When she was graduated the following year with a degree in art and anthropology and no matrimonial prospects, I wondered if we hadn't been too negative about her beaus, if maybe we had encouraged her to be so idealistic that nobody was good enough for her.

Martha did not share my concern. When she entrained for

Seattle the day after commencement to enroll in a summer linguistic course at the University of Washington, she was confident that the Lord had someone waiting there for her.

She was right. Before many days had passed, we received a letter in which she rapturously exclaimed, "I'm in love!" and triumphantly declared, "At last I've found someone you'll like!"; and added as a clincher, "You'll have to. He's just like Dad!"

I didn't cry at Martha's wedding. I suppose I let everyone down—my family, the guests, and tradition. I couldn't help it. I sat there smiling broadly and remembering.

I was recalling a pig-tailed tomboy who tenderly loved all of God's helpless creatures, bringing them home with her and asking each time, "May I keep this one?" I was remembering, too, a teenage charmer who had looked upon each boyfriend as a rehabilitation project needing her particular brand of solicitude. And I was comforted and elated by the knowledge that this time Martha had reached out—not down—for love.

The organist had just finished the Crimond version of the Twenty-third Psalm; and Martha, in a simple white frock and short veil, walked slowly down the aisle on her father's arm. For a brief second her eyes left Don's and met mine. She was smiling, too. This time she hadn't had to ask. She knew that we liked what she had found, that this one she could keep.

4

Moment of Truth

EVERETT'S MOMENT OF TRUTH was late in arriving. A man as well preserved as he is, who still takes the steps two at a time, is not ready to recognize the "bending sickle" even if it is poised right over his graying head. I'm afraid Everett had been lulled into a false sense of security by the frequent rave notices of those who refused to believe he antedates the airplane. I grant he is growing old gracefully, and that after a shave and a haircut and a good night's sleep he could fool even a carnival huckster whose business it is to guess weights and ages. His youthful appearance has deceived a good many people, including himself.

"I owe it all to eggs," he confides when his friends inquire about his abundance of energy and his *joi de vivre*. He does consume eggs at an alarming rate, averaging about three a day; and I have known days when that number has shot up to seven or eight. Cholesterol holds no terrors for him. At this writing, my calculations show that he has eaten a grand total of 78,840 eggs over the years; and during each of those years he has exhausted about four and a quarter hens—not ordinary hens, mind you, but jumbo layers.

Personally, I don't take much stock in the rejuvenating power of eggs, since I eat a fair share myself; and even after a facial and a hairdo and a good night's sleep, I not only look my age but quite often a little bit more.

No, I really can't go along with Everett's fruit-of-the-chicken theory. I'm convinced that his secret lies in his state of mind; he is a nonworrier. He was born to be content in whatsoever situation he found himself, and he has remained true to his calling. There were a lot of lessons he had to learn when he became a Christian, but contentment was not one of them. He calls himself a Calvinist; I call him an acquiescent believer. Be that as it may, one of the thousand and one things he has never fretted about is the problem of growing old. He was so indifferent to the "inevitable specter" that he didn't recognize its presence even when *Modern Maturity Magazine* appeared on the coffee table cheek by jowl with *National Geographic* and *Eternity*.

He seemed to possess a psychological shortsightedness that prevented his reading the signposts along the way. For example, he could never remember the name of the club that he belonged to, a group of local citizens who met every month in the town of Ellison Bay. There was a mental block, no doubt about it, that made it impossible for him to recall the name of that particular organization. A typical conversation would go something like this:

HE: We're having an auction sale at the next meeting.
SHE *(frankly puzzled)*: *Who* is?
HE *(after deep thought):* The people who meet at the schoolhouse.
SHE *(pretending innocence)*: What people?
HE *(beginning to fidget):* You know, the Tuesday afternoon group.
SHE *(pursuing relentlessly)*: How would *I* know. I'm in

Chicago on Tuesdays.

HE *(getting hot under the collar):* It's the group I joined last October.

LA BELLE DAME SANS MERCI: You've joined so many organizations, I can't keep track.

HE *(pleading):* You know I can't remember the name. It's the old people.

SHE *(helpfully):* You mean the Senior Citizens Club, don't you?

HE *(sighing gratefully):* Yes, that's it. The Senior Citizens.

There were other myopic indications along the way. He referred to a neighbor whom I had yet to meet as the "little old lady who lives down the road." She turned out to be a charming, intellectual, beautifully-groomed woman—silver-haired, true—but at least ten years Everett's junior.

"Well, she looks like somebody's grandmother," he insisted, defending his description.

Even the mutilations of the scythe Everett was able to ignore. "At your age—" the optician commiserated, and Everett came home with his first pair of bifocals.

"Whaddya know," he said that afternoon from behind the pages of the *Daily News,* "They've started using a different type. The print's larger and darker. I wouldn't have had to get these stupid glasses after all." He was dead serious.

The partial plate that followed soon after the bifocals was not due to aging, Everett hastened to explain. Years before, one of our children had playfully whipped back her head while sitting on his lap, cracking his front teeth above the gum line.

"Could happen to anyone," he reassured the family and himself.

Later, Everett claimed it was the hardware that anchored

33

the partial that contributed to the total breakdown. When the dentist said, "At your age, you've got to expect—", Everett cut him off with a choking sound, which was all he could manage around the dentist's knuckles, but which meant, "I'm too young to go the whole route, Doc."

His first bursitis attack sent Everett to the family physician with the story that he must have twisted his shoulder while lifting a heavy box at work. Plunging the needle into Everett's left deltoid, the doctor said, "Well, you know, at your age—" but he was speaking in the vicinity of my husband's left ear, which hasn't been functioning too well for the past few years and so the prognosis didn't register.

The eroding hairline was such a gradual change that it was almost unnoticeable; only comparison with the early family snapshots revealed the difference that time had wrought. Everett took care of that problem by stowing the daguerreotypes on an inaccessible closet shelf.

If the doctor, dentist, and mirror could not convince him, who or what could, I wondered. Not that I was out to cramp Everett's style, mind you. I just wanted to stop him from pushing neighbors' cars out of ditches, rescuing cats from trees, and volunteering himself into three-legged races at church picnics, that's all. I wanted him to slow down to a safe speed and conserve his energy before it ran out on him. Also, I was tired of my role of backseat driver, both in and out of the car; and I am certain he was just as weary of hearing "Take it easy," "Slow down," "Remember your shoulder," "You're not getting any younger," "Wear something warmer," et cetera—loving admonitions that went unheeded because Everett was confident they did not apply to him.

His quick and nimble footwork enabled him to sidestep the old-age issue for a long while, but then one day when his guard was down it hit him. His moment of truth occurred, as most revelations do, in a very ordinary and incongruous setting. For him it was the A & W lunchroom in Two Rivers. We had ordered our usual Momma- and Poppa-burgers; and while we waited, we discussed the witty signs posted on the walls.

When you have been married as many years as we have, you become grateful for any conversational assists you can get. Long silences are not necessarily strained; on the contrary, they are often quite comfortable; but in a public place you want to keep up the fiction that, old and married though you may be, you still find each other's company exciting and the dialogue fresh and sparkling—so much so, that the waitress approaching to take your order is an interruption and not a relief. Those are my sentiments. Everett would just as soon sit quietly and listen to his stomach growl.

I digress; but I do it consciously, in order to explain to those who haven't yet reached the stage of interminable companionable silences what desperate remedies we wives will take to keep up appearances. I read about a woman in my predicament—insecure and married to a taciturn male—who, when the conversation lagged, resorted to reciting nursery rhymes over the restaurant table. She would lean forward, eyes sparkling, face animated, as though she were about to impart some intimate and exciting confidence.

"Did you know that Mary had a little lamb?" she would ask breathlessly.

"Is that so?" her husband responded, trying to enter into the spirit of the game.

"Yes," she would aspirate excitedly "and its fleece was white as snow!"

Continuing to cooperate, her mate would ask, "Whatever happened to that lamb?

35

The waitress slipped up on us while Everett was responding in his best falsetto, "What? Lost their mittens? Those naughty kittens!"

"Well" was her response, accompanied by a shrug of the shoulders, "everywhere that Mary went, the lamb was sure to go."

"And what was Mary's itinerary?" he asked as though he really cared.

"It followed her to school one day—"

He raised his eyebrows disapprovingly and interrupted, "Wasn't that against the rules?"

"Oh, yes," she admitted. "But it made the children laugh and play to see a lamb at school."

Nobody at the surrounding tables would ever have guessed that they were an old married couple from the looks of them, this writer insisted. I thought it was worth a try. The waitress slipped up on us while Everett was responding in his best falsetto, "What? Lost their mittens? Those naughty kittens!"

We are back to long, comfortable silences and motto reading.

That's what we were doing the day that the scales fell from Everett's eyes, reading the writings on the wall. I pointed out a plaque that read, LORD, GIVE ME PATIENCE, SOON. Everett liked the one which read, DON'T CRITICIZE THE COFFEE. YOU MAY BE OLD AND WEAK YOURSELF SOMEDAY. We both laughed over PLEASE DON'T SHOOT THE CHEF. HE'S DOING THE BEST HE CAN!

We were halfway through our meal when Everett spotted another sign on the wall, an announcement posted behind the cash register. He began to read it aloud:

SENIOR CITIZENS
10% Discount
Monday through Friday
1-4 p.m.

"That's nice," he approved. "That's a nice thing for them to do," he added with only a faint trace of condescension. He bit into his sandwich then abruptly stopped, mouth open, eyes bulging, Adam's apple working. I was alarmed. The words "café coronary" sprang to mind. Before I could rush to his aid, he managed a whisper.

"That means me," he choked.

I patted his hand, relieved and sympathetic. "I know, Everett. I know."

We ate the rest of our meal in silence. The intensity of his preoccupation was evidenced by the fact that he neglected to filch half my French fries, and he refused a third cup of coffee. He was busy wrestling with the revelation. As we rose to leave, I was encouraged by the conspiratorial grin he gave me.

"Well?" I asked.

"I've decided," he winked, "that if you don't tell them, neither will I."

No matter that he kept his secret from the pretty young waitresses at the A & W—his moment of truth had arrived; he had recognized it; and things would never be quite the same again. Everett soon took to wearing bedroom slippers all day long, out in the barn, shopping, gardening, until a daughter told me how to remedy the situation. Hide the slippers. Then he began shaving only on alternate days. I considered hiding the razor since a beard seemed preferable to stubble. After further consideration, I decided to let him have that round, especially since he had given in on one of my major demands, retiring as neighborhood troubleshooter. Now, when the neighbors spin their wheels in the wet snow, he watches from the warmth and security of the house, hidden from sight behind the living room curtains, chuckling uncharitably.

And, oh yes, the mental block has disappeared. He remembers, without my prompting, that it's the Senior Citizens that

38

meet on the second Tuesday of the month. And that he is a member, not a mascot.

5

A Man and His Dog

WHEN I WALKED into the house one day with a pound and a half of Chihuahua in my purse, Everett demanded, "What have you got there?"

"It's a panacea," I hedged. "You work nights. I work days. I get lonesome."

"That's a poor excuse," he snorted.

"I don't think I need much of an excuse," I sniffed, huffily on the defensive.

"For a dog," he amended. "That's a poor excuse for a dog."

"She'll grow," I promised. "She's only six weeks old."

"She'll get sucked up into the vacuum cleaner first," he predicted. "What kind of dog is she supposed to be?"

"She's supposed to be—I mean, she is a long-haired Chihuahua. We'll get her papers in a few days."

"And the long hair? When will that arrive?"

"They told me she'll get her first full coat in about six months."

"Well, until then you'd better buy her a wig. She's shivering."

I couldn't blame Everett for his lack of enthusiasm. A man has dreams about the kind of dog he would like to own. He imagines himself donning a rugged mackintosh on a blustery

October evening and loping ankle-deep in fallen leaves with a well-trained Airedale at his heels, or clad in thick brogans and country corduroys striding over hill and dale with a brace of red setters frolicking on ahead, or driving down the crowded expressway in a station wagon with a Great Dane drooling over his leather-patched tweeds. Dreams like those die hard. There is no way a man can snap a leash onto twenty-four ounces of quaking dogflesh and manage to stride with dignity down the boulevard. But I had thoroughly researched the pet possibilities—a computer couldn't have been more objective—and for folks of our age, teetering on doddering; and our life-style, sedentary with frequent aberrations; and our living accommodations, rented city apartment on weekdays, mobile home in the country on weekends, a portable pup was indicated.

My one miscalculation had been not consulting Everett first, but that's my usual m.o., to confront him with the *fait accompli* and let the chips fall where they may. I have learned that my husband, who is able to argue all joy out of a proposal, bows gracefully to the inevitable, eventually.

The next morning at breakfast I attempted to get him involved. "The dog has to have a name," I reminded him.

He thought for a moment. "I have a suggestion," he said. "When I was a boy on the farm in Harrison Valley—"

"Here it comes," I groaned.

"—my brother and I had a pair of collie pups," he went on, ignoring my interruption. "Rudy called his You Know."

"And you named yours Guess," I supplied.

"That's right. And every time somebody would ask us what their names were, we'd tell them—" He couldn't finish; he was doubled over in laughter at the recollection. No matter how often he told that story—and he told it very often—it would break him up.

I waited for him to recover, and then I continued, "It should be a Spanish name. After all, she is of Mexican origin."

"That's no problem. How about Tortilla? Enchilada? Tostados? Taco?" he suggested, drawing upon his one excursion to an ethnic restaurant. "Don't laugh," he advised. "How much Spanish do you know?"

"Poquito," I admitted. "Which translated means 'not very much,' I think."

"Poquito," he said, trying it out. "Since she certainly isn't very much of anything herself, it ought to fit her perfectly."

Poquito, knowing no more about Spanish grammar than we did and aiming only to please, took to her name immediately. She also responded to such endearments as "Babydoll," "Sweetiepie," "Poochie," "good girl," and a casual glance in her general direction. Everett persisted in calling her "Hey, you!" and often just plain "dog," either of which sent her into ecstatic convulsions—to which he was impervious, I should add. To him she was a bit of ornamental fluff, a lady's lap dog. He would try to avoid inadvertently stepping on her or closing a door on her tail, but I was not to expect any more than that.

"You bought her," he reminded me the day I asked him if he would take her in for her shots. "You paid for her with your own egg money. So you walk her, and you take her to the vet. She's your dog."

He carefully avoided looking at Poquito while he issued the ultimatum. She was flopped across his instep, wagging her little tail furiously, eyes brimming over with liquid love.

"I can't, Everett. I can't bear to see the vet stick the needle into her. I couldn't stand it with the *other* children, either. Remember?" Fortunately, he didn't notice my slip.

He relented. "All right, just this once," he warned, tucking her under his arm and slipping out of the house after dark.

I hadn't anticipated it; but when they returned, I noticed a new relationship had sprung up between them—a camaraderie from which I was excluded. I suppose it was because they had shared a painful experience: she had been inoculated, he had paid the bill. Everett was not admitting a thing, however. He merely dumped her unceremoniously into my lap and retreated behind the evening paper.

A few days later, arriving home from work, I discovered that Everett had hung a tiny stuffed bear from the floor lamp for Poquito to bat and wrestle. He dismissed appreciation with, "She was bored, always pestering to get up into my lap."

The following week I walked into the house to find that a lookout platform had been installed on the living room windowsill so that Pokey could sun herself and bark at canine passersby. A padded ramp provided easy access. Ignoring the facts that it didn't do much for the decor and that it ended under the foot pedals of the piano, I praised the contraption.

"I can't keep getting up every time the mutt wants to look out the window," was his rationalization.

When spring arrived and we got our bicycles out of the barn for a trial run, it was Everett who decided that, if we didn't take Poquito along, I'd probably worry all the time we were away. He fastened a harness to a carrying basket and secured it to the handlebars of his bicycle. "She'll be safer with me," he explained, referring to my inability to get on or off a bike without incident.

Poquito, after a few minutes of anxiety, got into the spirit of the sport. Leaning into the wind, eyes squinted almost shut, ears folded back, she suggested a streamlined radiator ornament. It was on that maiden trip, however, that we discovered she was not merely decorative; she became a working member of the crew.

Heretofore, we had had to arm ourselves with rocks, spray

44

guns, aerosol whistles, and water pistols loaded with soapy water in order to repel vicious, cycle-chasing dogs. None of those weapons was really effective. But now, with Pokey in the vanguard, we were safe. Farm dogs, leaping from ambush and aiming for our ankles or calves, were suddenly distracted by Pokey's hysterical barking. They continued to pursue us, but they were no longer interested in hamstringing; they were infuriated by the taunting insults, the catch-me-if-you-cans emanating from our Mexican spitfire.

I don't know who enjoyed those encounters more—Poquito or Everett. Certainly not I, pumping furiously to keep up, lest the blood-thirsty hounds, unable to gain on their quarry, turn on me in their frustration.

It must have been Poquito's fierce Aztecan heart that was breaking down the last barriers of Everett's resistance, because when I suggested we leave her with one of the children while we took a trip to Arizona, he seemed a little put out. "There's no need," he said. "She's a good traveler." I wouldn't have been surprised by this time if he had added, "Besides, I want to show her the West. She's never seen it."

He built her a cushioned car seat and mounted it between us so that she had a clear view of Highway 66 all the way there, and I had a clear view of Everett only at gas and meal stops.

He had been right about her, though. She was an ideal traveling companion, thriving on doggybag meals and thrilled as a kid with each new motel room. Something we hadn't counted on was her social contribution. People found her so irresistible that we never lacked for company. Hardly anyone could pass by without asking about her lineage. Tourists paused in their inspection of the Grand Canyon to comment, "What a beautiful dog! What kind is she, anyway?" I rarely got a chance to tell them; Everett was right there to take full credit.

I pedaled furiously lest the blood-thirsty hounds turn on me in
their frustration.

The first few times he opted for accuracy. "She's a long-haired Chihuahua." Almost invariably the response was a skeptical "Izzatso? Never heard of it." Which meant that Everett had to prove his veracity and her purity by explaining that there is indeed such a breed and that in fact the AKC had our pup on file. It was a lot of trouble after the first twenty or thirty encounters. He decided finally that people would rather believe a lie—or at least hear one—and so he began to dream up weird answers. To the query "What kind of dog is that?" Everett, looking the interrogator in the eye, would reply, "She's a miniature Great Dane." The response was usually an indulgent laugh, which was preferable to a genealogical discussion.

Others would tell us, "She looks just like a young fox. What kind of dog is she? Oh, she's not a dog? She's a domesticated fox? Whaddya know!" they'd marvel, going along with the gag. Everett also tried shrunken sheltie, and dwarf caribou, dehorned, of course.

It was on that trip West that Everett learned that Poquito was a drawing card especially attractive to ladies, young and old. Consequently he exercised her to a frazzle.

Pokey had been with us for five years when she had her accident, a fall from a porch causing serious damage to a knee. She underwent surgery and was subsequently hospitalized for eleven days. We anguished a little, knowing how miserable she must be, and we plagued the vet daily with calls about her condition. At the same time we noticed a sense of liberation, not unlike the first months after our last child left the nest. Everett and I rediscovered each other; we began to communicate tete-a-tete in stead of via Poquito. ("Pokey, what's Mother fixing for dinner?" or, "Pokey, go tell Dad we'd like to go out for a drive.") We found that we were sitting closer

47

together on the sofa now that we didn't have to leave room for the dog. We held hands.

"Where have you been for the last few years?" Everett teased while we were watching TV on one of our nights alone.

"Just a dog's length away," I replied.

"Do you mean Pokey's been coming between us?"

"You'd better believe it! Every time you felt affectionate, you'd cuddle Poquito."

"Instead of you!" he said wonderingly.

"Instead of me," I agreed.

"We were such a happy threesome, I thought."

"More like a triangle," I countered.

"Why didn't you tell me I was neglecting you?" he demanded.

"I thought it was just that I was getting old and repulsive," I sighed.

"Nonsense," he reassured me. "From now on things will be different. We'll keep a proper perspective. We'll put Poquito to bed at an earlier hour. We'll hire a baby-sitter and go out more often."

The honeymoon and Everett's promises lasted until the day we drove to Green Bay to pick up our convalescent. She was emaciated and had a racking cough. Her shaved, stitch-puckered leg stuck out grotesquely from her body. I steeled myself. "A proper perspective," Everett had said. She was, after all, only a dog.

I started for the right side of the car, when Everett stopped me and snatched the ailing dog from my arms. "You drive," he ordered. "I'll hold the poor little thing."

That night I got out of bed around midnight to check on the patient. I had installed her in her cage a couple of hours earlier, wrapping her in a flannel blanket and laying her on top of my new heating pad. She was not there; the cage was empty and open. She and Everett were curled up sound asleep on the sofa. As I bent over them, Pokey opened one eye and closed it again. A slow wink.

"You little vixen!" I whispered, tucking the cover more securely around the two of them.

"Ah, well," I philosophized later in my lonely room. "I asked for it." How had Bernard, that wise and holy monk, phrased it? "Qui me amat, amat et canum meum."*

*"Who loves me, let him love my dog also."

6

So Much for Well-Laid Plans

PHYLLIS WAS COMING, and I was beside myself with joy. The cupboard was stocked with boxes of animal cookies and carmel corn; the freezer with three different flavors of ice cream; the refrigerator with chocolate milk and white, and a shelf of fruit juices and punch. The candy dishes were filled and placed at eye level—hers, that is; and there were strawberry tarts and sugar cones from Beil's Bakery.

"You will kill her with kindness," Everett warned.

"Oh, but I want her to remember this visit," I protested.

"Don't worry. She will. She's probably never in her young life seen a stomach pump or a dentist."

"You think I'm overdoing it?"

"Maybe just a little," he suggested. "I don't think she will be able to handle Christmas, Easter, and her birthday all rolled up into one."

"I want to make a good impression. I want her to like me."

"Listen, she liked you in San Diego when she was only a baby. She liked you last summer when she was only two. What makes you think she will suddenly dislike you at three?"

"She will be more discerning," I sighed. "She will recognize that I am a rank amateur next to her California grandmother."

"So that's why you're trying harder—you think you're

51

second best? Take my advice and relax. You don't see me wearing myself to a frazzle trying to compete with her California grandpa, do you?"

"You're right," I conceded. "As usual, I'm pushing too hard."

Everett started out the door.

"Where are you going?" I asked. "You promised to help with the dishes."

"Out to the barn. I've got to get Phyllis's bicycle seat finished; and the dining room furniture for the doll house needs a second coat of varnish."

"Well, don't work yourself to a frazzle out there," I admonished dryly.

I had begun my countdown about three weeks before, and now Phyllis was due to arrive the next day. In my enthusiastic planning I occasionally lost sight of the fact that she was going to be accompanied by her parents and infant twin brothers. I would be delighted, naturally, to see our daughter and son-in-law; and I was sure the identical twins would be fascinating and a joy to behold, but it was Phyllis for whom the strategy had been laid out.

I went to the closet to peek at the dress I had made for her; it was finished, all but the hem. Phyllis was such a little thing. How tall has she grown? I wondered. In my memory, she had held still. I rearranged the furniture in the doll house—a red, white and green Victorian mansion that Everett had completed since her last visit. Would she understand that it was still in the making, that it was only a promise as yet? I straightened the nursery rhyme and story books on the bedside table. Hans Christian Andersen! Whatever had possessed me? The stories would frighten her out of her wits. I removed that particular book and put it on a closet shelf.

Admittedly, I was anxious. It wasn't as though Phyllis lived next door or even in the same town and was running in and out the back door, on chummy terms with my cookie jar. We had seen our first granddaughter only twice, and to her we were but a legend. I wanted this visit to be a memorable one for her; I wanted her to take away enough vivid and lasting impressions to carry over until Christmas when we hoped to join her in Quebec.

I had made a list of activities that I thought might be exciting "firsts" for her—one for each day of the week that she would be with us. I planned toothsome dishes that I thought would be especially appealing. I shampooed and brushed Poquito as though she were going into the show ring, and I bought her a new collar.

"Phyllis is coming!" I sang to the bewildered pup as I whirled her around the living room.

They arrived in their VW camper the next afternoon, the parents weary, the boys hungry, and Phyllis shy. After a night's sleep, she trusted me enough to accompany me on a prebreakfast walk to a neighboring farm where she fed lumps of sugar to a spindle-legged colt. We spent the warm evening on a rocky beach tossing stones into the water, and she was persuaded to leave only by the promise that we would return the next night to finish the job.

Another day I took her to a nearby stable for her first pony ride. She was more impressed with the young boy who led her steed, but that's the way with a maid.

The waves were rough the day we went to Newport Beach, but she was not disappointed, content to build castles and canals in the sand.

I held her up high so she could feed soda pop to a black bear at the local outdoor zoo, and she stood breathlessly still while a

She fed lumps of sugar to a spindle-legged colt.

young buck ate from her hand at a deer preserve.

She licked frosting bowls and patted her own meat loaf into its doll-sized pan, stirred the jello and sliced the bananas, and dropped tidbits to Poquito.

She froze while the ruby-throated hummingbird paused on his way to the feeder to inspect the red ribbon I had tied in her hair. We crouched silently in the leaves to wait for my pet chipmunk to emerge from his underground home. We collected oval stones and painted faces on them and called them "Mommy," and "Daddy," and "Nathan," and "Ben," and told stories.

Too soon, it was time for them to leave. Everett, to give Martha and me time for a last chat, took Phyllis out to the yard to help with the raking. Martha and I sat as long as we could, making plans for a reunion at Christmas; it took some of the sting away from parting.

Then they were gone.

"Phyllis had a good time, didn't she?" I asked Everett, as we lolled in the lawn chairs, suffering from postvisit depression.

"The best," he replied encouragingly.

"I wonder what she liked the most? Do you think it was the pony ride?"

"I wouldn't be surprised. Although she sure did enjoy helping you in the kitchen."

I didn't have to wonder long. There was a brief tug-of-war over the first letter to arrive from Martha. "OK," I surrendered. "But read it out loud."

He glanced at the first lines, gave me a strange look, and then began to read, "Dear Folks. Thanks so much for the wonderful week. Phyllis really enjoyed herself. She hasn't stopped talking about—"

Everett hesitated, tried unsuccessfully to suppress a grin,

and began again, " 'Thanks so much for the wonderful week. Phyllis really enjoyed herself. She hasn't stopped talking about what fun she had helping Grandpa rake the leaves.' "

7

Roger

"IF YOU ARE RIDING on a Chicago bus after 3:00 P.M. on a weekday," an education professor once informed our class, "you can easily distinguish the teachers from the civilians. The teachers are the ones with the clenched jaws."

I recalled his remark as I stood on the Addison Street subway platform, sandwiched between the roaring traffic lanes of the Kennedy Expressway, at 3:30 on a Friday afternoon; a time when normally I would be home, stretched out on my La-Z-Boy with a bottle of cold soda pop at hand; but today some urgent errand was taking me to the Loop.

"Clenched jaws," the experienced instructor had said. I took my compact out of my purse and peeked. The description was accurate, if skimpy. He should have added "a drained and desperate expression around the eyes." My mirror reflected the look of a lost soul contemplating the third rail.

"Now pull yourself together," I told myself. "Throw back your shoulders, take a deep breath, and uncurl your toes. Remember, you don't have to re-enter the Coliseum until Monday. What's more, you don't have to talk to, smile at, or socialize with anyone under twenty-one all weekend."

The latter reminder did the trick. It dislodged the boulder from between my shoulder blades; it relaxed my eyeballs; it cleared my sinuses. It did everything but relieve my aching arches; those would have to wait until I snared a seat on the ride downtown.

Above my head, at the street level, a bus disgorged its passengers, and in a few seconds the more athletic came pelting down the stairs to catch the train that was just pulling into the station. Out of the corner of my eye I spied a vaguely familiar hulking figure topped by a friendly, open face and a mop of unruly black hair. I turned to take a second look and was instantly transported six years back in time to a seventh grade classroom where a certain Roger D—had harassed ten years from my life expectancy. This was Roger, no doubt about it, and instinctively, I looked for a way of escape. It was too late. Not only was I being swept forward by the boarding mob, but I had been discovered. Over the cataract roar of traffic and the throbbing of the train's motor, I heard the booming, slightly incredulous and more than a little triumphant, "Hey, Mrs. Reichel!" I turned a deaf ear and headed for the last remaining seat, hoping that some fellow traveler would fill the gap next to me before Roger could get there; but a couple of pivots, a stiff-arm, a crouching lunge, and he fell into the seat beside me.

"Boy, am I glad to see you!" he thundered.

I smiled weakly, since there was no rejoinder, both honest and polite, that I could offer. The feeling was not mutual. I remembered that the less I had seen of Roger, the happier I had been. His nearness now triggered a painful flashback: frantic notes scribbled almost daily to the third grade teacher across the hall. "Please, Betty, would you take Roger off my hands for a while so I can do some teaching!" Betty never turned me down; she had a Roger whose name was Greg, and I gave her equal time.

"There's something I gotta tell you!" Roger shouted as the train rumbled past the Belmont Avenue station.

Oh, Roger, there always was; and no matter where you were or what I was doing, you never were able to restrain yourself. In the midst of the pin-drop silence of a math test, you'd shout from your isolated corner of the room, "Hey, Mrs. Reichel! My pencil broke!" I'd point wordlessly to the windowsill sharpener; and you'd clump your noisy, cleated way over there, begin to grind, and then jar the class out of its resumed concentration with, "Hey, Mrs. Reichel! Kin I empty the pencil sharpener? It's running over!"

I'd rise from my desk, mayhem in my eye; and you'd take a feinting step away from the window. Only you wouldn't be finished with me. As soon as all the pencils were moving again; as soon as I relaxed, there'd be that pseudoinnocent, amoral, penetrating voice: "Kin I swat this wasp before it stings somebody?"

There isn't anything you can tell me now, Roger, that I'd be interested in hearing; but since I'm trapped until Lake Street, I'll make a show of civility.

"What is it?"

"Well, I been looking up all my old teachers—"

For what, Roger? To check the rate of survival? I'll wager you sent more than one teacher on a sabbatical leave. It was the year with you that made me switch to high school teaching—a compromise to satisfy my family who wanted me to quit altogether. So you're looking up your old teachers. Why? To deliver the *coup de grace?* Or are you selling vacuum cleaners?

"You see," Roger stumbled on. "I want to apologize."

Of course you do, Roger. Apologizing is your forte. Wasn't it you who spoiled the seventh grade class portrait with crossed

"What did Roger do today, Mom?"

eyes, protruding tongue, and horns sprouting from the crown of Mary Jane's head? And didn't you sit abjectly at your desk with tears cascading down your chubby face while I administered a verbal lashing?

And wasn't it you who sent the entire assembly into gales of laughter by dragging a half-beat behind on "Stodola Pumpa," at the same time puffing out your cheeks and pantomiming the motions of a slide-trombonist, safely out of my line of vision as I conducted but in full view of the audience, which that day included the music supervisor? And then later, while being barred from all future programs, didn't you flood the principal's office with evidence of your repentance?

Was there ever a recess—when you were allowed to go out, that is—that you did not return damply contrite, promising to pay for the torn shirt, the uprooted flowers, the broken window? Apologies, Roger, come easily to you. So what's new?

"Something happened to me, Mrs. Reichel."

I straightened up, suddenly interested, Did you finally get your due? Did a no-nonsense shop teacher threaten to run you through a planer? Did the history department gang up on you and put sugar in your gasoline tank? Oh, I could have gone on forever conjuring up punishment to fit Roger's crimes, but he cut into my pleasant reverie.

"I got saved!" Roger blurted out. "I'm a Christian now."

I looked at him, stunned, hardly comprehending. It was a solar plexian blow.

His words began to pour out and tumble over each other now that he had made his most important statement. He spoke about his growing conviction that he was "no good"; how an Awana leader had taken him home after a Friday night meeting—a meeting which Roger had tried to disrupt—and patiently and lovingly explained that God had cared enough

61

for him to send His Son to die for him, to redeem him from that "no-goodness"; that all he had to do was believe in Christ's atoning death and he would be cleansed from his sin and inherit eternal life. He accepted the Lord that night.

This boy who seldom opened a book in my classroom except to vandalize it related how he had been studying the Bible for the last two years "on my own, with the Holy Spirit teaching me."

Roger, thrown out of countless club meetings, described the joy he was experiencing as a leader in that same organization.

Irony of ironies, Roger, who had been returned to school more than once by truant officers, disclosed his plans to go into police work, counseling juveniles!

I sat there gaping, trying to keep up with his enthusiastic testimony. The words, "This is the Lord's doing; it is marvelous in my eyes," kept running through my mind.

Finally I interrupted the eager flow. "Roger, I'm a Christian, too." I wanted him to know that I understood and shared his happiness. It seems he was aware of my convictions, had been ever since I had mentioned during one of our frequent after-school conferences that I prayed for all the children in my class, especially for him.

"That really impressed me," he admitted.

Oh, I had prayed for him. Whether I was inspired by my instinct for self-preservation or by concern for his soul might be argued, but I prayed.

"It was when you sicced Dave onto me that I was really sure you were a Christian," he grinned.

I frowned, puzzled.

"David B—," he prompted.

It began to come back to me. David had been the most popular boy in the class, in spite of his perfect scholarship.

Certain candid observations he had made in his compositions had convinced me he was a Christian and active in his church. Taking him aside one day, I suggested to him that Roger needed a friend. Would he take an interest in him? I asked. Invite him to his home? To his AYA activities? Help him with his homework? I let it go at that. I was too bogged down with end-of-the-year duties to follow it up. This testimony of Roger's was the first indication that David had done his missionary work.

I wanted to hear more, but we were nearing my station. I gave Roger my phone number and urged him to call me soon.

When I arrived home that night, I sat down and wrote to my children. "Remember Roger?" I began. That was foolish, they were not likely to have forgotten him; they had had him for dinner five nights a week for an entire school year! "Well," I continued, "he's—" What should I say, I wondered. Redeemed? Transformed? Saved? Born again? "He's a new creature in Christ," I wrote. "Old things are passed away; behold, all things are become new."

Roger did call me and has come to visit us several times, always rejoicing in the Lord, never forgetting to apologize for "the monster I was in your class." On his latest visit he brought a trophy, a brand new convert, another boy from that same seventh grade class.

How grateful I am for that "coincidental" meeting on the subway! The problems I face now in high school teaching are far more complex and difficult to handle than any that Roger presented. I fight a daily battle against discouragement and depression. The Lord knew I needed a booster shot for my ebbing morale. He gave me incontrovertible evidence in Roger's transformation that He listens and "attendeth when I pray."

8

The Years Draw Nigh

EVERETT AND I don't like to admit to ourselves or to the world at large that we are running down. When our children and grandchildren spent their vacations with us in Wisconsin, we tended to set a pretty fast pace, trying to prove our eternal youthfulness and indestructibility. We shocked our offspring out of their sacks at sunrise with Sousa marches on the stereo; we bullied them into joining us for a swim in sixty-five-degree lake water; we dared them to explore new bicycle routes on hilly back roads; we challenged them to croquet tournaments after dinner; and then, at day's end, after we had gotten our second wind, we'd set up the Scrabble game for the survivors.

We did not sport sweat shirts emblazoned "CAMP AWANA" or wear megaphones around our necks, but I'm sure we came across as obnoxious and irrepressible recreation directors rather than the old folks at home.

Our children came to us from their respective concrete jungles pale and tired; they returned home peeling and spent.

They'll never make it to a ripe old age, we worried behind their backs.

"They have no stamina," I complained, not without a touch of smugness. "Why, anything they can do, we can do better, or

I'm sure we came across as obnoxious and irrepressible recreation directors.

earlier, or at least with more enthusiasm."

Well, all that was changed last summer. Somewhere between a 5:00 A.M. bird walk and an afternoon excursion to a deer preserve, I ran out of steam. I recognized the need for a long and quiet nap in a cool, shaded bedroom.

"Find the children," I urged Everett. "Tell them I'm canceling out for the rest of the day."

His jaw dropped, consternation in his eyes.

"What excuse will I give?" he asked. There was an uncomfortable silence as both of us tried to think of some nonsenility-connected disability that he could offer as an explanation for my sudden collapse. But neither of us is skilled at improvisations, or prevarications, for that matter. I decided candor was called for—candor and capitulation.

"Tell them the truth," I sighed. "Tell them the old *grandmère,* she ain't what she used to be!"

9

Silas Marner, We Love You

WE'VE ALWAYS BEEN READERS—the children and I. All of us passionately addicted to the printed page. Security in our nursery was not a fuzzy blanket or a teddy bear, but rather a book in hand, or at least within convenient grasp.

By the time they were ready to enter kindergarten, our youngsters had completed the Dick and Jane circuit; and they were standing on tiptoe to pay their own library fines at the age of six. The highlight, the peak of each week, was the Friday night trek to the Humboldt Park Library via our battered Radio Flyer wagon. Only measles, mumps, or blatant insubordination prevented any of the kids from participating in this excursion. To be left behind was heartbreak.

Oh, it wasn't that we were rearing a quartet of geniuses with built-in, insatiable curiosities. Not at all. Our children were quite average. What was not average were our circumstances. We were poor. "Poorer than average," I remind them now years later. They scoff; they remember only that they were happy.

"We were terribly poor," I insist. "As poor as the *Five Little Peppers*," I emphasize. "As poor as little Charlie Dickens in the blacking factory." They are unimpressed. To our four young adults, those were the "good old days."

The truth of the matter is, we taught our children to read when they were still lisping and barely off the bottle because of our straitened situation; we were prisoners in a third-floor, porchless, yardless apartment. We had no car— through circumstance. We had no TV—through choice. But books! Ah, we knew that books could become ladders and wings and magic carpets and frigates "to take us lands away!" We lived vicariously but richly; and the children, if I can believe their denials, were unaware of any deprivation.

Then one summer a friend loaned us her cottage located in the wilderness of Michigan's Upper Peninsula. Since Dad had to work and could not go with us, I was more than a little apprehensive about the venture. I am city-born and city-bred, with no Girl Scout training in my background. I knew that if I rubbed two sticks together, I would get nothing but slivers. Creatures that creep, crawl, or fly in my immediate vicinity can reduce me to a quivering pulp. However, the three oldest children—experienced campers—promised to protect me; and for their sakes I resolved to table my irrationalities for a few weeks.

The borrowed cottage, we had been told, was two miles from the nearest town and three miles from a beautiful lake, so we took bikes along—five of them. We packed linens, cooking gear, clothing, first-aid supplies, and some grocery staples. It never occurred to me to pack a few books. It occurred to the children; but, by the time they reminded me, the trunks had been packed, locked, and tied.

"Sorry," I apologized. "Anyway, there wasn't enough room."

Four pairs of eyes reproached me.

"Besides," I added, "we won't need books; we'll be too busy to read."

They were unconvinced.

"There'll be a library in town," I promised.

Everett drove us to the station in a rented panel truck, took care of our baggage, reminded us how lucky we were and how unlucky he was, and then, assuming the wistful mien of an abandoned husband and father, waved us off. I didn't feel fortunate at all; I felt scared and full of unreasonable resentment at being sent into exile.

We were met at the station early the next morning by my friend's cousin. He transported us and our belongings to the cottage. It was an enchanting sight from a distance: the rustic log house built against a hill and surrounded by dense woods. A huge barn, in a state of partial collapse, dominated the clearing; and a long way off—too long, I thought, for young children and frightened mothers—was the outdoor toilet.

There were adjustments to make. A primitive cookstove challenged my ingenuity. Our only source of light was a single kerosene lamp. Our water supply was an open well a couple of hundred feet from the house. The path to the privy was an obstacle course mined with sleeping garter snakes and a family of bumble bees that never slept. But the children's enthusiasm was encouraging.

"We must spring from pioneer stock," I wrote to Everett on the afternoon of the first day, proud of the children's resourcefulness and the fact that I had not yet come apart at the seams. "We are going to love every minute here," I assured my husband. "The tranquility of the place is unbelievable!"

Then night fell. There had been nothing in my experiential or vicarious background to prepare me for the "terrors by night"—the scrabblings, flutterings, squeakings, and moanings as the rodent-tenanted house came to life after dark. I was

71

horrified by the discovery that Tom, Debby, and Martha shared their attic bedrooms with a colony of bats. The children thought it was a "neat" experience. I remembered ghoulish tales of blood-sucking vampires.

Joanna and I slept on a sofa bed in the living room. The original tenants of that particular piece of furniture were resentful; there was ample evidence that they held nightly conventions on our covers trying to decide how to bell these particular cats.

The beagle that a neighbor loaned us for the duration, "to keep the bears at a respectable distance," was no help; he was just as "spooked" as I was. He snuffled and whimpered and howled and refused to act as escort to the outhouse, his intended function. On the third day he deserted us, and I couldn't say I was sorry. A dog that slept all day and carried on all night was of no use to me in my predicament.

If our nights were long, so were our afternoons. Hordes of insects sent us running for cover well before dinner time. "It would help if we had something to read," I decided. "Something to keep our minds off our before-and-after-dark visitors." Tom and Martha were given the assignment; bicycle into town, find the library, and ransack its shelves. While they were gone, Joanna plumped up the pillows, Deb started a batch of fudge, and I trimmed the wick and replenished the fuel in our one lamp. The anticipation was delicious!

Much too soon, however, we heard the rattle of returning bikes on the gravel road. Dust-covered and flushed with exertion, our two oldest stood before us—empty-handed.

"There is no library," Martha panted. We were stunned by the blasphemy. I remember looking around, surprised to see the snakes still basking, to hear the bees still buzzing in commerce. Surely, the world should have come to an end.

"There is no library," Tom echoed. "Only a post office, a depot, a Red Owl, and three taverns."

This is what comes of being a city girl, I thought—unbelievable naiveté! I had assumed that no town is without a library, a grocery store, and a soda fountain.

We had no choice but to carry on as usual, spending our days at the beach, our fun in the sun overshadowed by the knowledge that at four o'clock every afternoon, mobilizing insects would drive us indoors where we hid the key and twenty-questioned and charaded until exhaustion took over.

Then on the morning of the fifth day there was a shout from the barn. Tom came running toward the house, excitedly waving a small black object. It was a book! He was tackled and pummeled, tickled and spread-eagled by his three sisters until he relinquished his find—a mildewed but intact copy of *Silas Marner*.

"Is it a good book?" they questioned me. I was rescued by Tom's defiant "It's a book, isn't it?"

We began an in-depth study of the weaver of Raveloe. Chapters were rationed, one a day, and woe unto the greedy culprit who read ahead! At bedtime we gathered around for devotions, followed by an expository session on *Silas Marner*; that is, I read the day's chapter aloud for the benefit of six-year-old Jo.

We dispelled much of the boredom and ignored most of the terrifying "night music" as we dwelt among the "nutty hedgerows of Raveloe," absorbing Eliot's message of the transforming power of love. The night that we closed the book on Eppie's words to Silas, "I think nobody could be happier than we are," we were smitten with homesickness. We decided to start packing that night and return home the next day.

"Are we taking *Silas Marner* with us?" Jo asked.

Tom came running toward the house, excitedly waving a book.

"In more ways than you suspect," I answered, tucking the slim little volume in among the driftwood and agates.

Silas Marner now sits in obscurity on a crowded bookshelf in our living room, supported on one side by *Adam Bede* and on the other by *Mill on the Floss*. Whenever I feel the need for a bit of nostalgia—and that happens with more and more frequency of late—I reach for that particular volume and riffle the pages. Oh, I know it has to be imagination, but even after fifteen years the potpourri of mildew and mouse seems to waft upward and transport me back in time to that halcyon summer. I hear the rattling of our bikes on the gravel hills as we caravaned to the beach and back each day; the metallic reverberation of thunder during the night, so frighteningly unlike the sound of city thunder; the plaintive "Old Sam Peabody, Peabody, Peabody" of the white-throated sparrow, which Tom insisted was singing "Go, Lane, go, Lane, go"—his school song.

I can see ten-year-old Debby, addicted to Holloway suckers—those awful all-day caramel concoctions—pedalling madly home along the country lanes trying to outdistance the bees who shared her taste and wanted to share her confection. I remember how we would crowd together each night after dark at the little window in the loft after Jo discovered that from there we could see, for a few brief seconds, the lights of the Chicago-bound train as it skirted the far edge of Fish Lake. Oh, homesickness! And I shall never forget the sight of the three sisters, Anna, Alice, and Emma, walking out of the woods on a Sunday morning to drop in on us, for they had heard from their Chicago friends that we might be lonesome. What beautiful Christian hospitality these Finnish women offered us! They are still our friends.

My little copy of *Silas Marner* has strange powers—in my hands, anyway. It resurrects for me those dear dead days beyond recall, and as long as it can do that it will have its special place on my shelf as well as in my heart.

10

Thoughts on Moving Day

I DETEST MOVING. For weeks, even after the new curtains have been hung, and the dishes are arranged on the freshly-lined shelves, and all our mail has finally caught up with us, I still exhibit the restlessness of a cat in a strange attic. It takes a "heap o' living" in a house to make it feel like home to me. But worse than the ordeal of acclimation is the process of moving itself. With each successive uprooting it has become more burdensome, more expensive, the movers more independent, and I have become more vulnerable.

Our first relocation, post-honeymoon, was accomplished on a Saturday afternoon, on foot, with the help of a family friend. Contrast that with our latest move which required several weeks of packing, a consultation with a representative of the cartage firm, an enormous van, a team of piano-moving specialists, three husky weightlifters, and a crew boss. The accretions of thirty years and four children had been formidable; but because seventy-five percent of our worldly goods consisted of books, we hadn't anticipated any serious problems. Strange to say, therein lay the rub.

We had thought that any moving crew would appreciate the fact that our six rooms of furniture consisted mostly of reading material and the shelves on which to stack it. We were mistaken. We discovered that the moving trade has its prima donnas, sweatshirted and short-tempered, sensitive to the demands of their calling. Our men didn't complain about the oversized refrigerator that had to be inched and grunted along a narrow, twisting staircase to the third floor, nor were they at all distressed by the unwieldy hide-a-bed that began to unfold in their arms on the second story landing. They seemed to take delight, veins bulging, sweat popping, in wrestling the huge, old-fashioned kitchen range up the three flights and through the narrow doorways.

What did bug them were the more than forty boxes of books that had to be carried down from the flat we were leaving, loaded onto the van, unloaded, and then carted up to the new apartment. Running up and down stairs with Raggedy Ann and Seagram cartons, roped by Everett for easy handling and labeled by me for efficient unpacking, apparently embarrassed the movers. That kind of toting required no finesse, no expertise, and very little strain. They were disgruntled because it challenged their dignity and not their musculature.

With the portaging of the first few boxes, the men merely grumbled; then they sought relief in humor. They joked as they met on the stairs about how well educated they would be by the time they had completed this particular job.

"Hey, Mike," Steve yelled over the porch railing. "I just got done with a whole box of Greek!" He was referring to my husband's old textbooks.

"Izzatso?" Mike bellowed. "Me—I'm doin' a little research." He hefted a carton of encyclopedias onto his shoulder.

Steve spotted Dominic starting up the stairs. "Hey, Dom! What you got there?"

"You guys should be so lucky! Two boxes of 'Romantic Lit.'"

It was Dominic who later boasted at the top of his lungs that he expected to have twenty years knocked off his purgatory sentence since he was transporting a box of Bibles and concordances.

It was a warm spring day, windows were open, and I'm sure the neighbors on all sides knew before the morning was over not only the condition of our furniture but also the contents of our entire library, thanks to the running commentary of the men.

When Steve, the vociferous livewire of the crew, had set the last carton of books down on the living room floor, he decided to "take five." Mopping his face, he let his eyes travel over the cases of books that were stacked in the center of the room; then he gave me a quizzical grin and asked, "Seriously, lady, you people read all these books already?" When I answered in the affirmative, he shook his head incredulously. "Then how come you keep 'em?" he wondered. "I mean, like when I get done with a can of beer, I throw the can away."

I laughed. I had a sudden vision of America's highways littered with 'emptied' books; of recycling centers for paperbacks; of fliptop book covers.

I could see that Steve didn't really expect an answer. He had concocted the metaphor merely to poke a little gentle fun. Having gotten his laugh, he returned to work.

That night, lying awake uncomfortable in the strange house, I remembered Steve's question, "How come you keep 'em?" He had touched a sensitive nerve with his implied criticism. I had spent the first fifty years of my life collecting books, and I knew it was high time I began to reverse the process, especially if I wanted my children to mourn my passing fondly and in leisure and not be troubled by weeks of cataloging, inventory, and phone calls to the Salvation Army's pickup department.

My passion for books has caused Everett to refer to me more than once as "my wife, the bookkeeper." He is right. I operate on Ruskin's principle that "if a book is worth reading, it is worth buying. Nor is it serviceable, until it has been read, and reread, and loved, and loved again; and marked, so that you can refer to the passages you want in it."

My childhood copies of such books as *Black Beauty, Heidi, Jane Eyre, Little Women, Alice in Wonderland* fit Ruskin's description; they are dog-eared and spotted with peanut butter and jelly prints. They were on the shelves for years for my children's enjoyment, and now they are stored in the cellar waiting for the grandchildren to catch up with them.

Each spring Everett goes on a dig, foraging among the artifacts and crates in the basement attempting to eliminate and rearrange in order to establish a small work area for himself. Invariably he returns in a pet, frustrated and grimy, demanding equal space and warning that if he doesn't get it there will be a book burning that will light the sky for miles around.

"I declare," he pants at the top of the stairs, "you've got to do something. Those boxes of books are proliferating!"

"All right," I agree. "Let's start by getting rid of your *Greek Lexicon*, the *Matthew Henry Commentaries, Strong's Concordance*, and a few other textbooks left over from your student days—"

"Throw out *my* books?" he roars. "Over my dead body!" That challenge, emanating from a sexagenarian, is unfair and calculated to play on my sympathy; but it's effective and Everett knows it. He wins a compromise. We'll table the issue until next spring. "Soon," I assure him, "we can send the *Bobbsey Twins* to Phyllis and the *Sugar Creek Gang* to Ben and Nathan."

"Throw out *my* books? . . . Over my dead body!"

He's mollified but not deceived, knowing that by that time another fifty or sixty volumes will have been added to our bookshelves, necessitating the sending of a like number to the underground repository. My husband is familiar with my propensities; he learned early in our marriage that my idea of an exciting night on the town is a visit to a secondhand bookstore where I might pick up an eighty-year old edition of *Pride and Prejudice* for 50¢ or an authentic Horatio Alger for a quarter.

I have a handy defense for my obsession—I teach high school English; but my defense is an ostensible one, high school being what it is nowadays and students being what they are. My real reason for surrounding myself with the books I love, for not discarding them after one reading, for haunting book sales for coveted volumes, is that I find them a source of continual joy. I return to old books as to old friends—to recapture a mood, to quicken memories, to make new discoveries.

"How come you keep 'em?" the mover had asked. His question was contributing to my wakefulness. I decided to get up before I disturbed Everett with my tossing and turning. I groped my way through the unfamiliar darkness to the living room where the street lights shone in through the uncurtained windows.

I curled up in an arm chair and tried to pick up my thinking where I had left off. Poquito appeared from nowhere and jumped into my lap. "That makes two of us who are homesick, baby," I whispered. I comforted her for a moment with a little dog-talk and ear-scratching, and then the question returned and the soliloquy resumed.

How come I keep them? C. S. Lewis said, "An unliterary man may be defined as one who reads books once only." Well,

I shall need his and Ruskin's support if it ever comes to a showdown, I thought as I contemplated the stacks of boxes. Those two would appreciate my love affair with books. They would know what I mean when I say a book comes to life when I open the pages and read; just as a phonograph record is animated by the needle. They would understand me, all right, but would they sympathize with my moving and storage problems? Oh, Everett had a point there when he spoke of microfilming; only who can curl up with a good projector?

Far better to have a photographic memory, I would think. I recalled a futuristic novel that I had read a few months before. It concerned an authoritarian regime in which the leaders ordered the burning of all books, maintaining that reading only confused people and made them unhappy and rebellious. However, in remote areas of that fictional country there were individuals who spent every waking moment memorizing entire volumes before the books could be destroyed. These refugees from a godless society had mastered the art of perfect concentration, shutting out all distraction, in order to memorize the philosophies that they thought would be the means of salvation for future generations.

That's not unlike what God expects of me, I reflect. He wants me to hide His word in my heart, so that I can be a living epistle for all men to read. Oh, it's a good thing to study the classics, to commit to memory such passages as "Love is not love which alters when it alteration finds" from Shakespeare's Sonnet 116; or to learn "The world is too much with us . . . Getting and spending we lay waste our powers" from Wordsworth's "The World Is Too Much with Us"; or to recite "He who, from zone to zone, Guides through the boundless sky thy certain flight . . . Will lead my steps aright" from Bryant's "To a Waterfowl"; for these are reiterations of God's truth; but it is God's truth itself that must have the preeminence in my life. I must not lose my equilibrium.

Somewhere a dog howls, and Poquito's ears stand erect as she cocks her head at me for permission to respond. Not receiving it, she drops her head down upon her paws and resumes her napping. A good idea. Suddenly, I am tired enough to sleep. And I am impatient for tomorrow and the unpacking of my books—the surrounding myself with old friends. Shuffling back to the bedroom I bump awkwardly and solidly against a doorframe. Everett is awake, propped up on an elbow.

"I detest moving!" I grumble.

"You'll feel better in the morning," he promises.

11

Never Too Old

I TOOK MY FIRST DRIVING TEST when I was forty-five, and I failed. Through no fault of my own, I might add. Everett and the examiner were to blame; Everett for rushing me, and the examiner for rattling me.

I told Everett I wasn't ready.

"Nonsense," he contradicted. "You've had the best of teachers." He was referring to himself. "And you've driven hundreds of miles without an accident." He was referring to endless, vacant stretches of freeway west of the Mississippi. "And besides, your learning permit expires tomorrow."

"Do you really think I can pass?"

"I know you can."

"My parallel parking leaves much to be desired," I warned.

"Only when you park on the right side of the street. You're OK on the left."

"And I still can't back up in a straight line," I reminded him.

"Yes," he agreed. "I can't understand that. It's such a simple maneuver, too."

That "simple maneuver" had almost broken up our twenty-six-year-old marriage.

"Left! Left!" he would shout as I started to back down the empty alley behind our house.

"I am turning left!" I would scream.

"Not the steering wheel! The wheels!"

"Which wheels? The front or the back?"

"It's the front wheels that turn, sweetheart," he would remind me through clenched teeth.

"If you would just leave me alone and let me do it by instinct," I would plead. "It's when I think left and right that I get all confused."

"By the time your instinct takes over, you will have run over a halfdozen trash cans or flattened someone's garage."

It was at about this point in every lesson that I would throw in the towel.

"You hate me, don't you?" I would whimper.

"Don't be silly! I love you," he would bellow.

"Then why are you yelling at me?"

"I'm not yelling at you!" he would roar. "I'm just telling you what to do; and if you would do just what I tell you, there'd be no problem!"

"I'm not yelling at you!" he roared.

"It's no use," I would moan at the end of these sessions. "I'm just too old to learn."

"You'll do better next time," Everett would promise. But more practice was not the answer. My reversing deteriorated as rapidly as did our teacher-pupil relationship.

"This is ridiculous. I am not ready to take a test," I told Everett as we reported that morning to the Elston Avenue testing lanes.

"Think positively, and keep the wheel steady," he said, pushing me through the door.

It was early in the day, but even so there was a crowd of applicants and their sponsors already on hand. Everett pried my fingers loose from his arm and directed me toward a line where I was given a number and told to wait my turn. I found myself surrounded by teenagers. I envied them: their youth, their quick reflexes, their sharp eyesight, their insouciance. Envied? Let's be honest. I resented them with a passion.

The freckle-faced youngster next to me confided that she expected to fail her first time around. It was routine procedure, she informed me, to give sixteen-year-olds a hard time.

"Then what will you do?" I asked.

"Oh, I'll come back tomorrow. They'll pass me then."

I thought it over. If she expected to be failed because of her youth, then couldn't I expect to be slipped through without a hitch because of my maturity? I took heart.

The line, long though it was, moved rapidly, and soon it was my turn. I was turned over to an irascible fellow who grudgingly introduced himself. He did not look the type, I decided, to make allowances for crow's feet and hard knocks. His name was unmistakably Hibernian in origin, and he pronounced it with a heavy brogue. In a moment of weak-kneed disloyalty, I fervently wished the Bible on our dashboard would either self-destruct or turn into a plaster of paris St. Christopher.

"So you're a school teacher," he said, consulting my application. Something about his intonation told me that he had spent a disproportionate amount of his student days in the discipline office.

I pleaded guilty, adding with a smile, "Only until something better comes along."

Ignoring my pathetic attempt at humor, he ordered: "Repeat after me. 'I am in the left lane—lane number one. At no time must I leave this lane.'"

He had to be kidding, I thought, but I couldn't risk it. I repeated the promise, resisting the temptation to raise my sweaty right hand.

"Start the car!" he snapped.

I did, without a stutter. Betsy was eager to prove herself.

"Accelerate to thirty miles per hour and then put on the brakes."

My goodness, this is going to be easy, I thought. *Whatever had I been afraid of?*

I pressed down on the accelerator, reached the speed he had asked for, braked smoothly, and then waited for further instructions.

"Now," he said. "Back up slowly until I tell you to stop."

I did not imagine it; there was something ominous in his eye. *He knows*, I realized, my heart hammering in my throat. *He knew the minute he saw me. Maybe it's my weak profile, or the manner in which I grip the wheel, or perhaps there are vibes to which he's sensitive; but he's got me pegged as a loser, a nonreverser of the first order.*

I tried to suppress the mounting panic. What was it Everett

had said? "Think positively and keep the wheel steady."

I shifted into reverse. No problem there. I flung my right arm over the back of the seat and turned as casually as I could to look out the rear window. I knew my stance was correct; I had watched my husband do this a thousand times. I might even have been able to follow through, if I hadn't seen at that instant the cloud of witnesses, Everett among them, standing on the observation deck waiting for me to back down the course.

Unnerved, I stomped down hard on the gas and began what can only be described as a slalom in reverse. I lunged; I braked. I began again and overcompensated. I braked a second time, turned the wheel sharply to the left, saw it should have been right, overcompensated again—and wished I were dead! The hoarse "Stop!" of my passenger finally got through to me, and I shifted carefully into park.

There was a short silence. Before he could speak, I said, "Well, I guess that's that!" I opened the door and started to step out.

He grabbed my arm. "You'll finish the course," he said.

I got back in. I recognized a sadist. I resumed driving.

We hadn't gone very far when he said, "Lady, what side of the street are you supposed to drive on?"

I had to think. In fact, at this point I had to stop to think. I pulled over. He repeated his question. All my confidence had drained away.

"The right side?" It sounded like a question. It was a question.

"Then what are you doing on the left?"

I considered. Then I remembered.

"You told me to stay in the left lane," I accused him. "You said I was not to leave the left lane!" I repeated triumphantly. I had him there!

"That was back in the starting stretch," he snarled. "Now we're on a simulated highway."

We drove on. Now that I was beyond redemption, it made no difference that I did a beautiful parallel park that was better than the young boy ahead of me who knocked down the two markers. Nor did either of us care that I skillfully maneuvered the car out of the tight square, or that I parked correctly on the hill.

Everett was waiting for me at the end of the course. I slid over and let him take the wheel.

"Don't you want to drive home?" he asked. He's a bullet biter from way back.

"I'll never drive again," I said. I meant it. I had never known such complete humiliation.

He tried to revive my spirits. "Remember Mr. Jonas?" he asked. Of course I did. Charlie Jonas had been a retired army engineer who had worked on the Gatun Locks in Panama and also had had a hand in the construction of Bonneville Dam in Oregon. Single-handedly he had built a two-story home on the Oregon coast, even installing an elevator for his ailing wife. I knew what my husband was leading up to. Jonas, with all his intelligence and technical expertise, had become a legend around Nehalem because of his erratic driving. He drove on a provisional permit since he could neither parallel park nor back up. He also had a strong tendency to wander across the double yellow, a problem that proved to be his undoing—he died from injuries sustained in a head-on collision. "A natural death," the locals called it.

Everett believed—like Alice's Duchess, that "everything has a moral if only you can find it." He found one in the memory of Mr. Jonas.

"Your not being able to back up is not a sign that you are

90

mentally deficient," Everett stated pedantically. "On the contrary, it might be a mental block peculiar only to the very gifted."

"I'll go along with that," I responded when the tears had dried and my voice had steadied. "So I'm a gifted eccentric, but I'd much rather be a run-of-the-mill housewife with a driver's license."

For three years Everett tried to woo me back to the wheel, but I remained adamant. Even the inconvenience of trying to cash personal checks without a driver's license did not sway me; and as long as my husband and a few of my friends were willing to chauffeur me around the countryside, why should I place myself in double jeopardy?

I began to notice, however, a subtle change in my attitude; I became an insufferable passenger, wondering, sometimes aloud, how my card-carrying contemporaries had ever passed their tests. One crusty, silver-haired pioneer ignored a local stop sign and shot out onto the highway without a pause. Her excuse: "I was here before that sign was!"

I was occasionally chauffeured by a friend who pulled over to the side of the road—any road—in order to finish a sentence. "I can't talk and drive at the same time," she explained. When I was with her, I never initiated a conversation.

Another acquaintance, who was always willing to drive me to school events, could not drive without talking: about the tailgater behind her, the "turtle" ahead, the "demon" passing on her left, whether or not she could make the green light at the next intersection, the ambling pedestrian in her way, the sticky accelerator, et cetera.

But it was the elderly widow who thought that, because she had carefully braked at the stop sign, she was entitled to pull

91

out onto the highway without looking left or right—and whose assumption demolished our car—that made me reconsider.

I can do better, I thought. *At least not any worse.* I asked Everett if he would take me on again as a pupil. He accepted the challenge.

I passed my written test with a perfect score, obtained my learner's permit, applied myself with a fanatic, now or never zeal, logged umpteen hours of reverse driving, dragged myself out of a sickbed, and with a fever of 102, took and passed my driving exam without incident. I came close to throwing my arms around the examiner and giving him a grateful kiss.

For weeks I could not come down off cloud nine. I had not realized how intense was my feeling of ostracization from the human race until I earned my passport back—my driver's license. Who cared that it revealed my actual age and my approximate weight? I showed it to all and sundry who would hold still. I had not experienced such headiness since my husband, years before, had presented me with a Marshall Field's charge plate.

When license renewal time rolled around three years later, the Secretary of State sent me a safe driving citation. I was in the midst of hanging it in a prominent spot over the living room mantel when Everett walked in. He took a close look at it and snorted.

"A five-mile round trip to the laundromat once a week is not a true test of one's driving ability!"

I centered the matted and framed certificate and charitably chose to hold my peace.

"Especially," he continued, "since you stop driving at the sign of the first snowflake in November and don't take up the gauntlet again until the ice goes out of the bay in April."

I could stand the proud man's contumely. I knew what was

rankling him. During that same three-year period he had received several citations himself—of a vastly different nature. And it is difficult for a teacher to see himself overtaken by his pupil; most difficult when the pupil is also his wife.

It appears as though I may have to brave the elements and dent a fender or two before our old harmonious relationship is restored. I may even have to remove the "new driver" sticker from the bumper. The price of detente is exorbitant. I am willing to pay it, but not just yet.

12

The Doll House

WE CALL OURSELVES "semiretired." Meaning he is; I'm not. It happened three years ago when the Railway Express Agency transferred Everett's name from the payroll to the pension roll and handed him a handsome little box with a brass plate on the cover which read:

In Appreciation
from
REA Express
Upon the occasion of retirement
after 32 years of faithful and
conscientious service.

There was no gold watch inside. I looked.
"It's a beautiful box," I said. "It's mahogany, isn't it?"
"Just so long as it's not pine."
"What'll you use it for?"
Everett examined it carefully, inside and out.
"My dentures."

* * *

A couple of my cronies had warned me that I would have problems when my husband retired. I scoffed. Everett was a most adaptable and flexible person, and as for me, nothing would be lovelier than having a husband to come home to after a hard day's work. I anticipated nothing but a luxurious existence of being chauffeured, cooked for, cleaned up after, coddled, and constantly companioned. Just because it hadn't worked out well for some of my friends, didn't mean it wouldn't for us. And I was right—up to a point.

The chauffeuring, the cleaning, and the coddling I lapped up, being at heart a very lazy individual. It was the "constantly companioned" that was my undoing. Poquito, our Chihuahua, was ecstatic at having her master underfoot for twenty-four hours a day, but I wasn't. After seven hours of confinement each day in a high school classroom, I was accustomed to— and needed—time alone for quiet recovery, a private place in which to lick my wounds. Not getting it, I became a little short of impossible to live with. Everett, understandably, began to hobnob with bewitching Samantha Stevens and intrepid Chief Ironside and Gomer Pyle.

I suggested to my husband that he ought to pursue a hobby, one that would take him out of the house occasionally.

"I think," he said, "you are using the wrong verb. Don't you mean *get* me out of the house?"

I refused to spar. Instead I handed him a brochure advertising the adult education courses offered at a nearby school. I had encircled the woodshop class because I thought he had talent in that direction. Twenty years before he had nailed some boards together for a bookshelf, and it was still standing.

"It will keep your hands from mischief, and it will give me a couple of nights a week to myself," I encouraged.

He was reluctant; it meant sacrificing his favorite TV programs. I reminded him about summer reruns. It would tie him down, he argued. There were books he wanted to read, things he wanted to do.

"Me, too," I overruled.

He surrendered finally but conditionally, promising only to give it a try.

That first night I waved him off with my fingers crossed. It would not take much—a crowded parking lot, a snippy clerk, a flat tire—to send him home with a change of heart.

But circumstances cooperated. Everett got himself duly registered, sat through the introductory session, and returned enthusiastic, acting as though the whole idea had originated with him. I could see that this handyman of mine, who until now had lived by saw, hammer, and a pair of screw drivers, was captivated by the plethora of power tools that would be at his disposal, and, although he didn't say so, I knew he had been comforted by the presence of other senior citizens in the class. I was quietly jubilant. I thought it a little too soon to disclose my plans for a massive coffee table, a stately grandfather clock, and my long-suppressed desire for a doll house.

Those grandiose delusions suffered a slight setback when Everett brought home his first project, a pegboard game for which neither of us knew the rules. I admired it dutifully and at the first opportunity donated it to the local Lions Club garage sale.

His second offering was a colonial footstool, just the thing for a two-year-old granddaughter to push around from sink to counter to refrigerator.

A chess table modified into a night stand for the spare bedroom followed. So far, so good. He was improving. His work began to develop a patina of professionalism, and his conversation about woods and glues, lathes and routers rang with expertise. I bided my time. Let his enthusiasm and his

I waved him off to his first night of school with my fingers crossed.

confidence gain momentum, I decided, before I make my move.

I encouraged him to go ahead and design and execute a distinctive, varigrained fruit bowl. Next I OKed the expenditure of half a month's Social Security check for the forty feet of birch needed for a bookcase. The night that he finished fastening the last brass pull on a handsome bedside chest, I felt the time was ripe. I asked for my doll house. I didn't have to twist his arm. It seemed that his shop teacher had just completed a doll house for his wife. Within eight weeks I had my minimansion, six rooms and an attic, waiting to be painted, papered and furnished. I was enthralled. I had grown up without ever having a doll house—as inconceivable, I thought, as a boy without a bike.

I rushed home from work each day to varnish the floors, to paint the roof, to "plant" the flowerboxes, to hang the wallpaper; and as I decorated, I discovered that I was not alone, that there is an entire world out there dedicated to insuring the happiness of Lilliputian nuts like myself. I found shops and mail order houses that sell wallpaper, plain and flocked; carpets, oriental and rag; framed oil paintings, layer cakes and boxes of carmel corn; mice, and the traps to catch them; grand pianos that play and piano stools that spin; calendars, current and antique; Christmas trees and Easter bunnies; and, of course, dolls, three generations of them—all of these scaled down to 1/12 life size.

I was awed and tantalized by the amazing market in miniatures, but I could not in good conscience pay such huge prices for such petite merchandise. I would ask Everett to make most of the furniture and accessories, though I had doubts about his ability to work on pieces so tiny and detailed.

He was willing to try. The time seemed opportune. I was just beginning a year's sabbatical leave from teaching, and we were settling into our mobile home in Wisconsin. The summer before, Everett had erected a minibarn on the property, having no inkling then that it would become a factory, fittingly enough for minifurniture.

Every day my husband would disappear into the barn right after breakfast, emerging dusty and perspiring for lunch and dinner. I left him alone, but a neighbor across the road, his curiosity aroused by the piercing clamor of the circular saw, the lathe, the drill and sander, dropped in to see what was happening. From the fearsome din and the violent vibrations that threatened to lift the barn off its foundation he expected to find something monumental under construction—not the miniscule drop leaf table and matching kitchen chair that Everett held out for inspection on his outstretched palm. He was reminded, the neighbor told my husband, of Aesop's pregnant mountain that labored and brought forth a mouse!

Somewhere along the way "my" doll house became "Phyllis's" doll house. We realized we were getting ready to relinquish it to our granddaughter. We decided that once the last drape was hung, the pots and pans were neatly stacked in the kitchen cabinet, and the tiny flowers were stenciled on the cradle and wardrobe in the nursery, it would need a younger caretaker than ourselves; someone with tiny hands that could wield a four-inch dust mop, and squarecorner the sheets on a wee brass bedstead, and rock to sleep a palmsized baby in the diminutive cradle.

Phyllis was, and still is, impatient to move in. She asked her mother, "How come Grandma and Grandpa are keeping my doll house?"

"It's not ready yet," Martha told her. "Grandma and Grandpa still have a lot of things to do to get it ready for you."

What Martha didn't tell her, since it would have been a little difficult for her to grasp, is that at not quite four she was not quite ready for the doll house. But she believes, because she knows that we would not have told her so if we did not mean for her to have that magic, little house for her very own; and so her audacious assumption enables her to say "my doll house" while it is still a thousand miles away with Grandma and Grandpa.

My granddaughter's impatience reminds me, reprovingly, of a spiritual parallel: I am not nearly so anxious to possess the mansion that is being prepared for me.

"I wish," I confide to Everett, "that I had that same sanctified audacity, that child-faith, to believe Jesus' promise: 'I go to prepare a place for you.'"

"But you do believe it," he chides.

"Not the way I should," I confess. "Not to the point of unbearable suspense."

* * *

We don't bother to apologize for the fact that our own home is neglected while we work on Phyllis's doll house. "First things first," defends Everett. And neither do we make excuses for pursuing such a simple hobby. We've encountered too many envious friends. In fact, one of those friends, a person I had considered a confirmed spinster, says she is now on the lookout for a middle-aged, unmarried cabinet maker, preferably a man with a bit of whimsy in his makeup, so that he's not above carpentering a doll house. I suggested to her that she enroll in a woodshop class. Then, one way or the other, she'll get her petite *maison*.

101

13

A Glorious Way to Go

I REFUSED TO GO IN. My husband and I had been sitting outside a Chicago ski shop for an uncomfortable half hour while I dug in my heels and lifted my voice in protest. The whole thing had been my idea in the first place, he reminded me, and now I was balking.

"You know how you are," he argued. "We have to push you into the pool every summer and then threaten to pull the plug to get you out."

"This is different. Who ever heard of a fifty-year-old grandmother, and a three-time loser at Weight Watchers, taking up skiing?"

"It's only cross-country skiing," Everett reasoned. "You're not going to tackle the Swiss Alps!"

"I'm not in condition to tackle a waxed linoleum, and neither are you. You and I are old folks who should be at home. We're dentured, bifocaled, stiffjointed, dull of hearing. First time out, one of us will die in a tangle of splintered birch, impaled on our poles."

"It would be a glorious way to go," he grinned. "How many children can boast of a grandparent who perished in a ski mishap?"

I forced a tepid smile. "You really want to go through with this, don't you?"

He did. He pointed out that he was tired of losing to me at Scrabble; that bird-watching had begun to pall; and moreover, winter weekends were looming.

I capitulated. I left the warm security of our station wagon and with a little assist from Everett entered an emporium of instant intimidation. The ski shop reeked of youth and recklessness. It was unrelieved outdoorsman. It was no place for a bunioned, sinusitic hausfrau like myself.

The salesman, a lithe Jean-Claude in a turtleneck, did a doubletake at our entrance and then busied himself elsewhere. For this I was grateful. In Marshall Field's I could have pretended that I was taking a shortcut from housewares to gardening supplies by way of the sporting goods section, but in this watered-down Abercrombie and Fitch no one would believe that I was lost between escalator stops.

I tugged at Everett's sleeve. "If anyone asks, we're shopping for a gift for one of the children."

He didn't hear me. He was racing toward a rack of brightly varnished skis. It was apparent from his expression that he was entertaining visions of gemütlichkeit and fondues, apres ski togs and roaring fireplaces—all the romantic fantasies engendered by TV commercials.

Lifting a ski from the rack, he stroked it affectionately, turned it tenderly in his hands, ran a finger lightly along its bowed edges, and murmured ecstatically, "Look at the beautiful camber. These are the ones I want."

The only camber he knows anything about, I reflected disloyally, is found at the base of his Salem rocker.

The salesman returned; apparently his curiosity had won out. My husband shifted the ski he had been fondling and said with a *savoir faire* that was meant to impress—and a stilted

construction that immediately destroyed the impression—
"We would like to be outfitted with some cross-country ski
equipment."

"Well, then," the young man said, wresting the ski from my
husband's grip, "in that case, you'd better come this way.
You're looking at a downhill ski; the cross-country gear is on
the other side of the shop."

Our innocence had been discovered. From this point on we
were to be clay in the clerk's hands, and all three of us knew it.
He dispensed with a sales pitch. He didn't defer to our taste or
our intelligence. Rather, he prescribed: "You'll need this,
that, these, and those."

Within a half hour he had finished with us; and there it all
was, spread out on the counter and propped against the
register, the incriminating evidence that nothing can compare
with an old fool's foolishness. Our impedimenta consisted of
skis and bindings, boots, mittens, and one tin of wax.

"How long will this wax last?" Everett inquired.

"Oh, it will take you through the winter."

We trusted his judgment. At the time we knew no better. In
retrospect we can only assume that he was convinced the wax
would outlast our enthusiasm.

We began our adventure in a lonely picnic grove in Door
County's Peninsula State Park, an area sufficiently isolated
that I could lose my dignity and yet maintain my public image.
That we were far removed from phone and fracture ward
seemed of secondary importance.

We donned our skis. My husband, once. I, twice. No one
had told me that there were a right and a left ski! I leaned
heavily on my poles and watched Everett strike out on his
own. My heart sank. He was a natural! Swooping and gliding,
he rode his skis like a pro, albeit slightly pigeon-toed.

"Tremendous!" I shouted in a display of good sportsman-ship and immediately found myself spread-eagled in the snow, sans skis and sans poles. I floundered to my knees and after several spine-wrenching attempts managed to get myself back into my gear and on my feet.

Everett skimmed past. "Are you all right?" he asked, trying hard to appear solicitous.

"I'm fine," I shrugged, trying hard to appear nonchalant. Shrugging was a mistake. This time I landed on my face, with a ski tip embedded in my ribs. Again there was the frustrating, ankle-bending struggle to disentangle and reassemble—not only myself, but a right ski and a left ski, a right pole and a left pole, a right mitten and a left mitten.

"And a right and a left to the jaws of those outdoor evangelists who insist that anyone who can walk can most assuredly ski!" I muttered.

Those first few weeks I was never without a stiff shoulder or wry neck and sported contusions in various stages of absorp-tion. Let it be a matter of record, however, that I persevered. Each weekend I shucked the security of my orthopedic oxfords and became apodal: instead of on feet, I moved about on six-foot-long pedal extremities: "Skids," I labeled them. "Have to grease my skids," I would sigh, reaching for our tin of rapidly diminishing wax.

We measured my progress by the decrease in the number of falls; a no-fall weekend was a cause for celebration: marshmal-lows in my hot chocolate! Gentle genuflections that occurred on hummocks, and from which I could rise easily, were discounted. An experienced skier, trying to be helpful, suggested, "Tuck in your butt, suck in your gut, and plant your poles behind you." I put the vulgar little formula into practice, insofar as I was able, and found that it worked. Often.

106

We signed up for a series of lessons in January, ostensibly to encourage the young teacher. Actually, we wanted to enlarge our knowledge. That is, I did. Everett, already proficient, wanted to enlarge his audience.

Our instructor was a red-bearded, hollow-cheeked Mother Earth disciple named Steve. Our classroom was a cluttered combination bike, ski, and natural foods shop in Fish Creek. I inferred from the unwashed wok pans in the kitchen that it was also Steve's pad.

Our first lesson was concerned with the selection and care of skis. I braced myself for boredom. After all, we were veterans. But our guru-of-the-skis was a born teacher and had me spellbound from the start.

Steve sat on the floor, backlighted by the morning sun shining through a transplanted stained glass window, and led us step by step through the rituals of ski care. He demonstrated the laborious stripping of the lacquer from the new ski, then the fine sanding, next the sealing with pine tar using a propane torch, and finally, the waxing. *Mea culpa*. I gulped. We had done none of these things.

Arranging a palette of tins and tubes of waxes, Steve explained how they were color keyed to snow and weather conditions; how the right wax or combination of waxes made it possible to climb almost any kind of slope, to skim rather than plod, to avoid bogging down in wet snow on warm days.

Everett and I exchanged glances. We were both remembering the callous salesman who had sent us out into the world armed with a single tin of wax. Too, we were beginning to realize that it would take hours to get our skis into shape before the next lesson.

I had a sudden inspiration. "Wouldn't it be possible, Steve, for us to bring our skis in and have you recondition them?" I asked.

"It would," he answered. "But I don't recommend it." He paused, and his voice became gently reproving. "I think it's most important that a skier relate to his skis."

I blushed at my blasphemy and retreated into my corner as seven pairs of eyes, including Everett's, reproached me.

The lesson finished, Steve asked us to get our skis so that he could look them over. I felt suddenly ill. Everett and I hadn't related to our skis at all; in fact, we were guilty of ski abuse. We had scoured them on icy snowmobile trails; we had gouged them traveling over gravel-peppered snow on isolated back roads; we had splintered the edges climbing over tree stumps in dense woods.

I flinched as Everett handed our mutilated skis to Steve. I held my breath while his sensitive fingers moved gently over the pitted surfaces, tracing the cruel abrasions. Steve finished his inspection and then hesitated, searching for the right words. Then he grinned—warmly, admiringly. "Say," he said. "You folks have really been skiing!"

It was absolution and benediction all rolled into one! Tension snapped. Words poured forth. We backed Steve into a corner and related the story behind every scratch and scar. He listened, empathized, sold us a blowtorch and pine tar, scrapers and daubers, an assortment of waxes with a backpack to carry them in, and a copy of *The New Cross-Country Ski Book,* and sent us on our way—to sin no more.

The winter passed too swiftly. For the first time in our lives we were not anticipating spring.

"I think we are hooked," I confided to our children in our weekly newsletter.

"We rather suspected as much," my oldest daughter wrote caustically. "You keep forgetting to ask about the grandchildren until the postscripts."

We hadn't related to our skis at all. We were guilty, in fact, of ski abuse.

We realized the totality of our commitment on a Saturday morning in February when we arose, glanced at the thermometer that registered a plus five, listened unconcernedly to the winds howling about the eaves, and then without a backward glance, picked up our skis, and struck out on a prebreakfast tour.

We began to seek converts, even proselytized. A faculty crony, who happened to be an avid downhill skier, queried impatiently, "What do you see in crosscountry skiing?"

I chose to misinterpret her question and answered her literally. "One day we coasted down a forest trail and came face to face with a doe," I said. "We skim along beaches where sand has been crystallized into huge lumps of maple sugar. We pole our way along aisles of abandoned apple orchards where orange-hued, frozen fruit hangs from snow-laden branches—"

But I lost her. She is Physical Ed. I am English Lit. She cannot understand our fascination with the delicate traceries of rodent and bird tracks, hieroglyphics in the snow, or our excitement at hearing the distant thunder of ruffed grouse bursting into flight within arm's reach. And surely she would question my emotional stability if I confided that often, overcome by the grandeur of it all, I stop along the trail, breathless and teary-eyed, and whisper, "God, Your world is too beautiful today!"

Sometime around April the rains washed away the last vestiges of snow, and the ice moved out of the bays in our northeastern Wisconsin refuge, and we had to accept the fact that there was little chance of a late spring blizzard. Cantankerous as a pair of bears just out of hibernation, we took to our bikes to work off our frustration. Oh, how tedious and tasteless in comparison to skiing is cycling!

In May Everett persuaded me to store the skis in a closet,

promising I could take them out occasionally to do a little relating. The waxes, a dozen aromatic tins, I placed in my dresser drawer, like a pomander among my lingerie. I comforted myself with the knowledge that, since summer was almost upon us, winter couldn't be far behind.

"And if we become desperate in our doldrums," I joked, "there's a scuba diving school at Gill's Rock—"

Everett sat up, immediately captivated by the idea.

"Don't be silly," I headed him off. "Think of the absurdity of a fifty-one-year-old grandmother taking to the waves in flippers and goggles and a size twenty-and-a-half rubber suit. Why, the first time out, I'd get tangled in the seaweed and drown."

I knew what his retort would be, something about our grandchildren being able to boast about their grandparents dying romantically at sea. The dialogue was strangely familiar. This was where I had come in. The question was, Did I want to stay around and see if there would be any changes in the script?

Thirty years of married life have taught me that distraction is the better part of valor. "I'm about to bake a pie. Would you like cherry or apple?" I asked.

14

One Wife's Complaint

EVERETT IS ILL. Nothing serious, just a case of the flu. Not even a serious case, it merited no more than a "hot tea-aspirin-bed rest" prescription via telephone from our overworked physician.

"How is Dad?" a daughter calls to ask.

"How should I know?" I reply, a bit on the peevish side. "He's taken to his bed and barricaded the door from the inside."

"You should be used to that by now," she laughs. "Isn't that his usual pattern?"

It's his usual pattern, all right. The whole family—I'm the only holdout—accepts that fact that when illness strikes, Dad turns his face to the wall and asks for nothing more than to be left alone. He suffers in stoical silence behind closed doors and doesn't emerge until the malady has run its course.

They say I shouldn't complain; that I should remember all the women who have a different tale to tell, who are married to overgrown boys who demand intensive care for an ingrown toenail or who insist on round-the-clock nursing for a head cold. Well, for the record, let me say I envy those women. I would love to be able to identify with the compassionate ladies on TV commercials who spoon out cough medicine to their sneezing, raspy-throated husbands and are told, "You're a good wife, honey"; or with those who with healing in their fingers rub ointment into the aching shoulders of their appreciative mates; or with the efficient helpmates who keep a bottle of sleeping tablets handy in the bedside table for the insomniac husbands who have important business dates the next morning. But unfortunately for me, Everett concocts his own cough syrup out of a mixture of honey and lemon, and soaks away his muscular aches and pains in a steaming tub, and has never permitted a worry to rob him of a minute's sleep. There is nothing one can do for a do-it-yourselfer, except as Everett suggests, "take care of yourself, get enough sleep, exercise regularly and take a vitamin every morning, just in case."

"Just in case what?" I ask.

"Just in case I ever do need a nurse."

"Fat chance!" I reflect. Why, I haven't fluffed up his pillows, sponged his fevered brow, or prepared tempting invalid trays since the first year of our marriage when he came down with "la grippe." Looking back, I have to admit that I may have overreacted at the time, but I was motivated by fears of an early widowhood. Throughout the three-day siege I rarely left Everett's side, convinced that if I did, he would quietly slip away. When his temperature "soared" to 101, I begged to be allowed to summon a doctor, preferably a Harley Street specialist.

"Only if I take a turn for the worse," he smiled weakly.

I wrung my hands. "How will I know?"

"Keep an eye on my toes," he whispered. "They'll begin to turn blue."

He was needling me, of course, since I refilled the hot water bottle so frequently and enthusiastically that his nether

"Do I need all that for a sneeze?"

extremities were a permanent scarlet and threatening to peel.

To keep up his strength I plied him with gelatins and soft-boiled eggs and graveyard stews. "You have got to eat," I pleaded. "You'll feel better if you do."

He made the effort, but gave up, groaning, "You better. Me worse."

On the third day he staggered to his feet, claiming I left him no alternative: if he stayed in bed any longer, he would make medical history by dying of an overdose of TLC. That was his prognosis. It was my opinion that his rapid recovery was due to my dedicated nursing.

At any rate, he wasn't to receive such devoted care again for a long while. Our family began to grow, and any manifestation of illness that Everett displayed was quickly upstaged by the more dramatic chicken pox, mumps, measles, rheumatic fever, polio, rheumatoid arthritis, and the thousand natural germs that our children were heir to. I have shadowy recollections of Everett seeking medical treatment for a wrenched back, a sprained ankle, sporadic cases of the flu—but only out of the corner of my mind as I tended the children.

Then after twenty-seven years we were alone again, back where we had begun—in a strangely silent house with a medicine cabinet that was almost bare. It was an unhappy time of life for me, that anticlimactic period of despondency, that after-the-ball-is-over depression, when a woman becomes conscious of her supernumerary role. I needed to be needed. I would have welcomed a broken leg or a peptic ulcer if Everett had brought either home from work. I was ready to seize on a sneeze or gloat over a goutish digit to give meaning to my existence. Try as he might, Everett could not accommodate me. It was a period of unprecedented good health, until one day he came home with the news that he needed another hernia repair.

116

"How many is that?" I asked. "Your third, or fourth?" My vagueness was understandable since his previous surgery had been overshadowed by more demanding family emergencies. His third, he informed me; and if he had anything to say about it, it would be his last. And, since it was just a routine job of hemstitching, there was no cause for me to try to make an occasion of it or to become overly solicitous, he warned me.

His cautionary words had the opposite effect; they triggered an alarm. My suspicions mounted when I noticed he was cleaning out his dresser drawers and organizing his papers and prepaying some bills.

It was the fuses, though, that really sent me into a panic. "You ought to learn where the fuses are and how to change them," he said kindly but firmly, taking me down to the basement the day before he entered the hospital. *He is getting his house in order*, I thought. *He is concealing something far more serious than a recurring hernia*. But if he could be brave, then so could I. I stiffened my lip and listened to his parting instructions as attentively as I could under the circumstances—the circumstances being that his detailed directions sounded to me like deathbed dicta. There was nothing Everett could have said to me at this point that would have convinced me he was not riddled with malignancies.

I had promised that I would stay away from the hospital until the surgery was over and he was out of the recovery room. I had not, however, promised to abstain from besieging the switchboard with anxious queries. I suppose that's the reason they had the surgeon phone me with reassurances.

"Then it was only his hernia? You didn't find anything else?" I asked fearfully.

There was a long pause.

"What was it you had in mind?" the doctor asked dryly,

117

intimating by his sarcastic tone that, if I would be more specific, he might be inclined to go back and look.

"Nothing," I mumbled, thoroughly ashamed of myself. I hung up and returned to the bag I was packing for Everett with a few odds and ends I intended to take on my first visit: his Indian blanket bathrobe, flannel pajamas, a pair of down-at-the-heel mules, magazines, fresh fruit, and snapshots of the grandchildren. The latter item, the photos, were to remind him and the nurses that he was not as young as he looked.

That first visit lasted an hour. I had come prepared to spend the day: to coax him out from under the covers, to plump his pillows and to moisten his parched lips with a pipette, to complain about the lack of service in general and the shortage of blankets in particular, to crank the bed, to organize the clutter on the bedside table, to shave his jowls if necessary. But when I walked into his room, there was no neglected silent sufferer needing my ministrations. Someone had gotten there before me. My husband, clean-shaven and glowing, was sitting in an armchair, not much the worse for wear. I tried to conceal my disappointment.

"Say, am I glad you came!" he smiled, seizing my hand.

I brightened. He had missed me after all.

"I'm broke," he went on to explain. "I had to have the barber give me a shave, and I have to pay for my share of the TV rental, and the newspaper costs twenty-five cents a day, and they're taking up a collection for the head nurse, who's getting married next week."

Ah, well. I handed him my wallet and told him to take what he needed. "Just leave me bus fare," I asked. I started to unpack the goodies I had brought when we were interrupted by the entrance of a pretty librarian pushing a book and magazine cart. Everett checked out enough literature to last him through several operations.

No sooner had the bookmobile disappeared through the door when a pert young aid wheeled in a refreshment trolley. Everett helped himself to cheese and crackers and pineapple juice, "for now," he said, and a couple of cartons of chocolate milk "for later." Before I could begin to remonstrate, a kitchen staffer was at his elbow with the next day's bill of fare on which my husband was asked to check not only his preferences but the size of the portions, small or large. From where I sat, I could see that Everett did not intend to stint.

The beauteous and engaged head nurse dropped in next, yawning widely to emphasize her declaration that she was worn out attending one shower after another, and expressing regret that none of the afflicted in this particular ward would be able to attend the ceremony on Saturday. The four old men were charmed by her performance, which was interrupted by the arrival of a probationer come to take temperatures. We had barely begun to talk about the operation when a garrulous cleaning woman did a turn around the room with a dustmop. During all this activity I tried to keep a smile on my face and my feet out of the way.

"I guess I'd better start for home," I said making no attempt to disguise my desolation.

"You might just as well," he agreed, insensitive to my misery.

"The buses will be crowded," I reminded him, picking up the pair of shopping bags I had never gotten around to unpacking.

"Yes, they will," he nodded, impatient for my departure.

"Besides, my sinuses are killing me," I tried, knowing that was usually good for a comforting word or two.

"Must be the stuffy air. You'll feel better when you get outdoors," he hinted.

It was not the stale air. It was the head nurse's Shalimar perfume. I started for the door.

"Before you go, would you do something for me?" he asked.

I spun around. Would I? Just name it. Your slightest wish—

"Would you turn on the TV? Channel 2. 'Bewitched' has been on for the last couple of minutes." He couldn't eliminate the reproach in his voice. "Be a shame to miss it; especially since you're leaving anyway."

I rode down in the elevator with another hospital "widow."

"They have a much better system in Africa," I confided, still smarting from my rejection. "The family moves in with the patient."

"Oh, dear me, I wouldn't like that at all," she murmured. "I'm enjoying the rest."

I made another attempt on the crosstown bus. "It's inhumane," I complained to my seatmate. "What it amounts to is that the hospital has taken my husband into custody and I am allowed visiting privileges."

She said placatingly and with a sympathetic smile, "Well, he'll be home soon. Didn't you say it was only a hernia?"

"But he'll be practically well when he gets home—" I began, but her uplifted eyebrows stopped me. Clearly she had me categorized as an odd one.

I phoned my daughter when I reached home. "I don't think I'll go back for another visit. There's no need."

"That's good," she said. "Then there's nothing to worry about."

"That's the trouble," I wailed.

"That's the trouble," I explained to Everett when he had been home a few hours. "I'm being prevented from fulfilling my marriage vow: 'To have and to hold, to love and to cherish, in sickness and in health.' When you get sick you either go to

120

the hospital where you hide behind a half dozen antiseptic attendants or you stay home and lock yourself in quarantine!"

He said he saw my point, and he promised that he would put himself in my hands the very next time he fell ill.

I didn't have long to wait. That was the year of the Hong Kong flu. Everett, trailing his moth-eaten blanket robe, headed for the isolation ward. "Oh no you don't," I said, jamming my foot in the door, "I'm in charge, remember?"

I arranged the nostrums and various sickroom utensils on the dresser, a pitcher of lemonade and a box of tissues on the bedside table. I pinned a paper sack to the side of the mattress, lowered the shades, filled the icebag for his head and plugged in the heating pad for his feet. I dashed to the dime store and bought a small handbell that he could ring for service. When I wasn't in his room changing sheets or forcing liquids or taking his temperature, I was cleaning and polishing up a storm in the rest of the house. I was happily fulfilled—for one whole day.

Then on the morning of the second day I sat on the edge of the bed and said, "Move over, honey." I was burning up with fever. Every symptom that Everett had displayed, I had improved upon. We lay there, partners in pain, taking turns at squeezing lemons and filling icebags.

Eventually, my husband recovered. I didn't. I advanced to double pneumonia. That was all the evidence Everett needed to prove his point—that he was justified in keeping me out of the sickroom.

"From now on you will limit your practice to first aid," he ordered.

"Slivers?" I asked hopefully.

"Only those in inaccessible places," he qualified.

"Foreign objects in your eye?" I asked.

"Wednesdays and Sundays only."

I continued to haggle. "Temporary splints?"

He gave it some thought. "If we're miles from human habitation in the dead of winter, yes."

I decided to be content with the compromise and to table the topic of tourniquets until some future discussion.

Months have passed since our agreement; and while I have been assiduously studying my first aid manual, Everett apparently has been living more cautiously than ever, managing to avoid even such commonplaces as spattered grease burns and thumbtack punctures.

As I write this, he is lying in bed ill. Nothing serious. Just a mild case of the flu. It merits no more than a "hot tea-aspirin-bed rest" prescription via telephone. I decide to go out and have my hair done and do a bit of window shopping.

"Before you go," Everett calls from the bedroom, "come in here a sec." Wordlessly, he hands me the childproof aspirin bottle. I turn the cap till the arrows line up, press my thumb on the red dot, give it a half-twist to the left and pour out his dosage. Gratefully he pops them into his mouth and accepts the glass of water to wash them down.

"You're a good wife, honey," he murmurs, sinking back against the pillows.

"I know," I agree happily. It's so nice to be needed.

15

Of Benches and Pews

IT WAS ONLY NATURAL that my thoughts should turn to benches and pews this morning, for there had been a pleasant surprise, awaiting us in the little country church where we frequently worship. Handsomely covered foam rubber cushions had been installed since our last visit. For old bones, I muse; like Everett's and mine. And it's about time! Asceticism and austerity and hard pews were all right when I was young, but the ravages of rheumatism and old age have gradually transformed me into a voluptuary. I long ago turned in my haircloth and sandals for pile linings and crepe soles. I have become partial in my declining years to velvet housecoats and soft sweaters, electric blankets, air conditioners, and recliners. *I grab all the comfort I can get,* I reflected, as I settled back for a few minutes of quiet meditation before the morning service.

Ours is a mannerly congregation for the most part. The hellos are said and the news is exchanged in the vestibule; the sanctuary is what its name implies. My mind is free to wander undisturbed before the pastor mounts the pulpit and the Doxology calls me back to attention.

My reveries of late tend to be retrospective, one of the syndromes of advancing age that I am reluctant to accept, along with aching joints and graying hair. At any rate, this

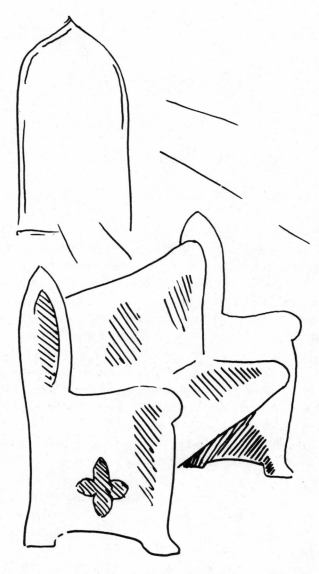

My moments of decision have come to me while I was sitting still.

morning I think of pews and benches, realizing with a shock of recognition that the crises of my life could be listed under the heading "Benches I Have Known." My moments of decision, my epiphanies, have come to me while I was sitting still.

No one will ever install a bronze plaque on a certain pew in Judson Baptist Church, a plaque reading: "Jocelyn Sat Here," but that's where it all began thirty-five years ago. "Strait is the gate and narrow is the way which leadeth unto life, and few there be that find it," was the text that morning. It was the minister's custom to give an invitation after each message. I didn't know that. As far as I was concerned, the whole event had been staged for my particular benefit: the setting, the songs, the sermon, and the invitation. I raised my hand, not quite certain what it was I was responding to but assured for the first time in my life that God loved me, that Christ had died for me, and that I was going to be one of those few to enter in at the "strait" gate. Nobody had ever been more ready to raise his hand at an invitation than was I. I didn't see it then (of course, I did later) that the Lord had been laying the groundwork for a long time. Small coincidences, chance acquaintances, and insoluble home problems—He was working these together for my good.

I was born into a nominal Roman Catholic home, lived in a Catholic neighborhood, and enrolled in a Catholic school; so it is not surprising that I was eleven years old before I had any real contact with a Protestant. Pauline was one of three non-Catholics in my sixth grade class, and she invited me over after school one day. I can still recall the cold, frothy milk in blue glasses; graham crackers stacked on matching plates; a lovely, friendly mother; and an air of order and tranquility such as never existed in my own home and which made me ache with envy. When they invited me to a children's evangelistic meeting, I accepted out of curiosity. I was allowed to go only after promising my mother I would not take an active part in the meeting.

During the prayers, I sat stiffly upright, eyes wide open, a superior smile on my face. While the others sang catchy choruses, I kept my lips tightly closed, unaware my swinging legs betrayed me. I recited a rosary to myself while a chalk talk was presented. At the end of the service I congratulated myself, convinced I had come away unscathed. I had not. A tiny chink had been made in my prejudice.

The chink widened, and a little more light penetrated a year or so after that. I was stopped near my home one afternoon by a bonneted, grandmotherly woman who thought she recognized me as one of the neighborhood children who relieved their summer boredom by singing taunting verses into the open windows of the Salvation Army chapel during the meetings. I refused to admit my complicity. If she had shown the least bit of malice, I might have boasted of it; but she was kind and soft-spoken and had smiling eyes. I resisted her seductiveness, maintaining stoutly, "I'm a Catholic!" as though that granted me a special dispensation and absolved me from all guilt. I ran from her presence and saw her no more, but let it go on record that I never again joined the neighborhood glee club!

In my junior year I transferred to a public high school. The reason I gave my family and myself was that I had my eyes on the editorship of the public school newspaper which had five times the circulation of the parochial publication. The real reason—the one that I was not at all aware of—was that God, who had begun a good work in me, was continuing to perform it. At the new school there was a student the Lord wanted me to meet.

Minette had the same inner peace, the same aura of tranquility that had filled me with such longing in Pauline's presence six years before. We became good friends. I respected her stand, but her low-keyed attempts to witness or to get me out to church were unsuccessful. I did not think the answer to my problems—and they were many and serious at the time— lay in a change of church address.

Then, shortly after high school graduation, while I was a probationer in nurse's training a hundred miles from Chicago, I began reading the Bible with a senior nurse, a Christian girl from Tennessee. I felt the first stirrings, the spiritual labor pains. I phoned Minette. "I am coming home this weekend," I said. "May I go to church with you Sunday morning?"

So there I sat, and the minister was faithful, and I raised my hand at the invitation, and everything began to fall into place. Spiritually, that is. Materially, my world fell apart.

"If you could have seen," someone asked me, "the inquisition that lay ahead, the harassment, the expulsion from school (justified because I was in a Roman Catholic institution on a scholarship), would you have made the same decision?"

"If I could have seen all that," I replied, "then I would also have been able to see the salvation of my mother, brother, and sister. I would have thumbed my nose at the sufferings of that present day," I laughed.

And besides, if it had not been for my experience in that church pew in the Chicago suburb, then there would never have been the bench in Humboldt Park two years later.

Everett and I were newly engaged. He had dropped in unexpectedly one afternoon carrying a paper sack containing a pint of strawberry ice cream.

"Get a couple of spoons," he ordered, "and hurry!"

I ran a comb through my hair, picked up the silverware, and

followed him at a breakneck pace down the stairs and onto a streetcar. In five minutes we were at the park, catching our breath on our favorite bench.

"A pint of ice cream for the two of us?" I gasped as he opened the bag.

"I didn't have enough money for a quart," he apologized.

"We make a pint do for the whole family," I went on to explain.

"Stop talking and eat," he urged. "It's melting fast."

I applied myself diligently for a while.

"How come this impromptu picnic? You're supposed to be studying for a test," I reminded him.

"We have something important to talk about."

"What?"

"Us." He assumed a stern expression that was not quite successful considering the dollop of ice cream on the tip of his nose. I started to reach for my hanky, then a premonition made me pause. Why was he so grave? Had he changed his mind about us? It would be understandable if he had, I admitted to myself. He was a Moody student, surrounded by the feminine cream of God's crop—girls who knew chapter and verse, proper skirt lengths, and cosmetic taboos—and I was a relatively new convert, unschooled and gauche in my Christian walk. "No, I can hardly blame him for reconsidering," I conceded grudgingly, deciding to let him go through the rest of the day with a frosted nose.

I braved the question. "What about us?"

"Our love," he said. "We haven't surrendered it to the Lord." My heart plummeted. It was true, I concluded. He had second thoughts. He wanted out. He was going to use a pious excuse to jilt me. I fought back the mounting panic and decided to argue my case.

"I prayed. For weeks after I met you, I prayed that, if God didn't intend us for each other, He would keep you from becoming interested in me." I didn't think it necessary to add that, while I was praying so selflessly, I kept sticking out my foot for Everett to trip over.

He considered, shifting the sodden ice cream carton in his hands.

"That's not quite the same thing. This is something we have to do together. We have to make sure this is what God wants for us; and if it isn't, we have to be willing to give it up."

I watched the ice cream dripping from between his fingers and onto his shoes.

"I think," I said, belaboring the only point that seemed worth discussing, "that you have discovered that you really don't love me. You bought the ice cream and dragged me to this idyllic setting in order to become disengaged or unengaged or whatever."

I got up and started to walk away—slowly—and he grabbed my hand. It was a sticky handclasp, but neither of us cared. Waxing eloquent, he convinced me that he did love me, but that he was very concerned about our rushing into the engagement without God's imprimatur.

I was loath to tempt God. At this point in my Christian experience I had no assurance that God wouldn't take away what He had given. I thought it over on the bench beneath the lilacs with bees buzzing around our carton of melted ice cream; and I calculated finally that my odds would be greatly increased if I let go, if I said, "Thy will, not mine."

We prayed, and I'm sure my words were as inadequate as my motive was imperfect, but the Lord made allowance for my immaturity and my lack of graciousness. I fancied I heard Him say, "There, that wasn't so bad, was it?"

129

He took nothing back, and He blessed what He had given us in the first place. I recognized this when I looked up at Everett after our prayer. I wanted to tell him that I had fallen in love all over again; that this was more of a betrothal than the night he had proposed and I had accepted.

"You have ice cream on the tip of your nose," I said instead; and moistening a corner of the hanky, I gently dabbed it away.

Then we were married, and then the children came, and there were other benches and pews, other surrenders and blessings. How often I longed for still waters and green pastures, but it was not to be.

Eight-year-old Tom was stricken with polio. He had been hospitalized for a week when the call came. A woman's voice, impersonal and harsh, ordered me to the hospital. "There's been a change in your son's condition. The doctor wants you to come in right away."

She could not answer my questions: "What's wrong?" "Is he dying?" She was programed to say, "I'm sorry. I don't know. The doctor will talk to you when you get here." It was not the kind of voice to which I could say, "But I am alone with a five-year-old and a baby, and Martha isn't due home from school for a half hour, and I don't know the neighbors well enough to ask for help, and I just put my hair up in curlers, and I know this sounds crazy, but I don't have a thing to wear on this unseasonably hot day in October." She would not have responded to my panic.

I phoned Everett at work. He could not be reached immediately. Was it urgent? They'd have him call me as soon as he returned. In the meantime I rehearsed my lines: "Something's wrong, Everett. They want us at the hospital right away. You'll have to go without me. There's no one to stay with the children." My speech was not quite true. I was afraid to go; I would clutch at every excuse, fabricated or real, that would justify my staying home.

The phone rang; it was Everett. I recited my lines. He said he would leave right away and call me as soon as he could. His voice was bleak.

I turned off the washing machine and carried the dripping clothes to the bathroom, where I dropped them into the tub. Removing my curlers, I tied my hair back into a damp ponytail. I called my mother; she promised to come to the house right from work. Then I threw a raincoat over my housedress and waited for Martha to come home.

There were three streetcars and a bus that I had to take to get to the Contagious Disease Hospital, and it was the rush hour, crowded and slow. People seemed to be staring at me, and I touched my cheeks more than once to see if I could be crying and not know it.

Everett had arrived only a few minutes before me and was sitting on a bench across from the second-floor elevator.

"I thought you weren't coming," he said, pulling me down beside him.

"I had to. Where's Tom? How is he?"

Everett pointed to a room a few feet down the hall. "In there. He's having trouble breathing. A doctor's on his way here from Michael Reese to operate on his trachea."

A nurse handed us wrinkled gowns and face masks, and took us to the cubicle where Tom was lying. "You mustn't go all the way in," she warned. "Just stand in the doorway."

Her admonition was unnecessary; there was no room for us. I had expected—I don't know what—but not this frantic scene. Six or seven whitegowned figures were leaning intently over the table, strained voices issuing commands and counter commands; there was an array of tanks and bottles and tubes, and the sound of suction. Somewhere in the center of all this desperate concentration was our son, but we couldn't see him.

We returned to the bench and I prayed. Such a pathetic prayer, an agonizing prayer! "Lord, not this one, please!" I heard Him ask, "If not this one, then which? Martha, your first born, your pig-tailed tomboy? Debby, just recovering from surgery and months in a body cast? Jo, the baby and Martha's shadow? I had no answer. I switched from bargaining "Not this one" to "Not now, Lord," and He asked me, "When?"

Our pastor arrived and sat with us on the bench. I told him I could not join him in a prayer of relinquishment. Speaking softly, with a Scottish burr, his voice lost occasionally in the noise of traffic going by and the opening and closing of the elevator doors, he asked me a question.

"Are you willing to be made willing?"

I caught my breath, surprised by his words.

"That's all God requires of you, you know; that's all He needs—your invitation to Him to come in and take over the battle."

That much of a concession I could make. That much of a prayer I could pray.

The surgeon finally arrived. After completing the tracheotomy he came and sat beside us. "We're doing all we can," he said. "Now it's in Someone else's hands." He seemed embarrassed by his admission, fumbling for words. "If you believe in prayer—"

Everett came to his rescue. "We do," he assured him, "and we have prayed."

Relieved, the doctor left.

We were told that Tom was still unconscious and that it might be quite a while before we could see him. Everett suggested we go out for a walk. It was nearly midnight; we had been sitting on the hospital bench for almost eight hours. He unwrapped a Hershey bar that he had bought in the hospital lobby, and we shared it as we walked up and down the deserted boulevard. I realized I was at peace with myself and God. At precisely what moment I had laid down my arms, I didn't know. It was like the tardy realization that an abscessed tooth has stopped throbbing or that a blinding headache is no longer there. Involuntarily, the words flashed through my mind: "Not my will, but thine."

When we reentered the hospital, a nurse met us at the elevator. "You may see your son for a few minutes." We donned fresh gowns and masks, and she led us to a room lined with iron lungs. There was an infant in one; a young, curlyheaded girl in another; a man our own age stared at us angrily from his respirator. In the farthest machine we saw Tom, whitefaced, his eyes fearful and bewildered. We spoke to him quietly, explaining what had been done to his throat and why; how the lung operated; why he couldn't speak. As we saw him gradually relaxing, we joshed him gently, "Look at it this way. It's a new experience." He grinned at the family joke, a slogan originated by five-year-old Debby to brace herself for everything from an unfamiliar dish to a first trip to the dentist. Before we left Tom that night, we told him, "You're going to be all right, you know." He believed us. That was not surprising; we believed it, too.

The organist ends her prelude; the carillon begins to chime. I am again where I began my reverie: the padded pew, the country church. I slip my hand into Everett's, glad to be back. The windows are open to the spring air, and the blended fragrance of lilac and apple blossoms is sweet and heady. A mourning dove, soft taupe of feather and gentle-eyed, alights on the window sill and surveys the assembly. Her mate calls plaintively from a nearby branch, and she flies off.

"O Lord, our lines are fallen unto us in pleasant places; yea, we have a goodly heritage," the minister proclaims enthusiastically. "Let us rise and praise God from whom all blessings flow!"

16

I Enjoyed You!

WE WERE RETURNING from our Christmas reunion in Quebec. To avoid a long stopover between trains in Windsor, we opted to do the final leg by Greyhound—a last-minute hectic switch. It was while sitting on the bus in the Detroit depot, attempting to cope with a hot beef dinner on a card-board plate—Everett's interpretation of "Just get me a hot dog and a Coke"—that I heard the words that have been haunting and convicting me ever since.

Two black women boarded our bus, a mother and her daughter. The younger of the two had come on board to get her mother settled, and having stowed the suitcases and packages above and around her, leaned over for a final embrace. The portly mother wrapped her arms around her daughter, kissed her, and said, "I enjoyed you, honey." The daugher, straightening up to leave, answered, "And I enjoyed you, Momma."

"I enjoyed you." My scalp prickled at the beautiful intimacy of the expression. I am accustomed to tossing off impersonal cliches at parting, like "I had a wonderful time!" or "It was awfully nice seeing you!" or "We must get together again soon!" Why, just sixteen hours ago I had said goodbye to my daughter and her family, whom I was not likely to see for another year, with a string of inadequate platitudes, when what I really should have said but didn't know how to pronounce were the words, "I enjoyed you."

We had stood in the overheated, crowded Ste. Foy terminal, our English conversation strangely alien in the babble of French that surrounded us. To ease the inevitable awkwardness that precedes parting, we talked of inconsequential things. Everett and I repeated our appreciation for the week of sumptuous dining: Martha and Debby had baked up a storm. We reminisced over the Christmas Eve supper and program at the Eglise Chretienne Evangelique, and the gracious *enchantes* as we were introduced to the Savards, the Funes, the Laforests, and the Desjardins—romantic appellations to provincials like Everett and me. We thanked the children again for the gloriously beautiful and bitterly cold tour of snow blanketed Isle d'Orleans on the morning after Christmas and for the caleche ride through old Quebec, viewed giddily through swirling snow, tucked snugly under fur rugs.

While we waited for our train, we rehashed things that had been said and said again. I wanted to slice through this repetitive circle of conversation to say, "I enjoyed your wonderful hospitality, but I enjoyed you more."

True, the elaborate meals were a treat for Everett and me, for we have begun to lean heavily on hamburger helpers and take-out chicken dinners; but better than the gourmet cooking were the hair-down sessions as we cleared the table and did the dishes, and the men took care of the children in the living room.

Isle d'Orleans I would not have missed for the world; I used up a roll of film on the snow-shrouded graveyards along the St. Lawrence, Everett informs me; but my happiest memory of that day is that of sitting uncomfortably in the back of the VW van, unable to see out of the steamed-up windows, with one of

We enjoyed each other in hair-down sessions as we did the dishes.

the twins—what difference whether it was Nate or Ben?—sleep-heavy in my lap.

And as thrilling as the caleche ride was, I enjoyed far more the morning that Martha took Debby and me on a shopping excursion, bravely asking directions of the mono-lingual bus driver, understood and understanding, getting us there and back successfully, arms full of cheeses and water colors, and the right change in our purses.

The fellowship on Christmas Eve with the French Christians was a once-in-a-lifetime experience for Everett; but he could not have enjoyed it any more than I enjoyed the late night vigil that Debby and I kept, alternating ginger ale and antacid tablets, waiting for the twenty-four-hour flu to have done with us and planning in those quiet hours the writing of this book.

"I enjoyed you, and all the short, short moments with you, and I left without telling you so. I promise myself that next time we will cut down on the sightseeing and concentrate on the companionship; and we will say goodbye from the heart."

*　*　*

"I enjoyed you." For a year I have not been able to put those words out of mind. It was inevitable that I should find in them a spiritual profundity. Hardly a day has passed since that time in Detroit that the Lord has not asked me, "Well, how about it? Are you enjoying Me?" Weak and human, with a more-than-average propensity for hedging, I reply, "I love Thy kingdom, Lord, and the house of Thine abode—"

"You know that's not what I mean," He chides. "Are you enjoying Me?"

"I enjoy reading the pundits," I plead. "C. S. Lewis and Francis Schaeffer. A person can't do much better than that."

"You're evading the question," He accuses. "Are you enjoying Me?"

I try circumlocution. "I'm only truly comfortable when I'm in the company of your people, Lord; my record collection is almost exclusively Christian artists; my radios are locked in to WMBI in Chicago and WRVM in Door County, so that I hear the finest of gospel music and the cream of the conference circuit; there are scriptural mottos on my walls and hymnals on the music rack; and two young orphans in Korea who call me momma—"

"Be still," He commands. "Stop your idle babbling and know that I am God, that I am here, that I am accessible."

"To enjoy?"

"To enjoy. I am so close you can hear My footsteps; they're only a pace ahead. So close you can reach out for My hand; it's at your side. So close you can whisper, and I will answer."

"Lord, I forget."

"You're too busy watching the scenery."

"I'll cut down on the sightseeing," I promise. "I'll concen-

138

trate on the companionship."

"You won't be sorry," He assures me. "In My company there is fullness of joy, and at My right hand there are pleasures forevermore."

CHRISTIAN HERALD ASSOCIATION AND ITS MINISTRIES

CHRISTIAN HERALD ASSOCIATION, founded in 1878, publishes The Christian Herald Magazine, one of the leading interdenominational religious monthlies in America. Through its wide circulation, it brings inspiring articles and the latest news of religious developments to many families. From the magazine's pages came the initiative for CHRISTIAN HERALD CHILDREN'S HOME and THE BOWERY MISSION, two individually supported not-for-profit corporations.

CHRISTIAN HERALD CHILDREN'S HOME, established in 1894, is the name for a unique and dynamic ministry to disadvantaged children, offering hope and opportunities which would not otherwise be available for reasons of poverty and neglect. The goal is to develop each child's potential and to demonstrate Christian compassion and understanding to children in need.

Mont Lawn is a permanent camp located in Bushkill, Pennsylvania. It is the focal point of a ministry which provides a healthful "vacation with a purpose" to children who without it would be confined to the streets of the city. Up to 1000 children between the ages of 7 and 11 come to Mont Lawn each year.

Christian Herald Children's Home maintains year-round contact with children by means of an *In-City Youth Ministry*. Central to its philosophy is the belief that only through sustained relationships and demonstrated concern can individual lives be truly enriched. Special emphasis is on individual guidance, spiritual and family counseling and tutoring. This follow-up ministry to inner-city children culminates for many in financial assistance toward higher education and career counseling.

THE BOWERY MISSION, located at 227 Bowery, New York City, has since 1879 been reaching out to the lost men on the Bowery, offering them what could be their last chance to rebuild their lives. Every man is fed, clothed and ministered to. Countless numbers have entered the 90-day residential rehabilitation program at the Bowery Mission. A concentrated ministry of counseling, medical care, nutrition therapy, Bible study and Gospel services awakens a man to spiritual renewal within himself.

These ministries are supported solely by the voluntary contributions of individuals and by legacies and bequests. Contributions are tax deductible. Checks should be made out either to CHRISTIAN HERALD CHILDREN'S HOME or to THE BOWERY MISSION.

Administrative Office: 40 Overlook Drive, Chappaqua, New York 10514
Telephone: (914) 769-9000